Gay Rights vs. Religious Liberty?

Gay Rights vs. Religious Liberty?

The Unnecessary Conflict

ANDREW KOPPELMAN

OXFORD
UNIVERSITY PRESS

Oxford University Press is a department of the University of Oxford. It furthers the University's objective of excellence in research, scholarship, and education by publishing worldwide. Oxford is a registered trade mark of Oxford University Press in the UK and certain other countries.

Published in the United States of America by Oxford University Press
198 Madison Avenue, New York, NY 10016, United States of America.

Library of Congress Control Number: 2020932761
ISBN 978-0-19-750098-9

1 3 5 7 9 8 6 4 2

Printed by Integrated Books International, United States of America

Contents

Introduction

Should religious people who conscientiously object to facilitating same-sex weddings, and who therefore decline to provide cakes, photography, or other services, be exempted from antidiscrimination laws? This issue has taken on an importance far beyond the tiny number who have made such claims. It helped make Donald Trump president.

Each side's position has become more unyielding. Many of the most sophisticated scholars are as rigid as the politicians and partisan commentators.

The dominant view, on both sides, is that this disagreement concerns a matter of deep principle. Religious liberty and nondiscrimination are each understood as moral absolutes. Compromise is perceived as an existential threat. Both sides feel victimized. Gay rights advocates fear that exempting even a few religious dissenters would unleash a devastating wave of discrimination. Conservative Christians[1] fear that the law will treat them like racists and drive them to the margins of American society.

The issue is one example of the polarization of American politics. A 2016 survey found Americans evenly divided on whether religious business owners should be permitted to refuse services to same-sex couples: 48% supported a right to refuse, 49% opposed it. Among churchgoing white evangelicals, 88% supported a right to refuse; among those who self-identified as having no religion, it was 34%. Among Democrats and those who lean Democratic, it was 30%; the corresponding number among Republicans is 71%. The Republicans were somewhat divided by age: exemption was supported by 76% of those 65 and older, but only 58% of those 18 to 29. Few Americans—18%—expressed sympathy for both points of view.[2]

Both sides are mistaken. Each invokes interests of a kind that can and should be balanced against others. Principles are a distraction, which make each side's claims seem more uncompromisable than they are.

This controversy has been a disaster for the Left. By pushing conservative Christians away from the Democrats, it helped elect Trump. (If Hillary Clinton had received Barack Obama's 2012 percentage of the white evangelical vote in Michigan and Florida, she would have won.) Trump has in turn been a disaster for the Right. The Republican Party, which once championed responsible conservatism, now stands for xenophobia, protectionism, isolationism, religious bigotry, kleptocracy, and racism—a transformation that is likely to survive his presidency. That in turn has been a disaster for American Christianity. The uncritical embrace of Trump by so many prominent religious leaders has persuaded many Americans, especially the young, that religion itself is a hypocritical sham.

Many on each side think that their counterparts are evil and motivated by irrational hatred—either hatred of gay people or hatred of conservative Christians. That is not only dangerous and false; it is profoundly illiberal in a free society where radical disagreement about moral fundamentals is inevitable. There are indeed extremists on each side with repressive aspirations, and each side is reasonably frightened by the worst and sometimes most visible representatives of the other. Most Americans, however, would like to live in peace with their fellow citizens, and are willing to consider and, if possible, accommodate other people's perspectives and fears. This is an issue that divides decent people who honestly hold radically differing views about what a good life requires. If the two sides have no sympathy with one another, this is largely because they do not understand one another.

The scholars, the activists, and the general public all include some who reject any compromise and others who are open to it. Of these, the moderates are visible and vocal mainly among the scholars. They publish in academic journals with specialized readerships. This book aims to present the case for compromise to a broader audience.

Conservative Christians and defenders of gay rights[3] can despise one another's views while respecting one another and sometimes joining as political allies. They can recognize one another's rights to live according to their principles. Religious toleration means, precisely, that we tolerate theological views that we regard as wrong and repugnant. The Establishment Clause of the First Amendment dictates that the state must remain neutral among such views.

Those theological disagreements should not be allowed to obscure the areas of agreement.

Secular liberalism and conservative Christianity alike condemn lying, cruelty, poverty, oppression, and prejudice. They need to unite against their common enemies. But before they can do that, they need to end this war.

"Freedom of religion and religion has been used to justify all kinds of discrimination throughout history, whether it be slavery, whether it be the holocaust . . . to me it is one of the most despicable pieces of rhetoric that people can use to—to use their religion to hurt others." So declared a member of the Colorado Civil Rights Commission, in denying the claim of a baker who claimed that the First Amendment protected his right to refuse to make a cake for a same-sex wedding. The Supreme Court overturned that decision on grounds of religious bias in *Masterpiece Cakeshop v. Colorado*. The statement, Justice Kennedy wrote, disparaged the baker's religion "in at least two distinct ways: by describing it as despicable, and also by characterizing it as merely rhetorical—something insubstantial and even insincere."

Alas, the Commissioner is not unique. There's quite a lot of this kind of talk. The baker's desire to be left alone is widely understood to be a demand to inflict harm. Some think the harm would be massive. "Gays would be perennial outcasts whose equality and dignity would always be subservient to the desires of religionists to brand them as abominable," Shannon Gilreath and Arley Ward write, "with the state giving religionists that license under the law."[4]

Prominent conservatives, too, perceive a malicious desire to harm—directed at *them*. Steven D. Smith, for instance, understands the application of antidiscrimination law thus: "People are using the law to crack down on a religion or a way of life that they disapprove of but that doesn't seem to be realistically harming them or interfering with their own lives in any obvious way. Why would they do that?"[5] He concludes that "the gravamen of litigation demanding redress for 'dignitary harm' is that same-sex couples are offended and hurt by the tacit or open communication of other citizens' beliefs regarding marriage. And the purpose of such lawsuits is effectively to censor or punish an objecting merchant for that communication."[6] Maggie Gallagher worries that those who oppose same-sex marriage will be regarded "as hateful bigots whose beliefs must be suppressed by operation of law."[7] Virginia state delegate C. Todd Gilbert said: "The activists who pursue same-sex marriage . . . are not satisfied with equality and they will not be satisfied until people of faith are driven out of this discourse, are made to cower, are made to be in fear of speaking their minds, of living up to their deeply held religious beliefs. They want us driven out."[8] Rod Dreher describes an emerging consensus "that the most important goal at this stage is not to stop gay marriage entirely but to secure as much liberty as possible for dissenting religious and social conservatives while there is still time."[9] David French reports that conservative Christians "have never felt more isolated and culturally vulnerable."[10]

Both sides thus understand themselves to be fighting in self-defense. The consequence, Jonathan Rauch observes, is that "an issue on which a few years ago there seemed to be reasonably good prospects for reasonable accommodations has hardened into legal and political trench warfare."[11]

Both sides are confused. Gay rights advocates have misconceived the tort of discrimination as a particularized injury to the person rather than the artifact of social engineering that it really is. Religious conservatives have failed to grasp the purposes of antidiscrimination law, and so have demanded accommodations that would be massively overbroad. They have also tried to enlist the Supreme Court to protect wedding vendors with some constitutional principle, but every principle that has been proposed would likewise be massively overbroad. That problem became clear in *Masterpiece Cakeshop*, in which lawyers, amici, and members of the Court proposed a bewildering array of possible rules, not one of which was workable.

Lawyers are trained to think about conflict resolution by devising abstract principles that should cover all future cases, and which incidentally entail that their side wins. But this is not the only way to think about conflict. Sometimes, the right thing to do is not to follow a principle, but to accurately discern the interests at stake and cobble together an approach that gives some weight to each of those interests. Ethics is not only about principles. There is a tradition in moral philosophy, going back to Aristotle, that holds that a good person does not necessarily rely on any abstract ideal, but rather makes sound judgments about the right thing to do in particular situations. Sometimes principles are overbroad generalizations from experience, and distract us from the moral imperatives of the situation at hand.[12]

The gay rights/religious liberty issue is not a question for courts. It is an appropriate occasion for legislative negotiation. Both sides ought to be looking for legislative relief. Discrimination against gays in public accommodations is prohibited in 21 states and the District of Columbia, with no religious exemption. Gay rights advocates sometimes forget that in most of the United States, there is no protection at all. Twenty-nine states have no such laws, and no new ones have been enacted since 2008.[13] "The near and intermediate future," Douglas Laycock writes, "appears to be religious dissenters getting crushed in blue states and gays and lesbians still discriminated against and denied protection in federal law and in red states."[14] In the present standoff, compromise is unthinkable, but how could protection-plus-exemptions be worse than nothing? The present paralysis is good for no one.

About a third of Americans think, most of them for religious reasons,[15] that homosexual sex is never morally acceptable.[16] The American Left increasingly has written them off as bigots whose votes are not worth pursuing.

In the 2016 election, Clinton received the smallest percentage of the white evangelical vote of any Democratic presidential candidate in history. She was the first Democrat since 2004 to lose the Catholic vote. There are many reasons for that, but a prominent one is that she made no effort to reach out to those voters. Evidently she and her campaign staff thought that there was no point. She still evidently doesn't think so, since, in her retrospective of the campaign, she doesn't even discuss these voters.[17] This isn't just about her. She typifies the American Left. What have we got to talk about with *them*?

I've been a gay rights advocate for more than thirty years.[18] This book is primarily addressed to those who share my views. It will, however, be of interest to religious conservatives as well, since it makes a case on their behalf that they can't make for themselves. I argue that even if they are absolutely wrong—and I do believe that—they still ought to be accommodated.

The toxic core of the conflict is the racism analogy: the idea that those who embrace traditional sexual morality are as bad as racists, and deserve to be treated like racists. That idea persuades gay rights advocates that any compromise would be morally repugnant, implicitly condoning evil ideas and bigoted people. It persuades conservative Christians that they face an existential threat.

Yet the analogy itself hasn't gotten much careful attention.

The comparison actually comprises several different analogies. Some of them are sound. But taken together they are misleading. They lead the spectator to the wrong conclusion: that all religious conservatives are malicious, hateful people. That makes the problem unsolvable. The religious traditionalists are right to feel threatened. The Left, which often prides itself on its attachment to science and rationality, is marching to war under the banner of a delusion.

When one says that opposition to homosexuality is like racism, one might be saying any of several things. One might be comparing their effects: the traditional religious condemnation has hurt gay people, a lot. One might be saying that both are grave moral errors. These, however, are not the analogies that matter. They are the stuff of ordinary disagreement. We're constantly arguing with people whose views we think are wrong and destructive, and we can try to persuade them without even getting angry.

The message the analogy usually conveys is more pointed. These people are evil! They ought to be stigmatized and shunned! Thus a majority of the US Commission on Civil Rights declared that proposals for religious accommodation "represent an orchestrated, nationwide effort by extremists to promote bigotry, cloaked in the mantle of 'religious freedom,'" and "are pretextual attempts to justify naked animus against lesbian, gay, bisexual, and transgender people."[19]

There is, of course, a certain charm in the suggestion that our adversaries know they are wrong and are just pretending to disagree with us because they are horrible people. However—and this is part of what makes the analogy misleading—that was false even of many white racists during the Jim Crow era. Many of them blindly accepted the poppycock they had been taught. This kind of demonization is likewise unfair to the millions of Americans today who hold conservative views about sexuality. The labeling of their views as "pretextual" seems to rely on the idea that no one could really believe this stuff. But that notion evades the familiar problem of religious diversity. Other people's religious beliefs often seem obviously bizarre to us.

Ryan Anderson and Robert George think it is important that their views at least be respected as rationally defensible:

> It is rational to support marriage as the union of a man and a woman, and supporters of same-sex marriage should stand up and say so, condemning attempts to disparage belief in marriage as a conjugal partnership as irrational—the moral and intellectual equivalent of racism, misogyny, and other forms of bigotry.[20]

This is too much to ask. It is also more than they need to ask. They presume that views that are not rationally defensible must be treated as bigotry. That doesn't follow. Many people think that others' religious views are not rationally defensible. Some even think that their *own* views are not rationally defensible, that they are matters of pure faith. In a free society, it is safe to hold views that others regard as rationally indefensible.

It is a truth universally acknowledged that there could not and should not have been religious exemptions from the Civil Rights Act of 1964. From this one might infer—many do infer—that those who refuse to facilitate same-sex marriages are not entitled to even the mild, defeasible presumption of accommodation that America has often extended to conscientious objectors. One might also infer that, as in 1964, the stakes are high enough to justify a state effort to stamp out the subculture that embraces these hateful views.

But this misunderstands the situation the country faced in 1964. One need not take heterosexism less seriously than racism in order to understand the uniqueness of our situation then.

America has a long tradition of accommodating religious dissenters. As a general matter, the law should not strive to stamp out any subculture and make its members outcasts. Racism has been so pervasive and destructive that these two principles are appropriately overridden. The civil rights struggle demanded coercive cultural reconstruction, especially but not only in the states of the former Confederacy.

The question is not simply whether people are acting on the basis of repugnant ideas. There are a lot of repugnant ideas around. It is whether there should be cultural war. That question, like any decision to go to war, depends on prudential assessment of likely consequences. In the case of race, there has been progress, but the war isn't over. Zero tolerance remains necessary. In the case of sexual orientation, war is unnecessary and unlikely to improve matters.

Another disanalogy is that unlike the white racists of the Jim Crow era, the conservative Christians are peaceful. The racism of the pre-1964 South was pervasively dependent on violence and the threat of violence. The religious traditionalists just want to be left alone. (There is, of course, a lot of violence against gay people, but it doesn't come from them.)

The wedding vendors might be able to be accommodated, in various ways, without defeating the point of the law. That wasn't possible in 1964; there were too many racists who would have invoked any exemption.

There has also, amid this conflict, been a distorted sense of priorities. The conversation has focused almost exclusively on discrimination. The most pressing gay rights issue today, however, is the terrifying environment that many gay teenagers face.[21] Religious parents, who often think they are doing the right thing, often drive their children away. There is an immense population of gay homeless youth. Parents need to be persuaded to change their treatment of their LGBT children, and the most credible sources of that persuasion are their own churches. The churches, however, need better information about what life is actually like for their gay teenagers. They can support LGBT youth and their families without abandoning their traditional sexual ethics. But in order to do that, they need to engage with gay rights organizations, and those organizations need to be willing to talk to them.[22] That won't happen while each side regards the other as too loathsome or threatening to talk to.

I've worked very hard to create a regime in which it's safe to be gay. I'd also like that regime to be one that's safe for religious dissenters. The notions that gay people are obligated to lifelong celibacy, or that marriage is inherently heterosexual, are grave moral errors. (I can't argue that here, though I have done so elsewhere.) But that does not mean that state power must unrelentingly be used to eradicate these ideas.

In the relatively bland religious environment we inhabit, we have forgotten what real religious diversity is. It was once widely agreed that there was only one true path to salvation, and that other people's beliefs were leading them to Hell. Toleration became the rule not because people no longer believed this, but because they became persuaded that the coercive use of state power wouldn't help: state religion is likely to be corrupted religion.[23] Religious liberty is fundamentally about tolerating ideas we regard as odious.

Both gay people and religious conservatives seek space in society to live out their beliefs, values, and identities.[24] Each side's most basic commitments entail that the other is in error about moral fundamentals, that the other's entire way of life is predicated on that error and ought not to exist. That was also true of the religious differences that begot the Establishment Clause of the First Amendment. Religious coexistence has nonetheless been achieved. The United States is a long-standing counterexample to Rousseau's dictum that "it is impossible to live in peace with people whom one believes are damned."[25]

Religious accommodation is a part of the reason for the success of the American regime. Quakers who resisted military service, Catholic priests who wouldn't reveal in court what they had learned in confession, Native Americans who use peyote in their services, and Muslim prisoners who seek to grow beards have all been granted dispensations from the law.

Our question, then, is whether accommodation is appropriate for a few businesses that hold themselves open to the public, or whether its costs are too high. In order to determine that, we must examine the purposes of antidiscrimination laws, and decide whether these would be frustrated by religious exemptions.

Some of the most important thinkers on both sides can't even think about this question, because they deny the validity of one of the considerations that have to be balanced. The most prominent exposition of the controversy is the book *Debating Religious Liberty and Discrimination*, by John Corvino, Ryan Anderson, and Sherif Girgis. Their presentation of opposing views on the question is valuable both for its philosophical sophistication and the civility with which they engage. Yet Corvino doesn't think it's ever appropriate to give religion special treatment, and Anderson and Girgis don't think it's ever appropriate to protect gay people from discrimination.[26]

This book aspires to a broad audience, but it also has something to say to the specialists. Any compromise depends on recognizing and accommodating the most urgent interests on both sides. I aim to describe those interests with more precision than has been done thus far, and in terms that both sides can recognize and appreciate. I analyze the aims of antidiscrimination law, with special attention to the idea of dignitary harm—a concept that has created considerable confusion on both sides. I explain why even those who do not regard religion as important or valid nonetheless have good reasons to support religious liberty. I show why those who regard religion as a value of overriding importance should nonetheless not want the law to give it the extravagant power that has been suggested in some Supreme Court opinions, which would amount to a right to inflict severe injury on others in the name of one's religion.

Antidiscrimination law has multiple purposes: amelioration of economic inequality, stigmatization of discrimination, and prevention of dignitary harm.[27] Consider them in turn.

Because antidiscrimination law's economic purpose is a response to pervasive discrimination, it is not thwarted by discrimination that is unusual. If gay people are generally protected, a few outliers won't make much difference. The reshaping of culture to marginalize antigay prejudice won't be stopped by a few exemptions.

Discrimination is also insulting. However, the dignitary harm of knowing that some of your fellow citizens condemn your way of life is not one from which the law can or should protect you in a regime of free speech. Even if they are wrong, free speech allows people to say things that no one should ever say to anyone. The dignitary harm that hurts the most is the wounding experience of personal rejection—or its anticipation, which is often a source of chronic stress—during what one reasonably expects to be the happy occasion of planning one's wedding. That can be avoided if the vendors are required, as a precondition for exemption, to make their objections to same-sex marriages clear to the public in advance.

The stakes of this dispute go beyond the gay rights issue. Resistance to religious accommodation has its source in the political left, much of which, largely as a consequence of disputes over sexual ethics, increasingly regards religion as a malign force in the world. Yet the American Left has never accomplished anything without religious allies. For those who are most concerned to ameliorate the growing inequality in America, hostility toward religion is a catastrophic error. (It also foolishly neglects the continuing activities of the very substantial religious left.) Accommodation would be a step in the right direction.

Many compromises are possible: an exemption for very small businesses, or for religiously oriented businesses, or expressive enterprises such as photographers. The specifics would have to be negotiated, and the negotiation would be different in different places.

The response I develop here is to exempt only those who post warnings about their religious objections, so that no customer would have the personal experience of being turned away. There is a cost to such an announcement: it will repel not only gay customers, but also that very large number of people who find discrimination repellent. For that reason, it's likely to be seldom used, and only by those with the most intense religious compunctions. A few dissenters, whom one can easily avoid ever meeting, won't undermine the equality of gay people.

Even this solution is not a panacea. This is not the kind of problem that can be solved by a professor sitting alone at his keyboard. The parties concerned have to talk to each other and work something out, something that can't be predicted in advance. What the professor can do is dispel the confusion that prevents negotiation from happening.

This book's focus is narrow. I will only address the issues raised by the cases involving wedding vendors—bakers, photographers, florists, and other providers of services for weddings. These have been the most fraught cases, because they are so stubborn about refusing to facilitate what they regard as a religious ceremony with a theological significance that they reject, and because the providers of such services are always small proprietors who make sympathetic Davids in the face of the state's Goliath. There are many other situations in which conservative Christians collide with the gay rights movement: religious adoption agencies, universities, providers of social services, private employers who object to providing spousal benefits to same-sex couples. If we can address the intractable public accommodations problem, that resolution will offer a model for dealing with these other cases.

The conflict this book addresses is commonly understood as a zero-sum clash of rights. It is not. To see why not, it will be helpful to clarify what a rights claim consists of.

Joseph Raz has argued that a right should be understood as an aspect of human well-being that "is a sufficient reason for holding some other person(s) to be under a duty."[28] If Raz is right, then rights are parasitic on interests. "The specific role of rights in practical thinking is . . . the grounding of duties in the interests of other beings."[29] Some interests are so important that others should help to realize them. That is what we are saying when we say there are rights.

The principles at issue here—religious liberty and nondiscrimination—may seem irreconcilable. *But they are themselves parasitic on interests.* The way to think clearly about the conflict is to look past the principles to the underlying interests. Discrimination harms its victims' urgent interest in equal treatment in public spaces. Religious liberty protects what many people regard as their deepest concerns. The legal rights in question are tools for protecting those interests.

Arguments about the gay rights/religious liberty conflict often talk past each other, because they often focus on one of the interests in question and ignore the other. The principles are in unresolvable tension. The interests are not. There are ways to ensure that all the relevant interests are accommodated. This may require some modification of the principles. But what ultimately matters is not the principles but the people. We only care about the principles because we care about the people.

The root of the problem is a philosophical confusion. No negotiation is thinkable, on any of these issues, if each side regards any deal as a betrayal of its deepest commitments. They think that because some of the best minds on their side have encouraged them to think that. They misunderstand their own ideals. Philosophy got us into this mess. Philosophy must get us out of it.

1

Liberals used to love religious freedom

Until very recently, almost all Americans were in favor of religious liberty. The idea had particular attractions for the political left. Religious minorities have always been among the oppressed. What was new about the New Left of the 1960s was its shift in the focus of its demand for social change on behalf of the worst off citizens, from economic deprivation to the cultural imperialisms of racism, sexism, and heterosexism. The defense of minority cultures has since broadened into a more general right to be weird. Religious freedom readily fit into that narrative.

Then gay rights and the contraception mandate came along. They engendered a new level of suspicion. "The phrases 'religious liberty' and 'religious freedom' will stand for nothing except hypocrisy so long as they remain code words for discrimination, intolerance, racism, sexism, homophobia, Islamophobia, Christian supremacy or any form of intolerance," declared Martin R. Castro, Chairman of the US Civil Rights Commission, in 2016.[1] Many now wonder what reason there could be for giving religion the special treatment it gets in American law.

Religious liberty has a long history. The way to begin to think about any tradition whose value has come into question is to learn how it developed and why it exists. It was brought into existence by people who did things for reasons. We have to know those reasons before we can decide whether we should preserve, modify, or discard what we have inherited. To what extent do their reasons make sense to us? Or are there new reasons for maintaining the old practices in some form? Some traditions, such as racism, will turn out to be rotten all the way down. Others will rest on once-valid reasons that are obsolete. But we can't know this until we investigate.

Liberalism is the political philosophy that holds the purpose of government to be not the dominance of one king, race, or nation, nor the promotion of religious, moral, or martial virtue, but rather peace, prosperity, intellectual progress, and above all personal liberty. Liberalism demands that each individual be autonomous within a certain sphere which government must not violate. The dimensions of that sphere have been understood differently at different times and by different people.[2] Most modern American political ideologies are variations on liberalism.

The gay rights movement, like many other social movements, is a demand that liberalism keep its promises. Liberalism, as it happens, began as an inference from religious liberty. The gay rights movement has been attacking its own grandparent.

The core idea of the Protestant Reformation was that each individual has a direct and unmediated relation to God. In the earliest proto-liberal texts, the sphere of individual autonomy that the state was obligated to respect was purely religious. The poet John Milton wrote the first major defense of freedom of speech in 1644. He argued that each person had to choose for himself to follow God. Even correct religious doctrine would not bring about salvation if it was the consequence of blind conformity rather than active engagement with religious questions. "A man may be a heretic in the truth; and if he believe things only because his pastor says so, or the Assembly so determines, without knowing other reason, though his belief be true, yet the very truth he holds becomes his heresy."[3] Religious salvation was to be achieved only by struggle against temptation. "Assuredly we bring not innocence into the world, we bring impurity much rather: that which purifies us is trial, and trial is by what is contrary."[4] What matters is not outward conformity, but adherence to the inner light. All that coercion can produce is "the forced and outward union of cold and neutral and inwardly divided minds."[5] For the same reason, he argued in *Paradise Lost* that God was right to allow the serpent into the Garden of Eden: people had to freely choose to do what was right. Authentic freedom required an environment in which our views are challenged and tested. The sphere of autonomy for Milton was entirely internal. He was no advocate of democracy. He was Secretary of Foreign Tongues for a military dictator, Oliver Cromwell. But he thought that the mind had to be free.

John Locke, writing 45 years later, similarly argued that "the Care of Souls is not committed to the Civil Magistrate, any more than to other Men."[6] He cited the limited responsibilities of the state, which exists for Locke solely in order to protect life, liberty, and property. He also insisted on the specifically personal character of religion: "No Man can, if he would, conform his Faith to the Dictates of another."[7] Coerced worship would be "Hipocrisie, and Contempt of his Divine Majesty."[8] Coercion of worship is absurd, because what it produces has no religious value. "Although the Magistrates Opinion in Religion be sound, and the way that he appoints be truly Evangelical, yet if I be not thoroughly perswaded thereof in my own mind, there will be no safety for me in following it. No way whatsoever that I shall walk in, against the Dictates of my Conscience, will ever bring me to the Mansions of the Blessed."[9] Locke thought that the state was generally incompetent to adjudicate religious questions: "The one only narrow way which leads to Heaven is not better known to the Magistrate than to private Persons, and therefore I cannot safely take him for my Guide, who may probably be as ignorant of the way as my self, and who certainly is less concerned for my Salvation than I my self am."[10]

Locke was concerned only with intentional religious persecution. He didn't think that religious scruples excused anyone from obeying otherwise valid laws.

From the beginning, however, American law often gave religion special treatment. Quakers and Mennonites were excused from the draft in colonial times. During Prohibition, Catholics were allowed to use sacramental wine. (The protection of religion was inconsistent: the practices of slaves and Native Americans got no respect, and the Federal government crushed Mormon polygamy.)

The early Americans did not rely on any abstract principle of religious liberty. They were addressing specific claims by specific groups, on an ad hoc basis. In each of these cases, accommodation made sense. There was no point in trying to draft Quakers, who would be lousy soldiers anyway. In a leading case, a Catholic priest turned in stolen goods, which he had extracted from a repentant thief. The court held that the state could not attempt to compel him to reveal the thief's name. It would have been futile and self-defeating to try to destroy the confidentiality of confession.[11]

The first time the Supreme Court considered an abstract principle of religious accommodation involved a Mormon polygamist, George Reynolds. He "asked the court to instruct the jury that if they found from the evidence that he 'was married as charged—if he was married—in pursuance of and in conformity with what he believed at the time to be a religious duty, that the verdict must be 'not guilty.'"[12] The precise question before the Court was whether the trial court had improperly refused to give that instruction. The Court accurately observed that the proposed rule would make every person who invoked religious reasons a "law unto himself." Religious claims would always win. The Court was correct to raise the issue of human sacrifice.

Nonetheless, legislatures continued to enact religious accommodations. Sacramental wine was permitted during Prohibition. The Catholic Church was and is exempted from employment discrimination laws when it denies ordination to women. Draft exemptions were expanded beyond Quakers.

The question of religious accommodation arises in cases where a law can allow some exceptions without undermining its purposes. Many laws, such as military conscription, taxes, environmental regulations, and drug laws, will accomplish their ends even if there is some deviation from the norm they set forth, so long as that deviation does not become too great.

In 1963, for the first time, the Supreme Court constitutionalized the exemption question. *Sherbert v. Verner* involved a modest and harmless claim: a Seventh-day Adventist, fired for declining to work on Saturdays, sought unemployment benefits. Her claim was denied on the ground that she had refused work without good cause. The Supreme Court, in an opinion by ultraliberal Justice William Brennan, held that accommodation was constitutionally required unless the state can show that the burden was justified by "some compelling state interest."[13]

The "compelling interest" test, in recent Supreme Court decisions, has meant a powerful presumption of unconstitutionality. In 1963, however, it referred merely to cost/benefit analysis. The Court normally doesn't weigh burdens against benefits, but merely rubber-stamps whatever the legislature has done. *Sherbert* meant that the Court would consider burdens on religion somewhat more skeptically.[14] In the religion context, it never stopped meaning that. One leading scholar concluded that in the free exercise context, it "amounts to little more than weighted balancing, with the scales tipped slightly to favor the protected right."[15]

Whatever its formal expression, the scrutiny was deferential. Before *Sherbert* was effectively overruled in 1990, the Court considered at least fourteen exemption claims under the Free Exercise Clause, but granted only five (four of which involved denial of unemployment compensation benefits).[16] In the lower courts, free exercise claims, by one count, had a success rate of 39.5%. After *Sherbert* was overruled, that success rate dropped to 28.4%.[17] Victories for religious claimants at trial were likely to be reversed on appeal. One study has reported that between 1980 and 1990 the federal appellate courts rejected an astounding 87% of free exercise exemption claims.[18]

The right to religious accommodation is a peculiar kind of right. It is sometimes suggested that it is in the nature of rights that they are trumps against the ordinary weighing of costs against benefits.[19] But a right to free exercise, if it includes any right to accommodation, can only be a right to a certain kind of weighing, in which religion is treated as a good that should be allowed to be pursued unless the marginal cost is too high.[20] The right is a right to have that marginal cost considered in individual cases—a favor that is not done for most of those who object to obeying particular laws.[21]

The argument for giving these judgments to the judiciary is that courts hear cases one at a time and so are confronted, as legislatures are not, with concrete situations. Courts are also committed to treat like cases alike. Legislatures often overlook the impact of rules on minority religious groups.

In 1990 the Court abandoned the *Sherbert* rule, in another innocuous case: Native Americans wanted to participate in traditional peyote rituals. Quoting *Reynolds*, the 1878 Mormon case, *Employment Division v. Smith* held that a right to accommodation would "permit every citizen to become a law unto himself."[22] This would be "courting anarchy."[23] In fact, cost/benefit balancing was not part of nineteenth-century jurisprudence, and was not even considered in *Reynolds*. The *Smith* Court thought that such balancing was not an appropriate task for judges, because it involved too much discretion: "It is horrible to contemplate that federal judges will regularly balance against the importance of general laws the significance of religious practice."[24]

Federal and state legislatures responded to *Smith* by attempting to reverse it by statute. Congress enacted the Religious Freedom Restoration Act of 1993 (RFRA), which provides that "Government shall not substantially burden a person's exercise of religion even if the burden results from a rule of general applicability," unless the Government "demonstrates that application of the burden to the person—(1) is in furtherance of a compelling governmental interest; and (2) is the least restrictive means of furthering that compelling governmental interest."[25] RFRA passed unanimously in the House and drew only three opposing votes in the Senate. It was not an issue that divided left and right. The Christian Coalition and the American Civil Liberties Union both supported it.

In 1997, the Supreme Court held that Congress had exceeded its constitutional powers by making RFRA applicable to the states.[26] (It remains valid as applied to federal law.) Even before that decision, religious claimants still lost most of the time.[27] Congress attempted to enact replacement legislation that relied on other constitutional powers, but by then the question of discrimination had already arisen, and the coalition for broad legislation was splintered. Congress managed in 2000 to enact the Religious Land Use and Institutionalized Persons Act (RLUIPA), which protected what the legislators could agree on: prisoners' religious activities and churches' land use decisions.[28]

Many state legislatures also responded to *Smith* by passing their own state-level RFRAs. These were not especially controversial either. Barack Obama, as a state senator, voted for one of the earliest ones in Illinois in 1998. There are now 21 state RFRAs.[29] Most of these came soon after the Court restricted the federal law, but interest in them waned. Only three were enacted between 2003 and 2013. Courts have not been overzealous in accommodating religion. Religious claimants invoking the federal RFRA and RLUIPA usually lose—over 70% of the time, according to one study.[30] State courts have often construed state mini-RFRAs so narrowly that they sometimes have no effect at all.[31]

Even given this limited role for the courts, there are legitimate reasons to worry about the judiciary engaging in this kind of prudential balancing as a matter of constitutional right. Any answer the courts arrive at will depend on a prediction about the effects of accommodation—for example, whether it is safe to let Sikh boys carry ceremonial daggers in school, or whether Amish children are harmed by allowing them to miss two years of high school for religious reasons. Sometimes courts guess wrong. In the last years of the Vietnam war the Court broadened military exemptions, and the draft was so impaired that in its last year more men were exempted than were inducted.[32] If a prediction turns out to be mistaken, it will be hard for a court to say that the meaning of the Constitution has changed.

The regime that RFRA aimed to restore was one in which courts are instructed by legislatures to balance on a case-by-case basis, but the results that courts reach can be revisited and overridden by legislatures—and so it answers the concern about unaccountable judicial power that played such a prominent role in *Smith*. This result plays to the strengths of both courts and legislatures. Courts get to decide, in the first instance, what to do in concrete instances of hardship that the legislature probably did not anticipate, but the ultimate tough calls are governed by the political process. The result is not all that different from the common-law regimes that already govern property, contract, and tort, where courts craft rules in response to specific disputes, but legislatures have the last word.[33]

Thus, when the Court construed RFRA to accommodate a tiny South American sect's use of hallucinogenic tea, and so to create an exemption from federal drug laws, it observed that "there is no indication that Congress, in classifying [the hallucinogenic ingredient as a controlled substance], considered the harms posed by the particular use at issue here—the circumscribed, sacramental use of [that substance by this small religious group]."[34] It concluded that "Congress has determined that courts should strike sensible balances."[35] The Court appeared determined to do just what Congress had told it to do—restore the modest balancing test used in the pre-*Smith* free-exercise cases. (At least until *Hobby Lobby*. See chapter 6.)

State RFRAs have also done some good. In Kansas, Medicaid refused to pay for a bloodless liver transplant for a Jehovah's Witness, because the state did not reimburse out-of-state procedures and the only facility in the area capable of doing the procedure was in Omaha. The Kansas Court of Appeals decided that there was no state interest that could justify the burden on her religion. (In that case, judicial intervention wasn't enough. By the time the woman won her litigation, her medical condition had deteriorated to the point that she was no longer eligible for a transplant, and she died soon thereafter.) In Texas, a school system insisted on cutting the hair of a Native American boy. The burden on his Apache religious beliefs was justified by claims of hygiene and safety (that would have had no weight if he were a girl). The Fifth Circuit, relying on the Texas RFRA, was unpersuaded. Religious liberty was the only available remedy for these and similar idiocies.[36]

Liberals have plenty of reason to support the protection of religious liberty. Muslims are the object of pervasive, ignorant hatred, made worse by Trump's despicable propaganda. Absent religious liberty protections, many communities would have a free hand to manipulate zoning laws to bar the construction of mosques. Or consider prison cases, which generally involve grooming and clothing, diet, group worship, and access to literature. The common thread is the weakness of the prisons' reasons for resisting the prisoners' claims. The Supreme Court rejected a preposterous argument that Muslim prisoners could not be permitted to grow half inch beards because they might hide weapons in them.[37] Jewish prisoners are entitled to kosher food. Normally, prisons can invoke security to justify doing whatever they want, and courts defer to weak security rationales.[38] Absent a discourse of religious liberty, it is hard to see how one could smuggle into American law the notion that convicts are human beings with rights.

2

But now they denounce it as a mere excuse for bigotry

In September 2006, Vanessa Willock sent an email to a business called Elane Photography, asking it to photograph her wedding. She indicated that she and her partner were a same-sex couple. (Same-sex marriages were not then legally recognized in New Mexico, but that didn't stop same-sex couples from celebrating their unions.) She received an emailed refusal, which explained that company policy forbids photographing same-sex weddings.

The company's owner, Elaine Huguenin, later testified that facilitating such a ceremony is contrary to her religious beliefs. Her objection, and the objection of other conservative Christian wedding vendors, rests on their belief that marriage is inherently religious. Civil marriage, in this view, implements the underlying religious institution. Facilitating a same-sex marriage would thus be participating in a religious ritual that they reject, one that their own religion prohibits. They did not object to serving gay people. She and her husband, she said in her legal papers, would "gladly serve gays and lesbians—by, for example, providing them with portrait photography—whenever doing so would not require them to create expression conveying messages that conflict with their religious beliefs."[1]

Willock complained to the state Human Rights Commission, which noted that she "thought that Ms. Elaine Huguenin's response was an expression of hatred."[2] New Mexico law prohibits discrimination, on the basis of sexual orientation, by businesses that offer their services to the general public. The Commission concluded that Elane Photography had violated the Act, and required it to pay more than $6,000 in attorney's fees and costs. The district court granted summary judgment for Willock, the state Supreme Court affirmed, and the US Supreme Court declined to hear the case in 2014.[3]

This produced consternation among religious conservatives. "Today's actions by the Supreme Court may unfortunately embolden some to expand their efforts to punish and humiliate publicly those who believe marriage is defined only as one man and one woman," declared Jordan Lorence, senior counsel for the Alliance Defending Freedom, which represented the photographer.[4] "Gay rights trump religious rights," Fox News columnist Todd Starnes wrote after the ruling. "I believe militant gay rights groups . . . will start targeting pastors who preach against homosexuality. And I believe they will go after individuals who attend those kinds of churches."[5] "This ruling is more in the spirit of Nero Caesar than in the spirit of Thomas Jefferson," said Russell D. Moore, president of the Southern Baptist Ethics & Religious Liberty Commission. "The Supreme Court did the wrong thing, and our cherished American principle of soul freedom is the victim of their neglect."[6] Huguenin herself said, "If it becomes something where Christians are made to do these things by law in one state, or two, it's going to sweep across the whole United States . . . and religious freedom could become extinct."[7] She began receiving threatening, anonymous phone calls. One caller said he would burn her house down while she and her children were inside. She evidently is no longer in the photography business.[8]

The movement for state mini-RFRAs was by that time nearly quiescent. But in 2014, the year that the Supreme Court declined to hear her case, there was a new wave of legislative initiatives. They brought the present conflict into sharp focus.

Religious liberty was cited as early as 1992 as a reason for giving gay people no protection at all from discrimination. A Colorado ballot initiative that year amended the state constitution to prohibit any law against discrimination based on "homosexual, lesbian or bisexual orientation, conduct, practices or relationships." The amendment responded to laws in Denver, Boulder, and Aspen that barred discrimination based on sexual orientation. It did not entirely repeal those laws: heterosexuals were still protected, but one had a right under the amendment to discriminate against gay people any time for any reason.

One justification for the law was that the city ordinances may "compel some individuals to violate their private consciences or to face legal sanctions for failure to comply."[9] The Supreme Court did not deny that this was a legitimate purpose. The law, however, was overbroad in its response:

> The primary rationale the State offers for Amendment 2 is respect for other citizens' freedom of association, and in particular the liberties of landlords or employers who have personal or religious objections to homosexuality. Colorado also cites its interest in conserving resources to fight discrimination against other groups. The breadth of the Amendment is so far removed from these particular justifications that we find it impossible to credit them.

The singling out of gay people for extraordinarily disfavored treatment—the law "identifies persons by a single trait and then denies them protection across the board"—led the Court to invalidate it. The law "classifies homosexuals not to further a proper legislative end but to make them unequal to everyone else." A legitimate concern had produced a blunderbuss remedy. Not for the last time.

The prima facie case for a religious exemption is simple: the burden on Huguenin outweighs the burden on Willock. Willock had no difficulty finding another photographer in Albuquerque. (For this reason, most Americans' sentiments were on Huguenin's side, though since then they have shifted dramatically.[10]) Maggie Gallagher states the point succinctly:

> Small numbers of unusually devoted Christians are just trying to feed their kids. I do not see who is benefited really by putting them out of business. . . . It is abstract justice versus real concrete and unreasonable harm.[11]

That argument persuaded a number of state legislatures, which began to enact remedial legislation. But this time even mini-RFRAs became hard to pass.

The first legislative response was Kansas H.B. 2453, approved by the state House in February 2014.[12] It was a blanket license to discriminate against same-sex couples. Unlike the mini-RFRAs that had been previously enacted, there was no weighing of the burden on religious belief against the burden on the couples; the couples would lose every time. Moreover, if a religious defense were successfully made against a suit, the defendant would automatically collect attorney's fees from the plaintiff, even though the plaintiff might have had no notice at the time of the suit that religion was even an issue. The law was so broadly worded that it would have protected government employees who refuse to do their jobs if that involves providing services to a same-sex wedding (and this was before the Kim Davis episode, to be discussed). The bill was widely condemned, and the state Senate declined to take it up.[13]

A less extreme response, also in February 2014, was S.B. 1062, an amendment to Arizona's mini-RFRA. The state legislature sent it to the governor that month. It provided that religion should be eligible for accommodation not only in disputes with the state, but also in private lawsuits, "regardless of whether the government is a party to the proceeding."[14] That language was obviously a response to the *Elane Photography* court's holding that New Mexico's RFRA had no application in private disputes, so that it could never be asserted against an antidiscrimination law.

The statute did not guarantee that there would ever be a religious accommodation. In keeping with the normal RFRA standard, accommodation would be denied if this were necessary to a compelling state interest. Courts would have to decide that on a case by case basis. It is not clear that Elane Photography would have prevailed had this bill been the law. It merely would have prevented Elane from losing before trial. In states with religious accommodation laws, courts have not been generous in granting such accommodations, and some have construed the statutes so narrowly that they have little effect.[15]

The New York Times declared that the bill "sends the abhorrent message that respecting the civil rights of all people interferes with religious freedom."[16] "This bill instinctively struck people as a violation of individual liberty," said Ari Fleischer, who had been White House press secretary under President George W. Bush. "The notion that because of your orientation or your religion that you can be denied food service because of someone else's sincere religious belief went too far."[17] The bill quickly was denounced by former Republican presidential candidate Mitt Romney, Arizona's US Senators John McCain and Jeff Flake, and the Arizona Chamber of Commerce. The National Football League threatened to relocate the Super Bowl if the bill became law, and other large businesses, including Apple, American Airlines, and Intel, declared that they might withdraw from the state.

Governor Jan Brewer vetoed it.[18] She was also under pressure from the national Republican Party, which was hoping to emphasize economic issues in the midterm elections and thought that the gay rights issue would not help them.[19] The isolation of religious conservatives became clearer as their party abandoned them.

Mississippi enacted a mini-RFRA in April, 2014. The state offered no antidiscrimination protection of any kind to gay people, so it had no effect at all on that issue. It was entirely symbolic. (One city, Jackson, passed an antidiscrimination ordinance in 2016.)[20]

The law made no mention of suits between private parties.[21] As originally introduced, it included language providing such a defense, but this was deleted from the final version signed by the governor.[22] The change, which removed any mention of discrimination, did not keep the law from being denounced as an "anti-gay segregation bill."[23] Professors Ira Lupu and Robert Tuttle, for example, opposed the Mississippi mini-RFRA because "the Bill's combination of context, timing, and specific provisions will send a powerful message that religiously justified refusals to serve particular classes of customers are legally superior to any state or local prohibitions on invidious discrimination."[24] (A second, more specific law was passed in 2016. I'll discuss it in chapter 9.)

The Oregon Family Council sought to place on the November 2014 ballot an initiative that would excuse anyone from any penalty for facilitating a same-sex marriage ceremony in violation of their religious beliefs.[25] This was the most narrowly targeted provision to date. It clearly had no application to ongoing same-sex marriages. On the other hand, it would not have prevented the ugly surprise that Huguenin got when she contacted Elane Photography.

The sponsors unsuccessfully attempted to title the ballot without reference to licensing discrimination. Once they lost that fight in the state Supreme Court, they stopped gathering signatures for the initiative.[26]

In December, CBS claimed—in a news story, not an op-ed, though it would have been silly even there—that a proposed RFRA in Michigan would allow doctors and emergency medical technicians to refuse to provide lifesaving assistance to a gay person.[27]

March 2015 was a busy month for RFRA laws, with prominent fights in Arkansas, Georgia, Oklahoma, and above all Indiana.

In Georgia, a RFRA closely modeled on the federal law passed the Senate but stalled in a House committee after an amendment was added providing that the law would not be a defense against antidiscrimination laws.[28] Proponents had insisted that the bill had nothing to do with discrimination, but the bill's author protested that this amendment "would completely undercut the purpose of the bill."[29] The bill's opponents included former state Attorney General Michael Bowers, who in 1986 had successfully defended the state's prohibition of sodomy before the Supreme Court and had once fired an assistant attorney general for participating in a same-sex wedding.[30]

The issue of religious accommodation from antidiscrimination laws became a national phenomenon because of Indiana. That state passed a RFRA that was substantially similar to the one vetoed in Arizona, including the provision making it applicable to suits between private parties.[31] It also expressly allowed for-profit businesses to invoke it as a defense in such suits.[32] Amendments considered and rejected by the legislature would have made the law inapplicable to antidiscrimination and civil rights laws,[33] declared that the prevention of discrimination was a compelling state interest,[34] and required businesses to post signs telling the public about their religious objections before they could invoke the statute as a defense.[35]

The reaction against Indiana's law was the most intense of any to date. In protest against the law, thousands of businesses displayed window stickers announcing "This business serves everyone."[36] At least ten national conventions, including GenCon, the world's biggest gaming convention, threatened to pull out of the state, the NCAA president expressed doubts about keeping the organization's headquarters in Indianapolis, Angie's List canceled plans to add up to 1,000 jobs in the city, and the CEOs of Apple and Nike condemned the law.[37] "As the son of parents who survived the Holocaust (and the grandson of some who didn't)," Forbes columnist Ben Kepes wrote, "this feels very much like a prelude to another Kristallnacht."[38] Governor Mike Pence had been considering a bid for the Republican presidential nomination. The controversy ended that ambition,[39] leading him to the desperate gamble of joining what seemed to be Donald Trump's doomed quest for the presidency. Hillary Clinton, on the other hand, tweeted, "Sad this new Indiana law can happen in America today. We shouldn't discriminate against ppl bc of who they love."[40]

At one point during the controversy, a TV reporter walked into a pizzeria to ask the owners what they thought of the religious accommodation issue, and they naively indicated that they would not cater a gay wedding.[41] It was a silly question—weddings are rarely catered with pizza—and they should have refused to talk to him. They were then subjected to a flood of vituperation and one threat of arson, which led them to temporarily close the business and consider leaving the state.[42]

Governor Pence quickly responded that the bill would be amended to clarify that it did not protect discrimination.[43] The amendment was hastily enacted and signed into law.[44] There is still no statewide antidiscrimination protection for gay people in Indiana, however; it only exists in 11 municipalities within the state.[45]

In Oklahoma, in March 2015 a bill was introduced that would specifically allow religiously based refusals to provide wedding services. A requirement to post a sign was proposed as an amendment before the bill was withdrawn without a vote.[46]

Also in March 2015, the Arkansas legislature passed a bill that was, in various details, even more favorable to religious claimants than previous state laws had been, because the state's burden of justification was described in even more demanding terms than in earlier state RFRAs: instead of showing that the burden is necessary to a compelling state interest, the state would have to show that applying the burden "in this particular instance" is "essential" to that interest.[47] It was immediately condemned by prominent businesses, most notably Walmart, the largest employer in the state.[48] The negative reaction, coming on the heels of the uproar in Indiana, led the governor to demand that the bill be amended to delete the provisions that did not mirror earlier RFRAs.[49] The legislature passed the revised bill,[50] which the governor quickly signed.[51] Ironically, the modification appears to have distracted attention from a much more important antigay law enacted earlier, which barred municipalities from giving gay people any antidiscrimination protection at all.[52] So long as that law is on the books, gay people can get no antidiscrimination protection anywhere in Arkansas, with or without the RFRA. The criticism directed at the state aimed at the wrong target.

On April 28, 2015, *Obergefell v. Hodges*, considering whether the Constitution required recognition of same-sex marriages, was argued before the Supreme Court. Justice Alito asked, "in the Bob Jones case, the Court held that a college was not entitled to tax exempt status if it opposed interracial marriage or interracial dating. So would the same apply to a university or a college if it opposed same-sex marriage?" Solicitor General Donald Verrilli responded, "it's certainly going to be an issue. I don't deny that."

Alito was referring to *Bob Jones University v. United States*, a 1983 case in which the Supreme Court upheld the IRS's decision to deny tax exemption to a school that banned interracial dating or marriage. To be eligible for treatment as a charity, an institution "must demonstrably serve and be in harmony with the public interest," and its "purpose must not be so at odds with the common community conscience as to undermine any public benefit that might otherwise be conferred."[53] Several scholars had worried about the question Alito asked.[54] Others (including me) doubted that the fear was reasonable: "At least so long as large and historically important churches refuse to recognize gay marriages, it seems . . . unlikely that the executive branch in any jurisdiction would try to revoke tax exemptions over the issue."[55] The pressure on religious entities not to discriminate wasn't contingent on recognition of same-sex marriage. The *Elane Photography* case happened before same-sex marriage was legal in New Mexico. Verrilli conceded Alito's point too quickly, and the concession quickly created alarm among conservative religious groups.

Bob Jones itself is a doubtful decision. It entitles government to withhold public resources from dissenters. John Inazu is right: "When the government offers generally available resources (financial and otherwise) to facilitate a diversity of viewpoints and ideas, it should not limit those resources based on its own orthodoxy."[56] But whatever one thinks of this precedent, its applicability to conservative Christians does not depend on the same-sex marriage question. The shape of antidiscrimination law is a separate legislative question.

In June, the Court held that same-sex couples had a constitutional right to marry.

While that case was pending, Kim Davis, the county clerk for Rowan County, Kentucky, warned the legislature that she would be unwilling to have her name appear on same-sex couples' marriage licenses, and asked that the statute be amended so that her name was not required. No action was taken, and for ten weeks after the *Obergefell* decision her office stopped issuing any marriage licenses. Litigation ensued, and she was jailed for contempt of court. Presidential candidate Mike Huckabee declared that this amounted to "the criminalization of Christianity." Eventually, a deal was reached whereby her assistants would produce the licenses without her name on them. The governor later issued an executive order to remove clerks' names from state marriage licenses.

Davis was a particularly ill-chosen poster child for conservative Christians. Rod Dreher observed that the prominence of her case meant that

> the cause of religious liberty will become synonymous in the public's mind with a government official refusing to obey the law because it conflicts with her Christian beliefs. . . . Many people, even many conservatives who may well oppose *Obergefell*, and who care about religious liberty, hold it to be unreasonable to expect state officials to reserve the right to decide which of those laws they will enforce. The political danger here is that when the public hears "religious liberty," they will think about Kim Davis and her special pleading for a right that, if it existed, would mean anarchy.[57]

Even with marriage registrars, the question persists whether they can be accommodated when there is someone else in the office who can do the job. The British counterpart of Kim Davis was Lillian Ladele, a registrar in Islington who was unwilling to officiate the registry of same-sex civil partners. The city's council had other registrars who could easily have substituted for her. Instead it fired her. The courts took it as tautological that nondiscriminatory provision of service necessarily meant that Ladele could not be accommodated. Of course it meant nothing of the kind. The unwillingness even to consider accommodation was remarkable.[58]

The combination of the Indiana controversy and that of Kim Davis radically transformed the national understanding of religious liberty. There was a surge in news stories mentioning religion, homosexuality, and bigotry together.[59]

The wedding vendor cases have dominated the popular imagination, and they are the focus of this book. There are, however, other, less prominent controversies, which were well known in conservative Christian circles.

Catholic Charities of Boston ran the largest adoption service in Massachusetts, and had done so for years. It did not place children with same-sex couples, in violation of a state statute. Its request for an exemption was rejected, and it shut down the service. There were similar closings of adoption services in Illinois and the District of Columbia. A quarter of the unrelated domestic adoptions in the United States are handled by private providers, many of them faith-based.[60] None has a monopoly of adoptions in its area.

The Christian Legal Society has chapters at 165 law schools throughout the United States. Its bylaws require members to refrain from any sexual activity outside of heterosexual marriage. Numerous universities have withheld recognition and funding from the organization because of this policy.

Christian schools themselves are endangered.

Gordon College, a conservative Christian school in Massachusetts, requires its students, faculty, and staff to agree to a code of conduct that bars sexual relations outside marriage and any homosexual practice. The school was threatened with the loss of its accreditation because of sexual orientation discrimination. The city of Salem cancelled a contract that allowed the college to help maintain the city's Old Town Hall, and that city's Peabody-Essex Museum also cut ties with the school. It retained its accreditation after a year-long review, but the issue is likely to arise again. Other conservative Christian colleges, which often have student ethics codes that ban sexual activity outside of heterosexual marriage, are likewise concerned about loss of tax exemption and accreditation, with which some of them have been threatened.[61]

California nearly enacted a statute that would have barred education funding to colleges that discriminate against LGBT students. "Discrimination" was defined to include schools with a code of conduct that prohibited any sexual activity outside of heterosexual marriage. Those codes are never enforced, but simply having them would foreclose funding. The schools could be sued if students were denied married student housing, dorms, or bathrooms consistent with their gender identities, or otherwise subject to rules of conduct that singled out their sexuality or identity. The provision was dropped after the schools objected.[62]

Marriage counselors, social workers, and psychologists may be denied licenses if they refuse to facilitate same-sex partnerships. Several social work schools have claimed that a person who cannot provide relationship counseling to any couple does not meet professional standards.[63] It is not necessary for every social worker to be willing to counsel gay couples, just as it is not necessary for every doctor to be willing to perform abortions. But these cases tended to be seen through the lens of Kim Davis: like her, these people were refusing to do their jobs.

The pattern was frightening. If conservative Christians conscientiously could not facilitate same-sex marriage, that "might well mean that they could not own and operate a large business or university, or work as a physician, pharmacist, wedding photographer, or landlord."[64]

Why do they get so worked up over what happens to such a tiny number of them? It isn't just about that tiny number. It is about the status of all of them.

The culture wars of the 1980s were especially fraught for gay people because they concerned whether they had any legitimate role in American society. Today conservative Christians are in the same position. The stakes for them are more personal than they were before.

It is because they felt threatened that they felt the need to turn to a strong protector. Even if he wasn't much of a Christian.

3

Worsening the divisions that helped elect Trump

Culture wars issues, such as religious accommodations from antidiscrimination laws, are an important reason for the country's political polarization. They have led the Left to regard conservative Christians as bigots whose votes are not worth seeking, and those Christians to regard the Left as an existential threat. The consequence is that a crucial part of the progressive coalition is split, creating the opportunity for a cruel authoritarian politics that was once unimaginable. The damage transcends politics: it threatens to give us a Trumpian Christianity.

White evangelicals are more than a quarter of the electorate. Yet Hillary Clinton made no effort to pursue their support. She got the votes of only 16% of them, the lowest of any Democratic presidential nominee in American history.

Michael Wear explains the consequence:

Though the national breakdown of the white evangelical vote and their percentage of the electorate were almost identical to 2012, there were some major differences in key battleground states. If Clinton had received Barack Obama's 2012 percentage of the white evangelical vote in Michigan (where she is currently losing by about 12,000 votes), she would have received more than 125,000 additional votes. In Florida, she would have received about 141,000 more votes, surpassing Trump's margin of victory in that state. Even in Ohio, if the evangelical breakdown of the vote between Clinton and Trump matched that between Obama and Romney, the margin of Trump's victory would have closed by more than 275,000 votes—much more than half of Trump's total margin. This story is replicated in states across the nation.[1]

She was similarly dismissive of Catholics. Her campaign chose not to send her to a St. Patrick's Day parade because, according to a news report, "white Catholics were not the audience she needed to spend time reaching out to."[2] She was the first Democratic candidate to lose the Catholic vote since John Kerry in 2004.

Her campaign was notably tone deaf to conservative Christian concerns. Clinton's first speech after the convention was at a Planned Parenthood event. This, Stephen Mansfield observes, "was guaranteed to distance religious conservatives, many of whom were uncertain about Trump and a portion of whom might have responded to a lean in their direction by Clinton."[3] As late as 2007, she repeated her husband's declaration that abortion should be "safe, legal, and rare." She dropped the "rare" and it played no part in her 2016 presidential campaign.[4] She called for the repeal of the Hyde Amendment, which barred public funding of abortions.

Some issues must divide us. Abortion, for instance. The abortion rate in fact had plunged during Obama's presidency, primarily because of a drop in the number of unintended pregnancies—something that all sides should celebrate. Yet Clinton did not want to say so, since that would imply that there was something wrong with abortion. The issue, made more salient by the Supreme Court seat left vacant by the death of Antonin Scalia, was a powerful mobilizing force for Republicans. She could have blunted it by showing some sympathy for their views.

Clinton grew up in a very religious Methodist family. As a Senator, she often invoked her faith. Responding to a repressive immigration bill: "It is certainly not in keeping with my understanding of the Scriptures. This bill would literally criminalize the Good Samaritan— and probably even Jesus himself." After John Kerry lost the presidency: "No one can read the New Testament of our Bible without realizing that Jesus had a lot more to say about how we treat the poor than most of the issues that were talked about in this election."[5] She is a member of the very large religious left, a group that is often ignored by the press and by activists on both sides.

Yet at the beginning of the 2016 campaign season, Clinton was perceived by 43% of Americans as having no religion at all.[6] Trump was able to say in June 2016, "We don't know anything about Hillary in terms of religion. Now, she's been in the public eye for years and years, and yet there's nothing out there."[7] That claim was easy to refute, yet little effort was made to refute it.

During the 2008 primaries, candidate Barack Obama gave an interview to the evangelical magazine *Christianity Today*. He spoke about his conversion, his longtime church membership, and his belief in "the redemptive death and resurrection of Jesus Christ." He said abortion should be less common and that "those who diminish the moral elements of the decision aren't expressing the full reality of it."[8] In 2016, the magazine repeatedly sought an interview with Clinton, who never responded.[9] She never gave a speech to evangelicals or met with evangelical leaders.

In his 2008 interview, Obama said:

> I think that there's been a set of habits of thinking about the interaction between evangelicals and Democrats that we have to change. Democrats haven't shown up. Evangelicals have come to believe often times that Democrats are anti-faith. Part of my job in this campaign, something that I started doing well before this campaign, was to make sure I was showing up and reaching out and sharing my faith experience with people who share that faith.

Clinton never showed up.

This isn't only about her. The entire Democratic Party is increasingly uninterested in the religious, regarding them as not worth reaching out to. They are the enemy. What could we have to say to *them*?

Rhetoric has always been attacked as a kind of dishonest manipulation. But in fact it is best understood as the enterprise of understanding one's audience and tailoring one's message in order to help them to perceive what is in fact true and right.[10] It thus has a moral dimension. The practice of rhetoric forces one to try to understand the deepest concerns of one's fellow citizens, and to respond to those concerns.

Too many liberals are profoundly ignorant of their rhetorical opportunities. Wear, who was White House director of evangelical outreach, recalls working with the 2012 Obama re-election campaign on a document aimed at people of faith. He headed one section, "Economic Fairness and the Least of These." A staffer deleted "least of these." Wear tried to restore it, eliciting the comment, "Is this a typo? It doesn't make any sense to me. Who/what are 'these'?"[11]

In the Book of Matthew, Jesus declares that on the day of judgment,

> "Then the King will say to those on his right, 'Come, you who are blessed by my Father; take your inheritance, the kingdom prepared for you since the creation of the world. For I was hungry and you gave me something to eat, I was thirsty and you gave me something to drink, I was a stranger and you invited me in, I needed clothes and you clothed me, I was sick and you looked after me, I was in prison and you came to visit me.'
>
> "Then the righteous will answer him, 'Lord, when did we see you hungry and feed you, or thirsty and give you something to drink? When did we see you a stranger and invite you in, or needing clothes and clothe you? When did we see you sick or in prison and go to visit you?'
>
> "The King will reply, 'Truly I tell you, whatever you did for one of the least of these brothers and sisters of mine, you did for me.'"[12]

The staffer evidently knew nothing of one of Jesus's best-known teachings, a phrase that Obama himself had used repeatedly.

There was no reason to concede the conservative Christian vote to a man who claimed to be religious but said he had never found any reason to ask God's forgiveness.

Trump's message was that Christians needed to suspend their moral compunctions about him (and his flagrantly authoritarian policy proposals) because they were endangered. When evangelicals of all races who voted for Trump were asked the most important reason for their vote, religious liberty was tied for the third most frequent answer (11%), ahead of limiting abortion, taxes, or LGBT rights, and behind only the economy and immigration. Among white evangelicals, both supporters and opponents of Trump, religious liberty was the fourth most frequent answer, slightly below national security, but again above abortion, taxes, or gay rights.[13]

The narrative of danger has long been a part of white evangelicals' identity. They actually think that in the contemporary United States, they face more discrimination than Muslims.[14] This helps to explain why, in the Republican primaries, they rejected their coreligionists in favor of someone who promised to be a tough guy, and then remained loyal to him even after he was caught on tape admitting to sexually abusing women.[15] "There is an assault on Christianity. . . . There is an assault on everything we stand for, and we're going to stop the assault."[16] Only the ruthless use of political power could save them: "We're going to protect Christianity, and I can say that. I don't have to be politically correct."[17] Politically correct he wasn't. To focus on one issue that got remarkably little attention, he embraced child murder as an instrument of policy. "When you get these terrorists, you have to take out their families," Trump said in 2015. He later asked the CIA why it waited until a terror target's family left a building before launching a drone missile strike against him.[18] Evangelicals continue to embrace Trump. Most of them were untroubled when his administration started seizing migrant children (including nursing infants) from their parents.[19] What mattered was that he responded to Christian grievances and reliably rewarded them for their political support.

This is a degrading spectacle. It makes Christians look like fools and hypocrites, and if it persists it will make them worse than that. Religion does not simply shape partisanship. Political partisanship sometimes shapes religious identity.[20] Loyalty to Trumpism is generating a new form of Christianity: unapologetically racist; indifferent to the habitability of the planet we leave to our children; gleeful about mass incarceration; despising the poor, the weak, the sick, the stranger and the foreigner.

They feel they have no choice. This time they really have something to be afraid of. The Democrats are committed to the idea that they are bigots whose beliefs need to be eradicated. So they end up acting politically with all the high principle of agribusinesses pursuing subsidies. David French observes: "The true tragedy of Evangelical support for Trump is that a group of Americans who have a higher call on their lives—and faith in a far greater power than any president—now behave (with notable exceptions) exactly like simply another American interest group."[21] The collective exercise of the franchise is necessarily inarticulate. It cannot generate a specific common will. But it does a fine job of registering pain. The overwhelming evangelical vote for Trump should be viewed in this light.

One may object that the growing Republican share of the evangelical vote has little to do with religious liberty issues, and is the product of the same racial anxiety that was the key to Trump's success with other Republican voters. Most white evangelicals regard immigration as a threat and say that America becoming a majority-nonwhite nation by 2045 will have a mostly negative effect on the country.[22] When asked what one issue they considered most important when voting, most cited the economy and national security. Only 10% said "Supreme Court nominees," 7% said "religious freedom," and a mere 4% said "abortion."[23]

On the other hand, these are the majority, not the entirety, of evangelicals. Those who waver will not be turned away from Trumpism by people who denounce them as bigots. They need to be offered an alternative vision of an America that has a legitimate place for them. That is not only an imperative of political strategy. It is necessary if Americans are going to have a common life together. Polarization and alienation are threats to the entire country, not just the Democratic Party.

Wear observes that because each side aimed only at mobilizing its own base, "in the 2016 presidential election, the morning after the vote half of the country was inevitably going to wake up feeling like they no longer had a place in their own country."[24] This type of political strategy is not only a recipe for electoral disaster. It poisons American political life.

Religious polarization is a distinctive aspect of contemporary American politics. In the 2016 presidential election, 56% of those attending church weekly or more voted for Trump, compared with 31% of those who never attend services.[25] That pattern has persisted for years.[26] The gay rights issue has played an important role in generating and sustaining the divide.

The proportion of Americans who report having no religious preference—statisticians call them the "nones"—has steadily risen, from 8.2% in 1990 (which had been its level for almost 20 years) to 14.1% in 2001, to 15.0% in 2008. By 2014, it had risen to 23%, including

35% of Millennials (those born between 1981 and 1996).[27] In 2018–2019 it was 26%.[28] About 27% of Americans do not expect a religious funeral.[29]

They aren't atheists. Among the "nones," 61% believe in God or a universal spirit; 37% pray at least once a month.[30] Eighteen percent describe themselves as "religious," and 37% as "spiritual but not religious."[31] More than half believe in life after death, about a third believe in heaven and hell, and 93% sometimes pray.

One study concludes that the newer "nones" are mostly "unchurched believers" who declare no religious preference in an effort to express their distance from the Religious Right.[32] When asked why they are nonreligious, about half say they dislike the positions churches take on social and political issues.[33]

Overwhelmingly, they vote for Democrats.[34] This is one face of American polarization: the sum of evangelicals plus the religiously unaffiliated was 30% of the population in 1973, but rose to 41% by 2008.[35]

Robert Putnam and David Campbell explain how this happened. The liberalization of sexual mores in the 1960s mobilized religious conservatives against the change, and they soon aligned with the Republican Party. From the 1980s on, "conservative politics became the most visible aspect of religion in America."[36] This produced a counterbacklash, especially among those who came of age in the 1990s.

Attitudes toward homosexuality closely track attitudes toward religion. Those with gay-friendly views "are more than twice as likely to be religious nones as their statistically similar peers who are conservative on homosexuality."[37] Almost half (48%) of LGBT Americans say they have no religious affiliation.[38] The gay rights issue is similarly potent for the other side. Among evangelical Protestants, 36% think homosexuality should be accepted, compared with 83% of the nones.[39] One widely publicized focus group study finds that American evangelicals feel a sense of deep cultural loss, centrally focused on homosexuality, which they regard as the harbinger of a culture that marginalizes and despises them.[40]

Alexis de Tocqueville observed in 1835 that anticlericalism had arisen in Europe because religion had become identified with a conservative politics. In America, on the other hand, religion was powerful precisely because it was not associated with any party. Modern secular Americans, like nineteenth-century secular Frenchmen, "attack Christians more as political than as religious enemies."[41]

The culture wars damaged the Christian brand. In 1990, 86% of American adults identified as Christian. In 2007 it was 78%, in 2018–2019, 65%.[42]

Conservative Christians feel besieged. A growing percentage of evangelicals say that it is becoming harder to be an evangelical Christian in the United States.[43] Almost half of Americans—and three quarters of Republicans, white Evangelical Protestants, and Trump supporters—say discrimination against Christians is as big a problem as discrimination against blacks and other minorities.[44]

As the gay rights movement consolidates its victories, the heat of this conflict could abate. The next generation of evangelicals will be far more accepting of the movement's claims.[45] But the identification of religion with bigotry isn't helping.

This battle offers the Left a satisfying narrative of the rationalists against the superstitious idiots. But it isn't true, and it has a political price.

At least in the United States, the alignment of religiosity with conservatism only began in the late 1970s. Before then, religion was a politically cross-cutting category.

The deepest roots of antislavery thought were religious. The Quakers and John Wesley condemned slavery just as Voltaire, Hobbes, Locke, and Montesquieu were devising clever new justifications for it.[46] The Second Great Awakening led courts to relax their rigid protection of vested property rights, allowing new morals laws to destroy the economic value of breweries and lotteries. Thus began the living constitutionalism that was the basis of the Supreme Court's decision to protect same-sex marriage.[47]

The Social Gospel movement of the late nineteenth century fought alcoholism, sweatshops, decaying tenements, business monopolies, and foreign wars. Without that movement and the influence of Catholic communitarianism, there would have been no New Deal: Catholics were as crucial a part of Roosevelt's coalition as evangelicals were of Reagan's.[48] The civil rights movement originated in African American churches. It was Martin Luther King Jr.'s adversaries who argued that religion had no place in politics.[49] In the 1960s, religious groups swung left, not only on civil rights but also the Vietnam war.[50] Liberal churches were an important part of the movement for same-sex marriage.[51] And, as already noted, there continues to be a large, but often neglected, religious left.

America is a religious country, and the American Left has never accomplished anything without religious allies. The most important historical effect of politically mobilized religion in American public life is the abolition of slavery. To the extent that it is motivated by resistance to political conservatism, militant atheism mistakes an historical blip for a permanent feature of the political world.

Religious people sometimes support legislation based on inarticulable moral intuitions, which grow out of their more general sense of the meaning of life. So do the nonreligious. Modern secularism, Charles Taylor has shown, began when medieval clerics started to worry about tensions between Christian benevolence and Christian doctrines and practices. It remains, in large part, a mutated form of Christianity. Intense concern about human suffering does not automatically emerge in the human psyche when religion is subtracted.[52]

We all have core convictions, and most of us are not moral philosophers. Either it's acceptable to legislate on the basis of these moral hunches or it isn't. Secularists and religious believers are in the same boat.

Those who regard religion as the enemy tend to be curiously unreflective about the basis of their moral commitments. Thus Sam Harris, the bestselling of the "new atheist" authors, after denouncing a few passages in the Bible that tolerate slavery (the abolition of which was unimaginable at the time it was written), explains that you don't need religion to deal with this issue:

> The moment a person recognizes that slaves are human beings like himself, enjoying the same capacity for suffering and happiness, he will understand that it is patently evil to own them and treat them like farm equipment. It is remarkably easy for a person to arrive at this epiphany.[53]

Aside from the naivete of the reference to "epiphany," this is remarkably blind anthropology. Slave-owners always understood that their slaves were human beings like themselves. That's what they liked about slavery. Orlando Patterson's comparative study found that in many slave societies, the principle function of slavery is not economic, but giving the masters people to bully and abuse. "The real sweetness of mastery for the slaveholder lay not immediately in profit, but in the lightening of the soul that comes with the realization that at one's feet is another human creature who lives and breathes only for one's self, as a surrogate for one's power, as a living embodiment of one's manhood and honor."[54] Harris's view of human nature is daffily optimistic: "Once you stop swaddling the reality of the world's suffering in religious fantasies, you will feel in your bones just how precious life is—and, indeed, how unfortunate it is that millions of human beings suffer the most harrowing abridgements of their happiness for no good reason at all."[55] No. A lot of people feel in their bones the pleasure of dominating others. Harris is feeling something other than human nature. He has been socialized into a tradition. And he doesn't know it.[56]

Consider one of the bitterest divisions in contemporary politics, the question of how, or even whether, the state ought to respond to the growing economic insecurity of the bottom half of the population. The Catholic Church has definite ideas about property: "Man should regard the external things that he legitimately possesses not only as his own but also as common in the sense that they should be able to benefit not only him but also others."[57] "If one is in extreme necessity, he has the right to procure for himself what he needs out of the riches of others."[58]

Churchgoing Trump voters part with him on some crucial issues. They have more favorable feelings toward African Americans, Hispanics, Asians, Jews, Muslims, and immigrants than nonreligious Trump voters. They care more about racial equality (67% versus 49%) and reducing poverty (42% versus 23%). Nonreligious white Trump voters are about three times as likely as churchgoing ones to say their white racial identity is "extremely important" to them (26% vs. 9%). The more often Trump voters attended church, the more favorable were their views on racial minorities, trade, and immigration.[59]

The Republican Party's growing, extreme libertarianism creates an enormous potential fault line, if only Democrats can exploit it. But culture wars issues, of which gay rights is among the most salient, keep them from seeing the possibility of common ground.

House Speaker Paul Ryan said that Ayn Rand's work is "the reason I got involved in public service," and he gave his staff copies of her didactic novel *Atlas Shrugged*.[60] John Galt's 56-page speech at the end of *Atlas Shrugged* declares that any redistribution of income benefits only "the weakling, the fool, the rotter, the liar, the failure, the coward, the fraud."[61] Rand's attitude toward the weak was nicely summarized in 1957 by her disciple, Alan Greenspan, later Federal Reserve chairman: "Parasites who persistently avoid either purpose or reason perish as they should."[62] (Ryan has said that as a Christian he repudiates her atheism. It is this pitiless contempt for the weak, not atheism, that is Rand's deepest inconsistency with Christianity.)

If Christianity has a core ethic, it is that it sides with the oppressed against the oppressor, with the weak against the strong. Its alliance with the present, Randian Republican Party is therefore unstable. The Left's hostility to religious conservatives is its indispensable mainstay.

4

Discrimination law can
tolerate exceptions

Although you might think that the gay rights movement has triumphed, being gay in contemporary America still has its inconveniences. Among these are a persistent worry about being beaten to death. The rate of violence against gay and transsexual people has risen in recent years. There is a murder every week, often with mutilation of the victim. Violence against gays frequently involves torture. The coordinator of one hospital's victim assistance program reported that "attacks against gay men were the most heinous and brutal I encountered."[1]

This is the tip of a large iceberg. According to Gordon Allport's classic study of prejudice, patterns of behavior rejecting out-groups form a continuum, from verbal denunciation (what Allport calls "antilocution"), to avoidance, to discrimination, to physical attack, to organized extermination. The milder forms of prejudice are the most common: "Most people are content to express their hostility verbally to their own friends and never go further. Some, however, reach the stage of active discrimination. A few take part in vandalism, riots, lynchings."[2] When violence does occur, it "is always an outgrowth of milder states of mind. Although most barking (antilocution) does not lead to biting, yet there is never a bite without previous barking."[3] The perpetrators of hate violence are predominantly young males, who are distinguished from their elders primarily in that they "have a thinner layer of socialized habit between impulses and their release."[4] Others, however, are likely to manifest similar attitudes in other, more socially acceptable ways. "Any negative attitude tends somehow, somewhere, to express itself in action. Few people keep their antipathies entirely to themselves. The more intense the attitude, the more likely it is to result in vigorously hostile action."[5] The violence is powerful evidence of a broader range of forms of mistreatment that are harder to detect.

Gay people still remember a huge range of other indignities, including being hunted down by police, driven out of their jobs, involuntarily committed to mental institutions, and lobotomized. These activities reached their peak in the 1950s. When one counts America's misdeeds, the antigay panic should take its rightful place beside the genocide of Native Americans, slavery, Jim Crow, and the internment of Japanese Americans. Many of these abuses were justified by citing morality and religion.[6]

Discrimination persists. Here is a summary of more than a thousand reports to gay rights organization helplines:

> Ranging from humiliating harassment to outright service denials, the reports describe discrimination by pharmacies, hospitals, dental offices, and other medical settings; professional accounting services, automobile dealerships and repair shops, gas stations, convenience stores, restaurants, bars, hotels and other lodging; barber shops and beauty salons; stores such as big box retailers, discount stores, pet stores, clothing stores, and toy stores; swimming pools and gyms; libraries and homeless shelters; and transportation services including busses, taxis, ride-shares, trains, air travel, and cruise ships. Discrimination reports included contexts with limited alternate options, such as by tow truck drivers, post office employees, and repair service technicians working in the homes of LGBT customers.[7]

There are stories of patients harassed in hospitals, parents turned away when they bring injured children for medical care, taxis ejecting passengers on the side of highways at night, couples thrown out of restaurants for minor displays of affection, a steady drumbeat of abuse. Discrimination is common enough that there is a genre of "gay-friendly guides" to goods and services, much like *The Negro Motorist Green Book*, which, before the Civil Rights Act of 1964, identified establishments that would serve black customers.

That's why antidiscrimination law is necessary.[8]

Religious opponents of antidiscrimination protection for gay people haven't confronted this evidence. Instead, they focus on the burdens that such laws would impose on *them*. A statement by more than 75 religious leaders, entitled "Preserve Freedom, Reject Coercion," opposes all legislative protection for sexual orientation because of its impact on religious liberty. It claims that those burdened are "people who serve everyone, regardless of sexual orientation or gender identity, but who cannot promote messages . . . that contradict their beliefs."[9] There is no acknowledgment that gay people are ever mistreated. Ryan Anderson similarly claims that antidiscrimination protections for gay people "seek to regulate decisions that are best handled by private actors without government interference," and asserts without evidence that "American business seldom discriminates based on sexual orientation."[10]

Twenty-one states and the District of Columbia have statutes prohibiting discrimination on the basis of sexual orientation. Such laws were first enacted in 1977. There have been no new ones since 2008.[11] Three states—Arkansas, North Carolina, and Tennessee—prohibit local municipalities from protecting LGBT people from discrimination.

The notion that gay people don't suffer discrimination is silly. The interesting question is whether, if the law forbids such discrimination, its purposes will be thwarted if religious exemptions are granted. In order to determine that, we need to consider what those purposes are.[12]

Antidiscrimination law is an exception to ordinary common law principles of property, contract, and freedom of association. Let's consider again the proto-liberalism of John Locke. The fundamental classical liberal rights, Locke observes, are those of bodily integrity, property and contract: "The business of Laws is not to provide for the Truth of Opinions, but for the Safety and Security of the Commonwealth and of every particular man's Goods and Person."[13] If they are respected, then conflict—and religious conflict in particular—is easy to avoid. If all associations must be based on mutual agreement, then in religious matters, "no man will have a Legislator imposed upon him, but whom himself has chosen."[14] Those who find one another's presence unendurable can stay apart. Discrimination thus facilitates peace and prosperity. Occasionally we will discover that our fellow citizens hold views we regard as loathsome, but that discovery is not the kind of injury that law needs to remedy.

Antidiscrimination law is inconsistent with these principles, which is why some libertarians (who tend to be neo-Lockean extremists) find it repugnant.[15] It is nonetheless justified by certain special conditions, patterns of exclusion with such deep cultural roots that the market is unlikely to remedy them.[16] In such cases, it is appropriate to create legal rights against discrimination. That is why the Civil Rights Act of 1964 was necessary, and why gay people should now be protected against discrimination. But notice that these legal rights are based, not on individual injury, but on the aggregate effects of the prohibited conduct.[17]

I've been arguing for years against doctrinaire libertarianism.[18] But any case for antidiscrimination law needs to take the libertarian position seriously enough to answer it.

Libertarians who address this issue tend to undermine their own credibility by overstating their case, rigidly opposing any protection against discrimination as an intolerable intrusion on liberty.[19] What they offer is, however, the appropriate baseline for regulation. Most of the time, property and markets ameliorate inequality and make everyone better off. Sometimes they fail. Antidiscrimination law is a response to market failure.

The 2016 US Commission on Civil Rights report, *Peaceful Coexistence*,[20] treats discrimination as the functional equivalent of a physical attack on the person:

> Civil rights protections ensuring nondiscrimination, as embodied in the Constitution, laws, and policies, are of preeminent importance in American jurisprudence. . . . Religious exemptions . . . significantly infringe upon these civil rights. . . . The First Amendment's Establishment Clause constricts the ability of government actors to curtail private citizens' rights to the protections of nondiscrimination laws and policies.[21]

Metaphors of violence do a lot of work in the various statements of the commissioners:

> Nondiscrimination laws stand as a bulwark against the assaults of intolerance and animus.[22]

Religious liberty was never intended to give one religion dominion over others, or a veto power over the civil rights and civil liberties of others. However, today, as in the past, religion is being used as both a weapon and a shield by those seeking to deny others equality.[23]

The First Amendment is a shield that ensures a diversity of religious views are allowed to flourish in the U.S. However, there are some seeking to make the right to exercise their religion a sword that can be used against others who do not conform with their interpretation of their faith.[24]

It is, however, confusing to treat discrimination as though it were an act of violence against the person. Law tolerates idiosyncratic discrimination, even unfair idiosyncratic discrimination, because in a free market it affects no one's life chances. (It may be insulting for me to refuse to hire anyone with large earlobes, but free speech protects insults.)

Pervasive prejudice is different. When black people traveled in the deep South before the Civil Rights Act, they had to pack food, because they could not be sure that any restaurant would serve them. They carried the *Green Book*. They could not be sure of finding shelter, bathrooms, or fuel. The market didn't fix that.

Even libertarians ought to endorse the project of transforming culture to eradicate the notion that some classes of persons are beings of an inferior order who have no rights. Such prejudices have typically meant that the law couldn't even be relied upon to protect their minimal entitlement to security of person and property. African Americans were lynched; violence against women was casually tolerated; police regarded assaults on gay people with indifference and sometimes perpetrated it themselves. A guarantee of Lockean rights demands a culture that respects those rights.[25]

Antidiscrimination law is an intervention that aims at systemic effects in society, dismantling long-standing structures of dominance and subordination. That overall aim involves the pursuit of a number of subsidiary goals.

The most basic of antidiscrimination law's purposes is the amelioration of economic inequality. A central purpose of the Civil Rights Act
of 1964 was to reduce black poverty, by making well-paying positions
available to black workers. It succeeded. In 1964, the median income of
nonwhite males was 57% of median white male income.[26] By 1985, that
proportion had risen to 66%.[27] The proportion of black men working
as professionals or managers relative to whites rose from 32% to 64%.[28]
The most dramatic progress came in the first ten years after the Act.[29]
Discrimination in public accommodations presented similar barriers.

The general rule that governs business transactions, both public
accommodation and employment, is contract at will. In many states,
most businesses have the privilege of refusing service to anyone for
any reason or no reason.[30] They need not justify these actions to any
official.

Antidiscrimination laws, such as the Civil Rights Act, are exceptions.
So long as an economic actor does not engage in the enumerated types
of discrimination, she has the privilege of being as arbitrary as she
likes. I can, for example, absolutely refuse to hire or do business with
anyone whose eyebrows are not at least three inches long.

It is important to understand the reasons for the rule of contract
at will, so that we can understand what we are doing when we depart
from that rule. One traditional justification is rights-based: people
have a right, it is sometimes said, to do what they like with their private
property. The bankruptcy of this claim became clear during the debate
over the Civil Rights Act of 1964, which then-presidential candidate
Barry Goldwater opposed on libertarian grounds.[31] The Civil Rights
Act is not an invasion of our precious liberties. On the contrary, it
diminishes the amount of oppression in the world. The idea of private
property is not as sacrosanct as it once was, because it is understood
that the uses of that property can have public effects that are legitimate
objects of legislative concern.[32] Even Goldwater eventually abandoned
the libertarian argument and supported antidiscrimination protection
for gay people.[33]

The more persuasive justification for the rule of employment at will
is efficiency-based. It would be a crushing burden on the economy
for government officials to have to approve every refusal of a contract
that takes place in the private sector. Moreover, there is little reason

to think that most types of arbitrary refusal can have much effect on anyone's opportunities. Although I may refuse to hire anyone whose eyebrows are less than three inches long, other employers will compete for the services of the short-eyebrowed, and so will bid their wages up to pretty much the same level that they would have been if I had been willing to hire them. And the market will also punish me for my foolishly discriminatory hiring practices, since competent short-eyebrowed workers will go to work for my competitors. My taste for discrimination means that I am turning away better workers and hiring worse ones. I will be similarly punished if I arbitrarily turn away customers. The overall tendency is for people like me to be driven out of the market.

Considerations of this sort led Richard Epstein to argue that the Civil Rights Act ought to be repealed, because it interfered with freedom of contract for no good reason.[34] In a free market, he argued, we can expect that blacks' wages (for instance) will be about as high as they would be if there were no discrimination.[35] Epstein did not persuade many people. The point most commonly made by his critics was that he had left culture out of his model. When the Civil Rights Act was enacted, his critics argued, racism was sufficiently ubiquitous and unapologetic to withstand the egalitarian tendencies of a well-functioning free market.[36]

Markets can fail in many ways. Prejudice is only one of them. Consider the curious case of discrimination on the basis of credit scores. There is no evidence that credit scores are a reliable indicator of job performance. But credit agencies marketed their product to employers, and a lot of employers bought it. In the age of the internet, delivering the information that the bureaus possess costs them essentially nothing, so they could provide this product at a low price. Credit checks were used by fewer than one in five employers in 1996. A majority was using them by 2010. Many people then found that because of poor credit scores, they couldn't get a job anywhere. Several state legislatures responded with statutes banning the use of credit scores in most jobs.[37]

The response to Epstein turns on the ubiquity of the discrimination that is at issue. Economic equality can be achieved even if there is discrimination, indeed even if there is a lot of discrimination, so long as the discriminators are a minor part of the market as a whole. (Sometimes they dominate the market. That's the part Epstein misses.) On the other hand, if the accommodation has the effect of being a free pass for any discriminator, and is frequently invoked, then the antidiscrimination law is effectively repealed.

That leads to the fear that any exception will become the rule. *Slate* columnist Mark Joseph Stern predicts that if there is any religious accommodation, "inevitably, it will soon stretch to restaurants, hotels, movie theaters—in short, to all facets of public life. A religious right to discriminate against gay people will lead directly to anti-gay segregation."[38]

But those who pursue exemptions are not asking for a general right to discriminate. The exemptions from public accommodation law they have pursued have arisen almost exclusively in the context of weddings. Conservative Christians do not believe that same-sex couples should not get ordinary goods and services. But they regard weddings as religious rituals, and they are unwilling to personally facilitate weddings they regard as immoral.

Some think that any accommodation presupposes a libertarian baseline in which businesses have a right to discriminate.[39] But if that were true, there would be no antidiscrimination law and so no claim for exemption. The exemption claim arises in a context in which most of the market is bound by the antidiscrimination norm.

Given that baseline, exceptions won't defeat the law. The 1968 Fair Housing Act includes the so-called Mrs. Murphy exemption, excusing dwellings with four or fewer units if the owner lives in one of the units.[40] Vice President Hubert Humphrey explained why it was there: "The relationships involved in such situations are clearly and unmistakably of a much closer and more personal nature than in the case of major commercial establishments."[41]

The provision of services to weddings is a fragmented and competitive industry. Consider retail bakeries.

In 2016, there were 6,756 retail bakeries (some with multiple locations) in the U.S. with $5.16 billion in collective sales. These retail bakeries tend to be small businesses; the average sales per retail bakery was $764,491. . . . "The retail side of the [baking] industry is highly fragmented: the 50 largest companies generate about 20% of revenue, and the typical company operates just one facility." Barriers to entry are virtually non-existent, ensuring rapid response to any exclusion. Estimates of startup costs for retail bakeries range from $2,000 to $5,000 on the low end to $10,000 to $50,000 on the high end.[42]

If such exemptions are rare, and there are plenty of other suppliers, then they can't do much harm to anyone.

One may respond that there are places in the country where a lot of businesses would assert an exemption. Those are precisely the places where discrimination against gay people is ubiquitous. One lesbian couple living outside Nashville, Tennessee reports that when one of them became pregnant, they were turned down by every midwife in the area. They were excluded from birthing classes because, they were told, other couples would not accept them. Their son was rejected by the childcare facility that his friends attended.[43] Stories like this one show that any accommodation should be narrowly drawn. A right to refuse to participate in a religious ceremony mustn't expand into a general right to discriminate.

Probably none of those places now have antidiscrimination protection for gay people, but a federal antidiscrimination law may eventually be enacted. A religious exemption could encourage the formation of new centers of resistance to the gay rights movement. It is even possible to envision a nightmare cascade scenario in which, once the accommodation is made available, its invocation becomes a sign of social solidarity, like the anticommunist blacklist in the 1950s or the Confederate flag in parts of the deep South today. Such a cascade would resuscitate attitudes that otherwise would have continued to steadily disappear.

There is no way to prove that this will not happen. If posting a notice will trigger an exemption, there will inevitably be more notices than there are now. The question is whether there will be enough of them to matter. The salience of the wedding vendor cases, in which otherwise decent people conspicuously face the loss of their livelihoods for doing what they think is right, threatens a different kind of cascade. Nathan Oman observes that "legally punishing religiously motivated conduct is likely to make it more, rather than less, salient for religious believers, as it plays into well-established narratives of religious persecution by the state."[44] Any prediction will necessarily be contestable. But that is a fact about religious exemptions generally.

Any religious accommodation rests in part on a bet that it will not be invoked so often as to defeat the purpose of the law. In this context, however, social attitudes toward gay people have changed so decisively that the trend appears irreversible. The kind of cascade just described would immediately be checked by the very negative reactions of openly gay people, their family members, and growing numbers of sympathizers. Businesses have a powerful economic incentive to avoid controversy rather than conspicuously take a side. That is true even in the places where antigay discrimination is ubiquitous.

One way of preventing the cascade, if it is regarded as a serious danger, might be to make the accommodations available only to businesses that were in existence at the time that the antidiscrimination law was enacted. A baker who specializes in wedding cakes might reasonably claim unfair surprise when he is told that he will lose his investment unless he serves same-sex couples, and so might reasonably ask to be "grandfathered." Once the law is in place, however, those who contemplate starting new businesses are generally expected to know the laws that apply to them.[45]

If we're talking about probabilities, it's worth noting that in 29 states, there is no law against discrimination on the basis of sexual orientation. The impossibility of compromise over religious accommodation is an obstacle to the enactment of such laws. It is hard to see how protection-plus-exemptions could be worse than no protection at all.

Look at the trends. In 1997, 27% of Americans supported same-sex marriage. In 2017 it was 64%.[46] Among Americans aged 18 to 29, in 2016 it was 83%.[47] It is only 34% of white evangelical Protestants, but even in that group, opposition has plunged from 71% in 2013 to 58% in 2017. Of white evangelicals aged 18 to 29, a majority—53%—are in favor. Majorities in every state, 69% of Americans overall, think LGBT people should be protected from discrimination in jobs, public accommodations, and housing.[48] In Alabama it is 58%.[49] Specific protection from LGBT employment discrimination is supported by 92%.[50] Among Americans who oppose same-sex marriage, 49% favor and 45% oppose such protection.[51] Four out of five Americans incorrectly believe that federal law already prohibits refusing to hire someone because of their sexual orientation.[52] In 2017, 63% of Americans thought that homosexual sex is morally acceptable, compared with 40% in 2001.[53] In short, there is a cultural cascade taking place, but it is in the opposite direction.[54]

Antidiscrimination law has a second, deeper purpose. It aims to reshape culture in order to eliminate patterns of stigma and prejudice that constitute some classes of persons as inferior members of society. This aspect of law is often unremarked, but it is indispensable if basic rights are to be guaranteed. Prejudice, if it is sufficiently deeply ingrained in a society, will prevent the state from even providing reliable police protection, a phenomenon that remains all too familiar to gay people in the United States.

One goal of antidiscrimination protection of gay people is cultural transformation: to stigmatize stigma, and make the pertinent prejudice into something that citizens instinctively reject.[55] The central triumph of the gay rights movement has been the spreading of that ethic across society, so that prejudice against gays is despised in the same way as racism.

That project of social reconstruction has multiple facets. It aims to reshape the beliefs and values that are shared by the members of the society; the practices that are constructed by (and, reciprocally, construct) those beliefs; and the distribution of wealth and power that emerges out of those practices. Thus, for example, the project of racial equality seeks to culturally marginalize the notion that African Americans are intrinsically inferior and unworthy. The consequences of that idea are also part of the evil to be eliminated, not only because of their intrinsic perniciousness, but also because they reproduce the idea itself. The desperate condition of huge numbers of black citizens would be a great evil for anyone, but the racial patterns, which reproduce themselves for generations, make the situation both more politically intractable and worse in itself. The injury of poverty is compounded by the insult of racism. Thus, the law of racial equality seeks to eliminate racial meanings, such as the belief that blacks are intrinsically inferior to whites; racially significant practices, such as school segregation and job discrimination; and racially tainted distribution, such as the existence of a large black underclass. Antidiscrimination law has an important role to play in this enterprise, but it takes its sense and purpose from the larger context in which it operates.[56]

The most sophisticated critiques of religious exemptions for heterosexist religion understand that the primary purpose of antidiscrimination law is to transform cultural mores. They fear that accommodation will impair that purpose.

Reva Siegel and Douglas NeJaime argue that while ordinarily religious scruples can be accommodated, allowing an exemption here would reinforce prejudice and defeat the purpose of the law.[57] Those who seek exemptions are not merely making "a simple claim to withdraw, conceding a new consensus in favor of same-sex marriage while preserving space for faith groups to maintain their religious views."[58] The exemption claims are "part of a long-term effort to shape community-wide norms."[59] Robert Post similarly argues against exemption "precisely because these claims derive so directly and obviously from the contemporary political arena. . . . When the faithful claim the right to exemptions as a means to undo in law what they have failed to achieve in politics, the stakes are the democratic process itself."[60]

The conflict between the norms of the religious dissenters and those of the majority is not peculiar to this conflict. It is present in any exemption case that involves a religion that makes universalizing moral claims. The Quaker conscientious objectors, for instance, did not seek merely to withdraw from military activity. They preached that military activity is always immoral. Their claim was not that Quakers must not kill. It was that nobody should ever kill anyone else.

Post is right: "Exceptions to the law can become neither routine nor commonplace without undermining the law's own force and authority."[61] But then the objection to accommodation depends on the contingent prediction that exemptions will overwhelm the law. The same prediction must be considered in any exemption case.

It's true that we're abandoning the opportunity to treat those who hold these views as outcasts. But that's what religious toleration is.

Louise Melling argues that exemptions for religious objectors "put the imprimatur of the state on an exclusion that stigmatizes."[62] Melissa Murray thinks that the state would be "deputizing private actors to express the kind of disapprobation and discrimination that the state itself is now unable to express."[63] But it depends on the description under which the exemption is offered. Property owners are allowed to exclude people from their land for discriminatory reasons, and that isn't seen as having the state's imprimatur. In the earliest recorded case of a judicially crafted religious accommodation, a Catholic priest was excused from having to divulge to the court what he had learned in confession, but the court emphasized that it was not endorsing Catholicism.[64] The state doesn't endorse minority religions when it accommodates them. They remain minority religions.

Both of these purposes of antidiscrimination law—opening economic opportunities and stigmatizing prejudice—are aggregative. The occasional exception will not impair them. On the other hand, as we've seen, discrimination is sometimes seen as an injury against the person. The Civil Rights Commission regards it as a kind of violence. There obviously can be no accommodation if discrimination is thus understood.

What kind of injury is this, though?

The injuries that law protects against generally have nothing to do with the kind of social engineering that antidiscrimination law attempts. The law of torts generally deals with remedies when one person hurts another. Its aim is to remedy that, to force the injurer to compensate his victim. It is about justice between these two people, not social or economic policy.[65] In the usual tort case, A has done something that would have harmed B if they were the only two people in the world.

Discrimination, however, does not fit easily into this common-sense understanding. Turning away a customer is not like breaking his leg. In refusing to deal, I make you no worse off than you would be if I had never been born. The normal rule of law in business and employment, once more, is contract at will: businesses have the right to refuse service to unwelcome customers, and employers may refuse to hire for any reason or no reason. Antidiscrimination law is an exception to that rule, created in response to circumstances that demand this peculiar kind of legal intervention.

The tort of discrimination makes no sense outside of a social context in which some particular group has been systemically wronged.[66] It is social engineering all the way down.[67] When this has not been understood, antidiscrimination law has sometimes been distorted at the core. Its ends are thereby frustrated more radically than they ever could be by occasional exemption. The wrong of racial discrimination, for example, comes to be seen as a kind of damage to the souls of white people when they act with impure hearts. Black unemployment, low incomes, de facto segregated schools, substandard housing, and disproportionate incarceration all disappear from view, because they are not the consequence of intentional discrimination by identifiable wrongdoers. Racial injustice becomes invisible.[68]

Imagining discrimination as if it were a bop on the head thus threatens to entrench the very inequalities the Left seeks to combat. It tends to imagine discrimination to be the conduct of a few bad actors rather than a structural wrong that demands structural remedies. If discrimination is fundamentally a harm to individuals, then group inequalities don't matter unless they are intended. Those inequalities, not individual acts of discrimination, are however the real evil that the law aims to remedy. Absent those inequalities, individual acts of discrimination would be mere refusals to deal, of a kind that are routine in a free market.

Three responses to this difficulty, defending the idea of discrimination as an individual injury, have been offered. One is to focus on the harms of face-to-face discrimination. A second is to say that the open display of discriminatory ideas is itself such a harm. And a third is to argue that the existence of discrimination anywhere damages the full citizenship of the group that is discriminated against. All of them have been characterized as "dignitary harm," but they are different kinds of injury.

Begin with the wrong of being personally turned away. Taylor Flynn argues that each individual act of discrimination constitutes "status-based harm to personhood."[69] Even if discrimination is rare, it still hurts. "When a same-sex couple is denied service," Ira Lupu and Robert Tuttle write, "the couple must absorb the full burden of such a denial—measured in the time and other expense incurred in locating a willing provider, along with the dignitary harm of being refused access to services that are otherwise available to the public."[70] A considerable literature documents the effects of "minority stress" on the well-being of people who experience discrimination, which has found that it can have a severe impact on gay people's mental and even physical health.[71] Doubtless a major component of that stress is the anticipation that one is in danger of losing real and important economic opportunities, and, as I've already argued, the degree of that danger is in dispute here. But the insult is itself a source of stress.

The availability of alternative providers does not cure this kind of harm. The Senate Commerce Committee report on the Civil Rights Act of 1964 observed:

> The primary purpose of . . . [the Civil Rights Act], then, is to solve this problem, the deprivation of personal dignity that surely accompanies denials of equal access to public establishments. Discrimination is not simply dollars and cents, hamburgers and movies; it is the humiliation, frustration, and embarrassment that a person must surely feel when he is told that he is unacceptable as a member of the public because of his race or color.[72]

The customer is induced, by a business that held itself out to the public and so invited her to contact it, to have this rejection be part of her experience of preparing for her wedding. The indignity here is much like what religious conservatives object to when they are asked to participate in the celebration of same-sex unions. It is a ritual that they are unwilling to participate in.

Bruce Ackerman has argued that the core of what public accommodations law prohibits is the "face-to-face insult in which the victim acquiesces in the effort to impugn his standing as a minimally competent actor within a particular sphere of life."[73] The humiliation of discrimination occurs "against the background premise of shared social competence." It "is institutionalized by social practices that strip an entire group of this ongoing presumption." Putting someone in this position "is wrong in itself, regardless of the psychological or economic consequences."[74]

That direct, personal insult is more wounding than the mere knowledge that there are people out there who do not want to deal with you. The anticipation that it could happen is yet another distinctive injury. "The question," Joseph Singer observes, "is not whether one can find a store willing to let you in and treat you with dignity. *The question is whether one has a right to enter stores without worrying about such things.*"[75]

There is an individual injury here, although, unlike physical assault, it is the cumulative effect of multiple episodes that would not mean much if they were never repeated. The expectation of possible discrimination is itself exhausting. It "results in a state of heightened vigilance and changes in behavior, which in itself can trigger stress responses— that is, even the anticipation of discrimination is sufficient to cause people to become stressed."[76] Apprehension about probable future threats can produce an increase in physical pain, and in fact perceived discrimination is correlated with chronic pain. The mechanisms are understood. Anxiety is "negative affect based on apprehension about anticipated future threats that have uncertain outcomes." This produces "hypervigilance" that "can result in neuro-biological changes that can result in hyperalgesia (increased sensitivity to pain)." This may be evolutionarily adaptive, because "heightened pain sensitivity allows potential threats to be detected more readily."[77]

Fear is one of the basic emotions. The mechanism of its arousal is based in the brain stem, a part of the neurological system we share with reptiles. The anxiety that is triggered can preoccupy a person long after the danger has disappeared. This is the most fundamental reason why threats are not protected speech.[78] The most destructive effect of discrimination is not the harm of the individual discriminatory acts, but the atmosphere of fear and stress that is the daily experience of those who are, at random and unpredictable times, its victims.

This is why it will not do to simply say that there are plenty of other bakers and photographers. The harm is not ameliorated because the injury does not invariably occur. The uncertainty is itself a harm.

The law should prevent such ambushes, and even the reasonable anticipation of such ambushes. But that does not preclude exemptions. It simply means that exemptions can only be granted under certain conditions, conditions that prevent the harm in question.

The approach I'll suggest here, and discuss in more detail in chapter 9, is to require those who seek exemptions to warn potential customers about the vendor's religious compunctions.

In the wedding photographer case, the New Mexico Supreme Court declared that "businesses retain their First Amendment rights to express their religious or political beliefs. They may, for example, post a disclaimer on their website or in their studio advertising that they oppose same-sex marriage but that they comply with applicable antidiscrimination laws."[79] A notice of refusal could be comparably brief: "We believe that marriage is exclusively a relationship between one man and one woman, and will not provide services for same-sex weddings. Please do not ask us to violate our religious beliefs."[80]

Few businesses would be willing to make such an announcement, which would keep other customers away. These then will be the vendors who have the strongest sincere religious compunctions, intense enough that they are willing to bear significant costs for what they believe. There are unlikely to be many of them.

The proposal to allow discrimination with prior notice raises concern about a second kind of dignitary harm, that associated with the notice itself. Just as a "Whites Only" sign does not make the discrimination nicer, so, Taylor Flynn objects, this would be "iconic of second-class citizenship."[81] She fears "a cascading effect that encourages additional claims for exemption as well as other acts of discrimination. Seeing the equivalent of 'no gays served here' affixed throughout town, all with the permission of the state, may spur further acts of discrimination or violence."[82] Justice Kennedy, in *Masterpiece Cakeshop*, thought it unacceptable that "all purveyors of goods and services who object to gay marriages for moral and religious reasons in effect be allowed to put up signs saying 'no goods or services will be sold if they will be used for gay marriages,' something that would impose a serious stigma on gay persons."

This objection runs into familiar free speech concerns. Free speech includes the right to say things that nobody should ever say to anyone. It protects insults, including the most vicious ones.[83] Religious diversity is relevant here: many religions include in their basic creed insulting denunciations of rival creeds.

Of course, the fact that speech is protected does not mean that the law should tolerate conditions likely to bring that speech into existence. But this concern also fails to account for ongoing cultural change. The likelihood of Flynn's scenario is quickly evaporating. At the time she wrote, just a few years ago, she could accurately report that "majority opposition to equal marriage is the nationwide norm."[84] Since that time, that opposition has collapsed, and a growing majority supports same-sex marriage. Reflect on the fact that this is the conversation we are having. The conservative claim has shifted from "stop same-sex marriage" to "let us retreat into our enclaves and be left alone."

A third formulation of the idea of dignitary harm is that one's full membership in society is placed in doubt when discrimination is allowed anywhere, even if one never confronts it oneself.

The writers who have described this harm most carefully have noted that it is based on a background norm of nondiscrimination in commerce. Joseph Singer writes:

> Our constitutional structure distinguishes between areas of social and political life where groups are presumptively entitled to be exclusionary (such as religion or political associations) and areas of life where access without regard to race or other caste designations is presumptively prohibited—and the main area of life to which the equal access norm applies is the parts of the economy that are open to the general public.[85]

From this it follows that there is a "right not to experience the humiliation of being turned away from a place open to all others because of characteristics about oneself that should be irrelevant to the opportunity to buy a shirt in a store."[86]

What same-sex couples seek, Elizabeth Sepper argues, is "universal recognition of their equal status as married or marrying." Were exemptions granted, "third-party recognition would no longer be automatic." Exemption "accordingly brands same-sex couples as second-class citizens."[87] Ira Lupu develops a similar argument:

> Their actual and perceived status as being married, with the identical social, moral, and legal force as different sex couples, is of profound

significance to their sense of equal citizenship. For a vendor, employer, or public official to discriminate against them with respect to their wedding or marital status is a deep assault on their full and equal place in American society.

It follows that "forcing [the vendors] to alter their policies, or to leave the relevant market, is the least restrictive means of furthering the compelling governmental interest of equal dignity for LGBT people."[88]

The argument depends on an account of the semantic meaning of refusal, and of the background norm it violates. More than that: it presumes a degree of cultural homogeneity sufficient for everyone to agree on what is being said. Sometimes the significance of an action is universally obvious. Any claim that segregated schools were not degrading to black children was so patently dishonest as to invite laughter: as one white Southerner wrote at the time, "it never occurred to anyone, white or colored, to question its meaning."[89]

The significance of the wedding vendors' refusals to serve, on the other hand, are objects of reasonable contestation. The violation of norms of citizenship depends on a shared understanding of those norms.[90] The vendors and their supporters don't believe that citizenship is at stake. Michael McConnell, for example, finds such refusals unremarkable: "It is a common feature of American life for people to refuse to do business with those with whom they have moral or ideological disagreements."[91] He cites, for example, the boycotts of Indiana and North Carolina after they enacted laws unfriendly to LGBT people. Russell D. Moore, president of the Southern Baptist Ethics & Religious Liberty Commission, similarly declared that Bruce Springsteen's decision to cancel performances in North Carolina to protest that state's transgender bathroom law was an exercise of the same right that the vendors are asserting.[92] Probably many gay people agree. They find the vendors' compunctions irritating, but shrug them off and move on.

Here I return to the point that antidiscrimination law is an intervention into culture. It vindicates equal citizenship by stigmatizing discrimination as evil and unclean. That is happening, and will continue to happen, whether or not there are exemptions. For law to declare that the bakers are attacking others' citizenship (whose, precisely, if gay people stay away?) is a distinctive intervention. That understanding of the meaning of such refusals is, however, not universally perceived.

Lupu argues that exemption proponents' failure to understand that citizenship is at stake is "spectacularly tone-deaf and insulting." The unwilling vendors "represent a continuing and profound insult to those whom they refuse to serve. Why they do not have a crisis of conscience about delivering that blow is a puzzle to me."[93] He is right about the significance of the refusals, to a large part of their audience. But it competes with a different meaning, the one that looms largest for the wedding vendors: the refusal to participate in a religious ritual that one repudiates.

My own view, for whatever it is worth, is that citizenship is not so fragile. It is jeopardized when discrimination is everywhere. It is not at risk if discrimination is anywhere.

Any legal resolution of this contestation about meanings will impose an interpretation on some who don't perceive it. Sometimes that is necessary, but there are costs. Drawing an exceptionless line at public accommodations means that it is the Christian wedding vendors who must acquiesce in their humiliation in face-to-face encounters. Ackerman notes "the importance of preserving spheres of private life reserved for free choices that seem arbitrary, and even despicable, to the citizenry at large. But over the course of the twentieth century, it has become increasingly apparent that only some kinds of private property are sites of truly personal relationships."[94] The line must be drawn with attention to "the real-world meanings Americans encounter as they move from sphere to sphere in everyday life."[95] There is no reason to exclude the meanings that the Christian wedding vendors perceive in their business activity. This controversy has made clear that some people perceive such religious significance in their business activity that they are willing to endure large pecuniary losses rather than do what they think is wrong. That real-world meaning should influence where we draw the line.

Singer is right that "we must define the parts of social life where we allow owners to exclude based on religion, political views and affiliation, or other associational interests, from the parts of social life where we require owners to open their property to anyone who is willing and able to seek their services in a non-disruptive manner." In jurisdictions with strong public accommodations laws, one might infer, as Singer does, that "stores that sell their wares to the public, which are not religious establishments, are firmly on the public side of the line."[96] On the other hand, such laws rarely require merchants to welcome all comers. Singer is right that the state could impose a general access policy on them. In most places it doesn't. Most public accommodations laws ban only certain categories of discrimination, leaving vendors free to reject customers for any other reason, however arbitrary.

Nathan Oman observes that the condemnation of discrimination sometimes presupposes "that ideally markets ought to embody the values associated with liberal democracy so that powerful market institutions should be treated as closely analogous to government institutions."[97] On that view, one should have the same rights in dealing with private businesses that one has in dealing with city hall. That idea sacrifices one of the great virtues of markets in a diverse society, that they facilitate peaceful cooperation among people who radically disagree about fundamental values. The ease of refusal to deal is part of what makes that work: gains from trade are available only if one can persuade counterparties, with whom one may otherwise have almost nothing in common, to freely agree to trade. The market thus stimulates, not only competition, but empathy. One must understand the desires of strangers well enough to attract their business, and transactions require the continuing unforced consent of those who participate.[98] Markets "cannot be made to instantiate the norms of deep, moral recognition or equality . . . without eroding their value as a sphere in which contestation over such deep political and moral concerns is muted."[99]

Antidiscrimination law is a limited intervention into markets in which, as a general matter, refusals to deal are permissible, commonplace, and devoid of public significance. The intervention is appropriate, but that is because the market is failing here to facilitate cooperation among diverse groups, not because people have a general nondiscrimination obligation.

If that intervention is worth doing at all, it must not be easily defeated by exemptions. Accommodation is thus acceptable here only if the nondiscrimination rule is adjusted in a limited and definite way, and the objecting wedding vendors are encysted in an economic niche that is clearly distinct from the norm. It would help if such an exemption were itself narrowly confined, for example only to the facilitation of wedding ceremonies. (That could be done by statute, but not by judicial declaration based on some abstract constitutional principle, which can't draw the lines in a definite and predictable way.) That would answer both sides' slippery-slope concerns, and (especially if coupled with a public announcement requirement) it would also help to ensure that exemptions would be rare enough to have little effect on anyone's access to goods and services. A liminal space between public and private is not unheard of: churches often have their doors wide open, inviting anyone to enter and hear their harsh and intolerant teachings.[100]

If the aim of antidiscrimination law is to guarantee full citizenship to everyone, then it is relevant that because of the uncompromising interpretation of that law that is now prevalent, conservative Christians may not be able to be wedding vendors, counselors, social workers, or psychologists, they may not be able to control the content or staffing of their educational institutions, and various other agencies face the denial of funding. Citizenship is at stake on both sides. The more general purport of this strict interpretation of the law is to feed the demonization of conservative Christians, officially assimilating them with racists as people who have intolerable views. If the law aims to end institutionalized humiliation, then this move is counterproductive.

One may object that this chapter's claims are inconsistent: there is a lot of discrimination against gay people, enough to warrant antidiscrimination protection, but I claim that if religious exemptions are offered, there won't be many takers. How can both of these things be true?

First of all, legislative accommodations can by their terms be narrowly restricted. For example, one could grant them only to wedding vendors, whose complicity claims are the strongest, who work in fragmented and competitive industries, and whose businesses tend to be small.

Far more than in the Jim Crow South, alternative vendors are available. The injuries of antigay discrimination are not the absolute unavailability of goods and services, or even the difficulty of finding them (the *Green Book* situation), but the anticipation and pain of rejection. That can be prevented without denying all accommodation.

In the deep South in 1964, black travelers seeking food and shelter could anticipate being rejected by almost all of the establishments they might visit. They faced a united front, backed by violence. The trick was finding any services at all, which was what the *Green Book* was for. The situation is not comparable for gay people today even in the most hostile regions. The poll data from Alabama and Mississippi suggest that even those places are deeply fragmented: people who support antidiscrimination protection for gays are, at least, less likely themselves to discriminate. And that means that in those places, openly discriminating has a cost. "Whites only" signs were good for business then. "We don't do gay weddings," not so much. There may be rural pockets where this is not true, and where such signs will proliferate. Should that defeat any possibility of exemption?

When evaluating any legislative proposal, you need to compare it, not with an ideal state of the universe, but with the world as it exists before the legislation. In the places with the worst discrimination against gay people, right now there is no legislative protection. None. If any is to be enacted, it will probably have to include some religious accommodation. Today's politics are such that no such accommodation is thinkable. In the states with the worst discrimination, gay rights advocates should not be defenders of the status quo.

5
Free speech principles are barely relevant

Thus far we've been considering this conflict through the lens of religious liberty. But there is another argument on behalf of the wedding vendors, thus far neglected: that they are protected by the right to free speech. This was presented to the Supreme Court in 2018 in *Masterpiece Cakeshop v. Colorado.*

This is, however, not a plausible solution to our problem. Free speech arguments can be stretched to protect some wedding vendors, but will arbitrarily favor them over other equally worthy claims. The argument will protect businesses that produce material that is generally expressive, such as wedding photographers. Others with equally pressing conscience claims, however, can't be shoehorned into this category. Bakers are among the losers. Food preparation is not conventionally an expressive medium, whatever particular bakers may intend.

In *Masterpiece Cakeshop*, a bewildering proliferation of free speech claims were made on behalf of a baker who would not sell a wedding cake to a same-sex couple. For our purposes this is useful, because the briefs in this case pretty much exhaust all the free speech arguments that could be made. The lawyers were thorough. Here we will sort them out.

There's a lot of confusion, some of it intentional, over what that case was about. Here are the basic facts. Charlie Craig and David Mullins visited the Masterpiece bakery and looked through a photo album of custom-designed cakes. When the owner, Jack Phillips, greeted them, they told him (according to his own testimony) that they "wanted a wedding cake for 'our wedding.'" Phillips told them that he did not create wedding cakes for same-sex weddings. They left immediately without discussing any details of their proposed wedding cake. The entire exchange lasted 20 seconds. Craig and Mullins then sued Phillips for violating Colorado's antidiscrimination statute. Phillips claimed that he was protected by freedom of speech and freedom of religion.

To clarify the issues, it helps to contrast *Masterpiece Cakeshop* with a case that was pending simultaneously in the United Kingdom Supreme Court. Asher's Bakery in Belfast, Northern Ireland, refused on religious grounds to make a cake iced with the slogan "Support Gay Marriage in 2014." It was sued for discrimination. The bakers testified, and the trial court accepted, that they would have supplied the cake if there had been no message and that they would have refused to produce the message even if the customer had been heterosexual. The court nonetheless found that refusing to write words supporting same-sex marriage was itself discrimination based on sexual orientation. The Northern Ireland Court of Appeals thinks you can commit antigay discrimination *against a heterosexual customer* by refusing to produce a message supporting same-sex marriage. (Britain's Supreme Court ultimately overturned that decision.)

This is a bizarre interpretation of antidiscrimination law. It also would clearly violate the First Amendment if it were adopted by any jurisdiction in the United States.[1] One cannot be compelled to say what one does not believe. The Supreme Court so held in 1943, when it decided that children could not be required to say the Pledge of Allegiance: "If there is any fixed star in our constitutional constellation, it is that no official, high or petty, can prescribe what shall be orthodox in politics, nationalism, religion, or other matters of opinion or force citizens to confess by word or act their faith therein."[2] The Court has since explained that a person cannot be compelled to be "an instrument for fostering public adherence to an ideological point of view he finds unacceptable." When the state does that, it "invades the sphere of intellect and spirit which it is the purpose of the First Amendment to our Constitution to reserve from all official control."[3]

But this was not the issue in *Masterpiece Cakeshop*. Unlike Northern Ireland, Colorado did not tell Phillips what words he must put on his cake. It merely told him that if he sells any products to heterosexual couples, he must sell the same products to same-sex couples. He is free to refuse to write "Support Gay Marriage" on any cakes that he sells, so long as he refuses that to both gay and heterosexual customers.

Much of the argument on behalf of Phillips mischaracterized the facts to make his case look more like *Ashers Bakery*. He cited evidence that Craig and Mullins wanted a "rainbow-layered" cake. "Given the rainbow's status as the preeminent symbol of gay pride, Craig and Mullins's wedding cake undeniably expressed support for same-sex marriage."

Phillips had no idea what they were going to ask for. He refused service before he found out anything about what Craig and Mullins wanted to buy. The arguments on his behalf—which have since been expanded into a general free speech argument on behalf of dissenting wedding vendors—were a series of elaborate pirouettes around this inconvenient fact.

The brief for Phillips most directly addressed the problem this way: "When he heard [that the cake was for a same-sex wedding], Phillips immediately knew that any wedding cake he would design for them would express messages about their union that he could not in good conscience communicate." The conduct of baking a cake has a conventional meaning. It expresses the celebration of a union. So the law was forcing him to express a message with which he disagrees.

The Supreme Court came close to embracing this kind of logic in *Boy Scouts of America v. Dale*, which declared in 2000 that forbidding the Boy Scouts to expel a gay scoutmaster "would, at the very least, force the organization to send a message, both to the youth members and the world, that the Boy Scouts accepts homosexual conduct as a legitimate form of behavior." The Court's extension of the compelled-speech doctrine in this offhand sentence, from the use of words to behavior that is meaningful to some audience, has absurd implications. Federal regulations now require cars to have airbags. The federal government adopted these regulations despite the resistance of automobile manufacturers. When new cars conspicuously have airbags, this is reasonably understood as sending a message that airbags are necessary to make cars safe and that their inclusion is cost-justified. The car manufacturer may dissent from that message, but does the company have an argument that its First Amendment rights are being violated by requiring airbags? Although the Court could reinvigorate the principle it stated in the Boy Scout case, the consequence would be anarchy. It would allow anyone to violate any law if obeying it would conventionally be taken to convey a message with which the objector disagrees.[4]

The compelled speech doctrine means that a person may not be required to personally generate words with which he disagrees.[5] That would arguably demand an exception to Colorado's antidiscrimination law if a baker were asked to write the words "God Bless This Wedding" on a cake for a same-sex wedding. In that narrow case, he would be constitutionally entitled to decline to sell a same-sex couple the exact same cake that he would produce for a heterosexual couple (and, for whatever it is worth, he would have the same right to refuse an interracial or Muslim couple). But that is no help with the more pertinent case of the unmarked wedding cake.

Even if one embraces the anarchical principle that one may refuse to engage in conduct that has a conventionally understood semantic meaning, this is no help to Phillips. The conventions aren't the ones he needs. One doesn't ordinarily think that a professionally made cake conveys any message from its paid preparer.

He also claimed that the state was discriminating on the basis of viewpoint because the antidiscrimination law, as applied, "favors cake artists who support same-sex marriage over those like Phillips who do not." He cited the case of William Jack, who had requested that several Colorado bakers create cakes decorated with biblical verses and images that condemned homosexuality. Each baker refused, and Jack unsuccessfully claimed religious discrimination: the cakes reflected his religious beliefs, and so rejecting the cakes discriminated against those beliefs. The Colorado courts rejected the claim. The discrimination here was not on the basis of religion, because the bakers would not sell these cakes to anyone. The law makes no reference at all to viewpoint. It just prohibits discrimination. It is true that the law favors those who oppose the conduct it prohibits over those who would like to engage in it. But that is true of *every* law.

Similarly with his religious freedom claim. That claim was a desperation move: after its 1990 decision in *Smith*, the Court has no authority to carve out religious exceptions to state laws. On the other hand, states must not discriminate against religion. Phillips claims that because bakers who support same-sex marriage have been permitted to refuse to make cakes quoting Biblical passages condemning homo-sexuality, the law "applies different rules to all expressive professionals depending on their views about same-sex marriage: supporters get a pass, but opponents get punished." But this again confuses the facts of *Masterpiece* with those of *Asher's Bakery*. Phillips never found out what message (if any) he might be asked to convey. Two law professors, Thomas Berg and Douglas Laycock, tried to defend the claim of reli-gious discrimination in somewhat different terms: "The conscience of bakers who support same-sex marriage, or refuse to oppose same-sex marriage, is protected. The conscience of bakers who object to same-sex marriage is not protected."[6] But this same description is available for any legal regulation that generates a conscientious objection. The existence of the objection does not make the law discriminatory.

Phillips made yet another claim of bad motive: because Craig and Mullins easily found another baker, they must have been illicitly motivated by the desire to punish him for his ideas. But even if this were true (how could he know that?), the questionable motives of a plaintiff aren't relevant to adjudication. If you negligently ding my car and I sue you, the court won't care that I'm motivated by racism or other vicious motives. Even if the plaintiffs in some of these cases are trying to compel affirmation of what the Christian merchants do not believe, this has nothing to do with their legal claim.

Other arguments in Phillips's brief framed his case more narrowly. Phillips's business is not just a bakery, but "an art gallery of cakes." He "has been an artist using cake as his canvas with Masterpiece as his studio." "The cake, which serves as the iconic centerpiece of the mar-riage celebration, announces through Phillips's voice that a marriage has occurred and should be celebrated. The government can no more force Phillips to speak those messages with his lips than to express them through his art."

The argument here is that *custom* cake decoration is inherently ex-pressive. According to this argument, the result should be different if Craig and Mullins had requested a premade cake.

Here again the facts intrude. Phillips had said in his adver-tising: "Couples may select from one of our unique creations that are on display in the store, or they may request that I design and create something entirely different." When he denied service to the couple, he had no idea which choice they would have made. Evidently, he deems "customized" the production to order of cakes that he has previously designed. When he had his very brief conversation with Craig and Mullins, they were looking at a book of such designs. Would the identical cake be "customized" if Phillips baked it in the afternoon, knowing what it would be used for, but not "customized" if had been made in the morning, before they walked into the store?

If "customization" means unique work made to order, many kinds of work are customized. Auto repair is unique work made to order. If the wedding limousine has engine trouble, would a mechanic have a First Amendment right to refuse service? How about a caterer? A hairdresser?

His artistic freedom argument was similar to one that had been developed in the earlier *Elane Photography* case, on behalf of a wedding photographer, by professors Eugene Volokh and Dale Carpenter: "If the government may not suppress photographs, it may not compel their distribution or display, either."[7] The application of public accommodations law to the photographer, they argued, unconstitutionally compels her to speak. "A writer must have the First Amendment right to choose which speech he creates, notwithstanding any state law to the contrary. The same principle applies to photographers."[8]

But in a second amicus brief, in *Masterpiece*, Volokh and Carpenter made clear that this logic could not apply to cakes. Speech, they argued, is protected if it "falls within a generally expressive medium,"[9] a medium that "has historically and traditionally been recognized in the law as expressive."[10] Writing, singing, and photography are inherently expressive. Cake-making is not. If free speech is deemed to protect conduct whose significance one disagrees with, they conclude, the law would embrace what the Court has specifically rejected, "the view that an apparently limitless variety of conduct can be labeled 'speech' whenever the person engaging in the conduct intends thereby to express an idea."[11]

The power of their free speech argument was evident in a later case, in which a company that made custom videos was told by the state that if they "enter the wedding-video business, their videos must depict same- and opposite-sex weddings in an equally 'positive' light."[12] The law of free speech has to bar the state from this kind of viewpoint censorship. But that doesn't mean that the Volokh/Carpenter argument is an adequate tool for addressing the conflict that concerns us.

The moral reality is that the videographer and the baker are making exactly the same kind of claim: they conscientiously object to participating in a ceremony that they do not regard as a real wedding. Yet the law, as construed by Volokh and Carpenter, treats them differently. This—which is the most that one can get out of a free speech claim—is not a good solution to our problem.

So none of Phillips's own arguments worked. He got some sophisticated help, however, generating even more distinctive free speech arguments. The surprising election of President Donald Trump was followed by the unsurprising decision of the Department of Justice (DOJ) to file its own brief supporting Phillips's claim. The lawyers in the Solicitor General's office are far more skillful than those of the Alliance Defending Freedom, which represented Phillips.

The DOJ brief ignores every argument that Phillips makes and starts all over with an entirely new theory of the case. The brief acknowledges, what is settled law, that the First Amendment is not violated by content-neutral laws that incidentally affect speech. For example, newspapers are not immune from antitrust laws. That means that bakers are not immune from antidiscrimination law, either.

But then the brief proposes a new proviso: "Public accommodations laws compel expression—whether speech or expressive conduct—when they mandate the creation of commissioned goods or the provision of commissioned services that are inherently communicative." The theory follows Phillips's brief in drawing the line at customized work, though its formulation is more deft and careful. Why the line is drawn there—and what counts as customized work—is still not explained. Food preparation is not inherently communicative. A cake is not a newspaper.

The DOJ brief offers another, independent theory: "A public accommodations law exacts a greater First Amendment toll if it also compels participation in a ceremony or other expressive event." The fact that it's a wedding raises a special free speech issue. The logic now seems to extend to premade cakes—and "participation" includes the sale of goods, hours before and miles away from the event. The Solicitor

General tries to limit the scope of this point: "Whether governmental compulsion creates an association with an unwanted message depends on a reasonable observer's perception of the relevant expression."

But how is a reasonable observer to know whether a cake is custom-made? Or who made it? Wedding cakes aren't normally accompanied by signs explaining the history of their preparation, such as whether they were based on customized designs. A wedding is not an art museum.

The claim that what matters is the "deeply expressive" character of a wedding has broad implications that DOJ does not notice. Lots of services that can be the basis of discrimination involve deeply expressive events: funerals, theaters, concerts, private schools, pregnancy and childbirth.[13] Courts would have to decide which of these is "deeply" expressive. Would classical music concerts count, but not light pop music? Getting the courts into the business of drawing such lines has troubling free speech implications. If the "deeply" proviso is dropped, then free speech will protect all intentional conduct, since intentional action always expresses *something*.

Anyone who participates in these events in any capacity, expressive or otherwise, would have a First Amendment right to refuse—even if they were motivated by pure, unapologetic bigotry. (If you think such bigotry has become marginal, talk to any American Muslim.)

At the oral argument, the Justices saw the problem. Much of the argument consisted in a fruitless struggle to figure out where a line could be drawn. Justice Stephen Breyer worried that if the Court rules in favor of Phillips, "we would have caused chaos with that principle across the board because there is no way of confining an opinion on [the baker's] side in a way that doesn't do that." Without definite boundaries, the argument would "undermine every civil rights law." Even Justice Neil Gorsuch, generally sympathetic to the baker, said "I'd appreciate a more abstract general rule than the government suggests."

Solicitor General Noel Francisco made a new suggestion in response to Gorsuch: to find out whether conduct, such as food preparation, is protected speech, "you analogize it to something that everyone regards as traditional art and everyone agrees is protected speech." A nice job to give to trial courts. No one would be able to figure out what is and what is not immunized from antidiscrimination law. It wouldn't help the bakers, either, because they would not know what the law required of them.

Justice Sonya Sotomayor observed that in some places, such as military bases far from cities, there might be a very small number of providers, so that the service would be absolutely unavailable. Solicitor General Francisco responded that "that is precisely a situation where the state would be able to satisfy heightened scrutiny because their interests in providing access to goods and services would be narrowly tailored." But notice how impossible this makes the burden for the discrimination claimant: now, in addition to proving the discrimination, the complaint would have to survey the neighborhood to prove that no substitute was available, which would mean contacting every other service provider to ask what they would have done. (And hope for truthful answers: those who intend to discriminate often don't want to advertise that fact.)

Justice Gorsuch, casting about for some theory that could help Phillips, noted that the Colorado Commission ordered training for the bakery staff—a common remedy in discrimination cases. "Why isn't that compelled speech and possibly in violation of his free-exercise rights? Because presumably he has to tell his staff, including his family members, that his Christian beliefs are discriminatory." The state's attorney correctly responded that all the baker must teach his staff is how to obey the law.

When the case was decided, the press reported that Phillips had won. That is technically accurate but misleading.

The Court seized on one detail in the record.[14] One of the members of the Colorado Civil Rights Commission had declared: "Freedom of religion and religion has been used to justify all kinds of discrimination throughout history . . . to me it is one of the most despicable pieces of rhetoric that people can use to—to use their religion to hurt others." Justice Kennedy's opinion for the Court observed that this disparaged Phillips's religion "in at least two distinct ways: by describing it as despicable, and also by characterizing it as merely rhetorical—something insubstantial and even insincere." The language, which neither the other commissioners, the later court rulings, nor the state's brief disavowed, "cast doubt on the fairness and impartiality of the Commission's adjudication of Phillips' case."

One sees a lot of this kind of rhetoric on the Left. It is unfair and contributes to the political polarization that gave us Trump. Kennedy was right to denounce it. (Whether it justified reversal by the Court is more doubtful.)[15] State officials have no business deciding which religious beliefs are despicable or hypocritical.

So Phillips got the decision against him reversed.[16] What he (and other wedding vendors) did not get was what he was seeking, the right to turn away same-sex couples. As we shall see in chapter 9, his troubles weren't over.

Two of the justices, Clarence Thomas and Neil Gorsuch, wanted to go further, to announce general principles that would govern all future wedding vendor cases. Those arguments, however, have implications that even those justices could not accept.

Their argument begins with Jack Phillips's claim that he did not, after all, discriminate on the basis of sexual orientation. Phillips had said, "I will not design and create wedding cakes for a same-sex wedding regardless of the sexual orientation of the customer."[17] Similar claims are common in the wedding vendor cases: the discrimination is said to be not on the basis of anyone's identity, but rather on the basis of the event that the vendor is unwilling to facilitate, or on the basis of the message sent by that facilitation, which the vendor has a free speech right not to endorse. Event-based and message-based discrimination, we are told, is not discrimination on the basis of sexual orientation.

The Court could not adopt that argument, of course. It is a question of Colorado law, and Colorado's courts have the last word about what Colorado law means. But Justices Thomas and Gorsuch attempted to mutate the argument into a constitutional claim, in different doctrinal forms.

Justice Thomas argued that the baking of wedding cakes is inherently expressive: "A wedding cake needs no particular design or written words to communicate the basic message that a wedding is occurring, a marriage has begun, and the couple should be celebrated."[18] If Thomas is right, then Colorado was exceeding its legitimate authority by stretching its antidiscrimination law to cover protected expression.

Justice Thomas is right that many actions have communicative significance. The Court has, however, rejected "the view that an apparently limitless variety of conduct can be labeled 'speech' whenever the person engaging in the conduct intends thereby to express an idea."[19] Government can regulate conduct that communicates if its interest is unrelated to the suppression of the message, and if the impact on the communication is no more than is necessary to the government's purpose.[20] Discrimination laws easily satisfy these requirements. Discriminators do not get a free pass whenever they mean to communicate something by discriminating.

Thomas has two responses to this difficulty. One is to claim that in this case, compliance with the law amounts to a kind of compelled speech: "Forcing Phillips to make custom wedding cakes for same-sex marriages requires him to, at the very least, acknowledge that same-sex weddings are 'weddings' and suggest that they should be celebrated— the precise message he believes his faith forbids." The language here appears to be modeled on a key sentence in *Boy Scouts of America v. Dale*:[21] the Court declared that requiring the Boy Scouts to accept a gay member "would, at the very least, force the organization to send a message, both to the youth members and the world, that the Boy Scouts accepts homosexual conduct as a legitimate form of behavior."[22] Both sentences have unacceptable implications. It can't possibly be true that one has a right to disobey laws whenever compliance would be taken to convey a message.[23]

Every time a vendor provides someone with goods and services without discriminating, that's an event that has communicative significance. You can't carve out an event-based or message-based exception to antidiscrimination law. The exception will swallow the rule. There will be no violations of the law that do not fall within the exception.

Take the familiar case of the restaurant that would not serve black customers. It's the paradigm of wrongful discrimination, the core case of what the law prohibits. We generally think of that as status-based discrimination. But it is also conduct-based: the black customers want to *do* something, something that white people are already permitted to do. The presence of black people eating lunch at Ollie's Barbecue in Birmingham in 1965, sitting at a table next to white people, was an event that Ollie didn't want to facilitate, and it sends a message that

Ollie didn't like. Neither conduct nor event nor message can provide a workable distinction between what Phillips did and the paradigmatic discrimination that the law prohibits.

There was one case in which the Court considered and rejected a claim of a right to discriminate, for religious reasons, on the basis of race.[24] There were many who sincerely believed in such a right, and in the religious reasons.[25] Their claim would not have been stronger if it had been framed as a free speech claim. The Court would not have accepted a claim that the owner would refuse without discrimination to sell "racially integrated dining," or "food that expresses approval of integration."

Thomas's second strategy is to emphasize that the normal rule, of deference to regulations of expressive conduct, "does not apply unless the government would have punished the conduct regardless of its expressive component."[26] The injury the state aimed to prevent was not absolute unavailability of wedding cakes to gay couples—other bakers were available—but the "humiliation, frustration, and embarrassment"[27] of being turned away on the basis of a protected characteristic. That has been a settled purpose of antidiscrimination law for half a century, but Thomas thinks it is impermissible: "States cannot punish protected speech because some group finds it offensive, hurtful, stigmatic, unreasonable, or undignified."[28]

Thomas misdescribes the injury that discrimination law aims to remedy. The humiliation engendered by discrimination is not merely the offense of encountering unwelcome ideas. As we saw in chapter 4, it has to do with one's physical well-being and one's status in society.

If Thomas's argument is accepted, then it is equally applicable to race discrimination. There is almost certainly nowhere in the United States where, if all antidiscrimination laws were repealed, goods and services would be absolutely unavailable to African Americans. Would a restaurant have a free speech right to maintain separate dining rooms for white and black customers, so long as it served the same food in both? If noneconomic harms may not count, then antidiscrimination law, both state and federal, would be invalid today in nearly all its applications.

Justice Gorsuch had a more complex theory of the case, one that partakes of both free speech and religious freedom. He claimed that religious objectors to laws were being treated worse than other objectors. The basis of his claim was religious neutrality, but it depended on a view of expressive conduct much like that of Thomas.

Recall the case of William Jack, whose request for cakes with antigay inscriptions was refused. The Colorado courts rejected his claim of religious discrimination, because the bakers in his case would not sell such cakes to anyone. Gorsuch, however, thinks that Phillips's case is just like Jack's:

> All of the bakers explained without contradiction that they would not sell the requested cakes to anyone, while they would sell other cakes to members of the protected class (as well as to anyone else). So, for example, the bakers in the first case would have refused to sell a cake denigrating same-sex marriage to an atheist customer, just as the baker in the second case would have refused to sell a cake celebrating same-sex marriage to a heterosexual customer. And the bakers in the first case were generally happy to sell to persons of faith, just as the baker in the second case was generally happy to sell to gay persons. In both cases, it was the kind of cake, not the kind of customer, that mattered to the bakers.[29]

Gorsuch observes that Phillips is happy to sell his products to gay people. He just won't engage in conduct that endorses same-sex weddings. A "cake celebrating same-sex marriage" is part of an event in which he is unwilling to participate. This bears an obvious affinity to Justice Thomas's formulation, that what Phillips would not sell to anyone was "custom wedding cakes that express approval of same-sex marriage."[30] Gorsuch, however, is not making a free speech argument; he is claiming that because Phillips and the bakers who refused Jack's order were alike declining to send messages, their different treatment reveals discrimination against Phillips's religion.

Justice Elena Kagan responded that what Phillips refused to sell "was simply a wedding cake—one that (like other standard wedding cakes) is suitable for use at same-sex and opposite-sex weddings."[31] Jack's case is different, because the bakers would not have sold the cake he requested to anyone. Those cakes manifested his religious views, but there is no obligation to sell products that manifest religious views. A vendor of hats is permitted to omit yarmulkes from its inventory.

The reason why discrimination on the basis of some activities, such as participation in a same-sex wedding, is LGBT discrimination, is because such participation is a near-perfect proxy for the protected class. A merchant who won't admit customers wearing yarmulkes is discriminating against Jews. A merchant who won't sell cakes to same-sex couples is discriminating against gay people. Protection from LGBT discrimination must rely on such proxies, because being gay is a concealable identity. Before there can be discrimination, the victim must voluntarily do something to identify herself as gay. The Vatican in 1992 opposed antidiscrimination protection on this basis:

> An individual's sexual orientation is generally not known to others unless he publicly identifies himself as having this orientation or unless some overt behavior manifests it. As a rule, the majority of homosexually oriented persons who seek to lead chaste lives do not publicize their sexual orientation. Hence the problem of discrimination in terms of employment, housing, etc., does not usually arise.[32]

The discrimination can then be described as being based on conduct, not status: "I'm happy to serve gay people, just not the ones who unrepentantly, publicly identify as such."

If antidiscrimination protection of gay people has any point at all, it is to prohibit this kind of discrimination. It exists in order to remove the pressure on gay people to hide their identities. The conduct is the object of protection. The case is similar with the prohibition of religious discrimination. One can't know that a target of discrimination is Mormon, for example, unless that person discloses that he is one. Discrimination against those who wear yarmulkes and hijabs is religious discrimination, even though the wearing of those items is conduct and not status.

Gorsuch does not dispute this. Rather, he claims that this is why William Jack's case is analogous to that of Phillips. A same-sex couple, asking for a cake with a message that manifests their sexual orientation, is protected by Colorado law, but Jack, asking for a cake with a message that manifests his religion, is not. The treatment of these cases, Justice Kennedy wrote for the Court without further explanation, "could reasonably be interpreted as being inconsistent as to the question of whether speech is involved."[33]

Justice Gorsuch elaborated the purported inconsistency: "Just as cakes celebrating same-sex weddings are (usually) requested by persons of a particular sexual orientation, so too are cakes expressing religious opposition to same-sex weddings (usually) requested by persons of particular religious faiths."[34] Gorsuch evidently thought that if Colorado was going to construe its antidiscrimination law so expansively on behalf of gay people, in fairness it also must do so for religious conservatives like Jack. His formulation, however, manipulates the level of abstraction by specifying that the comparator expresses "religious opposition," rather than just "opposition." Opposition to same-sex weddings is not characteristic of any specific religion, however, so failing to accommodate such opposition does not discriminate against any specific religion.[35]

Religious views are always expressed by persons of particular faiths. That tautology doesn't mean that the prohibition of discriminatory acts, which happen sometimes to be motivated by religion, is motivated by hostility to those religions. Aztec human sacrifice was always practiced by persons of a particular religious faith, but the homicide laws do not discriminate against the Aztec religion. Put another way, homicide is not a near-perfect proxy for the Aztec religion. Most killers don't know or care about the Aztec religion. Nor is discrimination against gay people a near-perfect proxy for conservative Christianity.

Gorsuch thought the state was playing games with the level of generality at which it understood the two cases:

> If "cakes" were the relevant level of generality, the Commission would have to order the bakers to make Mr. Jack's requested cakes just as it ordered Mr. Phillips to make the requested cake in his case. Conversely, if "cakes that convey a message regarding same-sex marriage" were the relevant level of generality, the Commission would have to respect Mr. Phillips's refusal to make the requested cake just as it respected the bakers' refusal to make the cakes Mr. Jack requested. In short, when the same level of generality is applied to both cases, it is no surprise that the bakers have to be treated the same. Only by

adjusting the dials *just right*—fine-tuning the level of generality up or down for each case based solely on the identity of the parties and the substance of their views—can you engineer the Commission's outcome, handing a win to Mr. Jack's bakers but delivering a loss to Mr. Phillips. Such results-driven reasoning is improper.

This reasoning overlooks the level of generality at which Colorado law actually operates: "If a retail bakery will sell a cake of a particular design to some customers, it has no constitutional right to withhold that same cake from others because of their race, sex, faith, or sexual orientation."[36] The bakers Jack approached would not have sold the cakes he requested to anyone. "But businesses do not violate public accommodations laws when, relying upon general terms of service, they decline to sell products with particular designs to all of their customers. Businesses trigger those laws only when they refuse to sell a product to customers because of their protected characteristics, despite selling the same product to others."[37] Phillips would have sold the identical cakes to heterosexual couples.

If you omit, and keep the reader from thinking about, the level of generality at which laws actually operate, you can easily do what Gorsuch does. Change the facts a bit and the confusion becomes manifest. Every state's laws prohibit human sacrifice but permit homicide in self-defense. If "homicide" were the relevant level of generality, then those who kill in self-defense would have to be punished. If "killing for reasons that the perpetrator thinks morally justified" were the relevant level of generality, both would have to be excused. Only by adjusting the dials just right can you engineer the outcome that American law reaches. It's unfair to the Aztecs!

The only First Amendment theory that can help any of the wedding vendors is Volokh and Carpenter's argument, which has not been adopted by any court but coherently could be. One could protect wedding photographers and wedding singers, because they work in media that are generally expressive. But the argument can't be expanded to food preparation, such as cake-making, without assuming that all intentional human conduct expresses something and is protected by free speech. That implies anarchy. The claims of the wedding photographer and the baker ought to stand or fall together. The free speech argument arbitrarily separates them.

The impulse to constitutionalize religious dissenters' claim to accommodation is understandable and in some ways admirable. Where they are denied accommodation, they are an unpopular minority of just the kind that the judiciary often protects, and they reflect the kind of moral disagreement that must be protected in a liberal society. The protection of that kind of disagreement is one of the purposes of free speech. Nonetheless, none of the doctrinal free speech arguments make sense. This is a job for legislation.

6

"Religion always wins" rules are bad for religious liberty

As we have seen, the basic idea of religious accommodation was always to exempt religious objectors *when that could be done without impairing legitimate state purposes.* That was what Congress was trying to codify in the Religious Freedom Restoration Act.

The Supreme Court has now abruptly lurched into an entirely different regime, one Congress never intended. Justice Alito's opinion for the Court in *Burwell v. Hobby Lobby*[1] contemplates a regime in which religion will be accommodated, even if the consequence is serious injury to nonadherents, so long as there is some *imaginable* less restrictive means for preventing that injury—and it does not matter whether that is a realistic possibility.

The Court seized on a limited religious accommodation that the Obama Administration had devised, and vastly expanded it. The decision has important implications for the gay rights/religious liberty controversy—so important that this chapter will need to explore at length a different controversy, that over employer funding of contraception. The way the Court addressed that issue has made it more difficult to compromise the one that this book is concerned with. Legislators trying to make a deal can't be confident that courts won't again change the deal's terms, skewing it in favor of the religious.

The Court's eagerness to protect religious liberty is ironic. What it describes will sometimes amount to a right to hurt people who do not share one's religious views. If this is now to be the authoritative meaning of that liberty, then the long-standing, broad consensus that supported it will inevitably collapse.

Hobby Lobby was not a gay rights case. It presented the question whether a for-profit employer could be exempted from the requirement to provide health insurance to its employees that included coverage for contraception. It is, however, the Court's most important recent pronouncement on religious accommodation.

In the United States, most health insurance for the nonelderly is provided through employers. Employer-based coverage has the economic advantages of economies of scale and the creation of natural risk pools. It is also encouraged by the tax code.[2]

Health insurance need not come from employers. The government could provide it itself, as it does for veterans, and in a different way for the elderly with Medicare. But a wholesale overhaul of the American health care system is politically impossible. The failure of Bill Clinton's plan showed that any health care reform that transforms most people's coverage will run into insuperable political obstacles. Most people like the coverage they have. So Obama worked within the system as he found it.[3] Part of the mess he inherited was that many employers were dropping their health care coverage, particularly among the lowest paid workers.[4] Obama sought to reverse that trend.

The Affordable Care Act of 2010 (the "ACA") seeks to approach the goal of universal coverage by (among other innovations) expanding employer health insurance, with a requirement that large employers provide their employees with such insurance or pay a penalty. The requirement would, of course, accomplish little if the law said nothing about what must be covered by the insurance. So a minimum benefits package is specified.

Among other things, the ACA mandates that insurers cover "preventive health services" without additional charge—that is, without copayments, coinsurance, deductibles, or the like.[5] Such deductibles discourage people from using health care, but it makes no sense to reduce spending on preventive care. That spending saves money in the long run by keeping patients healthy and detecting illness early.[6]

Before the ACA, insurance often excluded coverage of women's specific medical needs, making them bear higher health care costs than men—as much as a billion dollars a year more in the aggregate.[7] Women of childbearing age spent 68% more in out-of-pocket health care costs than men, largely because of the costs of reproductive and gender-specific conditions, including the costs of contraception.[8]

Some contraceptive methods are not medically suitable for women with particular medical conditions or risk factors, and certain more expensive methods are more effective at preventing pregnancy than less costly alternatives.[9]

Women take account of costs when deciding whether to use contraceptives.[10] Without insurance coverage, the affected women will incur significant out-of-pocket costs or forgo contraceptives altogether.[11]

Unintended pregnancies comprise nearly half of all pregnancies in the United States.[12] Women with unintended pregnancies are less likely to receive timely prenatal care, and are more likely to smoke, consume alcohol, become depressed, experience domestic violence during pregnancy, and terminate their pregnancies by abortion.[13] Pregnancy may be dangerous for women with serious medical conditions, such as pulmonary hypertension, cyanotic heart disease, and Marfan syndrome.[14] Unintended pregnancies also obviously prevent women from participating in labor and employment markets on an equal basis with men. The children of unintended pregnancies are at greater risk of preterm birth and low birth weight.[15]

Accordingly, the Department of Health and Human Services issued the "contraception mandate," a rule that defines all FDA-approved contraceptives as preventive services. The mandate improves the health of pregnant women and newborns, reduces the disparity in health costs between men and women, and most importantly, allows women to determine the course of their own lives.[16]

Some forms of contraception sometimes prevent the implantation of fertilized eggs. Many regard this as the killing of young human beings. Some employers objected to the mandate because they understood it to require that they pay to kill babies.

Churches and other nonprofit religious entities have employees, and thus are within the ambit of the contraception mandate. They asked to be exempted from the requirement. So did some for-profit employers.

The Obama administration handled those objections clumsily. The solution that the Supreme Court devised could have come from the administration. In the event, in response to resistance from religious groups, it adjusted the mandate at least eight times.[17] Some in the administration affirmatively wanted conflict: one senior political advisor thought "the bishops' complaints could bolster a useful campaign narrative: that supporters of their view, including Republican Mitt Romney, held anachronistic views about women and family planning."[18]

The mandate accommodated religious organizations,[19] but refused accommodations to for-profit businesses. Those businesses employed enormous numbers of women who do not share the employers' religious beliefs. Hobby Lobby alone had more than 13,000 full time employees at the time.[20] Litigation followed. The store won its exemption, but not the relief it was asking for, which was to absolutely cut off its employees from coverage for the expensive forms of contraception that the employer found objectionable.

The burden on the employers was significant. Douglas Laycock observes that with the mandate, "for the first time in American history, government required adherents of the nation's largest religions to violate core religious teachings."[21]

The question before the Supreme Court was whether, under RFRA, this burden was necessary to a compelling government interest.

In some ways, the Court's decision was very good news for the women who would have been deprived of contraception by their employers' choices.[22] Under RFRA, any burden on religion must be the least restrictive means for achieving a compelling government interest. Hobby Lobby claimed, and many lower federal courts agreed, that the government's interest in guaranteeing cost-free access to contraceptives was not compelling. Some of those courts said that religious liberty could not be outweighed by a vague, generalized interest in "the promotion of public health."[23] One court was clueless enough to conceptualize the problem as one of determining the harm to the *government* if the exemption were granted.[24] The government did not focus its argument on the women who would have to endure higher costs and unintended pregnancies.[25] It was only in response to aggressive criticism that the administration, and eventually the Court, began to emphasize that.

Justice Alito, writing for the Court, deflected one of Hobby Lobby's principal claims by assuming, without deciding, that the government's interest was compelling. Doubtless some members of the five-judge majority disagreed with that, but Anthony Kennedy's separate concurrence signaled pretty clearly that he thought so, and Ruth Ginsburg's dissent, for four justices, was even clearer. That's a majority of the Justices. So what could have been a disaster for women's equality suddenly became a victory.

Having assumed a compelling interest, the Court moved on to least-restrictive burden. It noted that the administration had crafted a clever solution for religious nonprofit employers not already categorically exempted as churches or religious congregations, such as religiously af-filiated hospitals, universities, and social service organizations.[26] Those companies' insurers were required to provide contraception in separate policies, for free—something the insurers were happy to do, because even expensive contraception for all covered women is cheaper than childbirth for a few. Extending the same accommodation to religious for-profit employers was a less restrictive means to get the contracep-tion to Hobby Lobby's employees, so the Court ordered that. The effect on those employees, the majority declared, "would be precisely zero."

That's the good news. But the Court also offered some ominous speculations about other less restrictive means.

The Court declared that the "most straightforward way" of providing coverage "would be for the Government to assume the cost of providing the four contraceptives at issue to any women who are unable to ob-tain them under their health-insurance policies due to their employers' religious objections." The Court rejected the claim that "RFRA cannot be used to require creation of entirely new programs."[27] Although "we do not doubt that cost may be an important factor in the least-restrictive-means analysis," it observed that "the cost of providing the forms of contraceptives at issue in these cases (if not all FDA-approved contraceptives) would be minor when compared with the overall cost of ACA," which is "more than $1.3 trillion through the next decade."[28]

This calculation makes even a multi-million dollar program look like a trivial burden on the government. It is not clear why the entire ACA budget is the denominator in terms of which costs are to be cal-culated. If the determinative number is the entire set of conceivable government resources, then why not the whole federal budget, or the gross national product of the United States?

The majority opinion also included a footnote broadly dismissing the relevance of burdens on nonadherents, saying that it is not necessarily a burden when a religious entity merely refuses to provide a benefit to a third party. This adopts a libertarian baseline for harm that assumes out of existence much of modern law, including almost every regulation of the employer/employee relation.[29] And of course it would do away with antidiscrimination law as well, since discrimination leaves its victim in the same position as if the discriminator did not exist.

The Court's decision had limited scope, but the limit—Justice Kennedy's reservations about the majority's formulation—offers little reassurance. He was skeptical about "imposition of a whole new program or burden on the Government." In *Hobby Lobby*, he declared, there happened to be "an existing, recognized, workable, and already-implemented framework" for accommodating the religious objection. This fact "might well suffice to distinguish the instant cases from many others in which it is more difficult and expensive to accommodate a governmental program to countless religious claims based on an alleged statutory right of free exercise." On the other hand, he joined the majority opinion in full, and he did not make clear in his concurrence whether the "difficulty" that he would consider in deciding whether a less-restrictive alternative is "available" would include political difficulty. And Kennedy is no longer on the Court.

When government burdens religion, it will often be possible to imagine a less restrictive means for accomplishing what government wants, particularly if that means involves spending money. Even a religious group that routinely steals money from nonadherents could argue that government could compensate its victims, and if the group is small and only steals small sums, it could also argue that the cost of doing so will not be exorbitant.

Because the alternative that is the basis for religious accommodation need not be politically feasible, the consequence of this new interpretation of the statute will be that in practice, RFRA exemptions will sometimes impose severe costs upon identifiable and discrete third parties.[30]

The dangers of the *Hobby Lobby* spending dictum have since been realized. Two federal district courts have cited the possible provision of services by the government as a less restrictive means of advancing the interest in antidiscrimination laws.[31]

No antidiscrimination law could survive this logic. Even with the Civil Rights Act of 1964, government could have set up its own network of public accommodations, and could have made itself the employer of last resort for African Americans who could not get good jobs. And those hypotheticals would have meant that every racist who articulated a religious motive—and that was almost all of them—would have been exempted. The law would have been a dead letter.

Another innovation of *Hobby Lobby* was the Court's embrace of a less restrictive alternative that was not proposed by the party seeking the exemption. Hobby Lobby didn't care at all about women's access to emergency contraception, and was untroubled that the RFRA exemption it sought would wholly deny them this coverage.[32] The Court devised its solution on its own. The upshot is that now, when government resists a religious exemption claim, it will not be enough for it to show that the alternatives proposed by the claimant are not feasible. It will need to rebut every imaginable alternative.

Justice Sotomayor writes, in a more recent religious liberty case, that the Court has not said that "officials must refute every conceivable option." On the contrary, "the government need not 'do the impossible—refute each and every conceivable alternative regulation scheme' but need only 'refute the alternative schemes offered by the challenger.'"[33] Her reading of present law may be too charitable.

The broad reading of RFRA makes it more difficult to reach a legislative compromise of the gay rights/religious liberty question. Ira Lupu explains the problem:

> In light of *Hobby Lobby*, LGBT rights proponents will be rightly concerned that any specific exemption or accommodation for some religious interests will put a significant burden on the government to explain why the accommodation should not be extended to other religious claimants, business firms or others. For supporters of LGBT rights, *Hobby Lobby* has made the bargaining chip, represented by specific exemptions, far more dangerous or expensive to play.[34]

It is no longer possible for a legislature to enact exemptions only for nonprofits, for example. Any such exemption might be judicially expanded. Thus, for example, the Employment Non-Discrimination Act, a ban on employment discrimination based on sexual orientation or gender identity, had been on the Congressional agenda for years. It had always included a broad exemption for religious employers.

After *Hobby Lobby*, a number of groups supporting ENDA withdrew their support because of the exemption.[35] The Court is now pushing Congress away from religious accommodation, because it has made accommodation threatening in a way it never was before.

The root of the problem is the Court's implausibly broad reading of RFRA. Here we must digress to examine the Court's approach to the interpretation of statutes.

Statutory construction—the rules for reading enacted laws—is a less prominent topic than constitutional law. But it matters just as much. A fear that looms over constitutional discourse is the "countermajoritarian difficulty," the concern that unelected judges will distort the law to defeat the will of the people. It is equally present when courts distort the meaning of statutes to reach political outcomes they like. Whatever Congress might do, the courts will get to say what the law means. This creates opportunities for abuse. Congress never intended the extravagant regime that *Hobby Lobby* proposes.

Perhaps it is because *Hobby Lobby* is a statutory interpretation case that in it the Court abandons the judicial restraint that guided its constitutional interpretation in *Smith*. The Court has developed an impressive array of techniques of statutory distortion. These include wrenching terms out of context in order to contradict the statute's purpose, relying on presumptions that are so strong that they defeat express statutory language, aggressive use of preemption doctrine to defeat state regulatory laws that Congress had no intention of disturbing, devising new interpretive approaches and applying them retroactively to laws already in existence, and minimizing the effect of corrective legislation that overrides the Court's misinterpretations.[36]

Hobby Lobby is best understood as standing in this tradition, using vague legislative language as an opportunity to craft a new statutory scheme that is radically at variance with what Congress had in mind.

Congress passed the Religious Freedom Restoration Act precisely to *restore* the abandoned, deferential pre-*Smith* free exercise jurisprudence. That's why the law has its name, the original statute expressly said so,[37] and its congressional proponents were at pains to assure RFRA skeptics of that.[38] The Court, however, rejected the argument that RFRA "did no more than codify this Court's pre-*Smith*

Free Exercise Clause precedents."[39] We are now in unknown territory, which Congress never imagined.

If government refusals to accommodate are viewed with the kind of skepticism that the Court displays in *Hobby Lobby*, then claims of accommodation will nearly always be supported by some imaginable less restrictive means, even if its enactment is politically impossible. The consequence in practice will be an interpretation of religious liberty in which adherents get to harm nonadherents, in which some are forced to pay for the religious exercise of others. Religious liberty here would mean the right to impose your religion on other people who don't share your views. RFRA, as construed by the Court, is an injury-generating machine that will produce a growing class of persons who have been harmed, perhaps severely harmed, in order to accommodate the religious scruples of another, more favored class.[40]

This activism sits uneasily beside the conspicuous judicial restraint of *Smith*. The Court can, and sometimes does, say that its interpretation of a statute is vindicated by the fact that Congress has let its decision stand. But changing statutory law isn't easy. The Court craves democratic legitimation, but evidently bogus legitimation will do.

One of the principal attractions of the idea of religious liberty has always been that the exercise of one person's religion doesn't hurt anyone else. In Thomas Jefferson's classic formulation: "It does me no injury for my neighbour to say there are twenty gods, or no god. It neither picks my pocket nor breaks my leg."[41] But paying for contraceptives that should be covered by insurance is exactly like having one's pocket picked, while involuntary pregnancy is worse than a broken leg.

The Court evidently thinks that it is helping the cause of religious liberty by construing RFRA very broadly. It may have lost sight of the fact that RFRA is a *statutory* accommodation, and *Hobby Lobby* is a mere *statutory* interpretation that Congress has the power to undo. The existence and vitality of RFRA—and other statutory accommodations of religion—ultimately depends on the sufferance of Congress and the voters who elect it. How likely is it that those voters will support religious claims that manifestly hurt innocent people, or pay in perpetuity to subsidize religious practices they do not share and may find politically or morally repugnant? The idea of religious liberty is in trouble.

The Court seems determined to confirm militant atheists' ugliest stereotypes of what religious citizens want.

Religion has been a great force for good in the world, but it is hard to see that when this becomes its most prominent manifestation. If this is to be the official meaning of religious liberty, than the broad acceptance of religious liberty will fade.

7

A right to be weird is a good reason to give religion special treatment

So what should the law of religious liberty look like? Is there any good reason for specifically *religious* accommodation? Is there any reason for nonreligious people, a growing proportion of the American population, to support such special treatment?[1]

The extraordinary privileging of religion in *Hobby Lobby* is not peculiar to the Court. Many distinguished scholars argue that religion ought to be treated as more important than almost all other state concerns. They have claimed, moreover, that this privileging is the original meaning of the First Amendment.

These claims are as giddily extreme as the Court's position in *Hobby Lobby*.

Many liberals have taken a comparably extreme position on the other side. It is wrong to single out religion for any special treatment at all. The entire American tradition of religious accommodation is a mistake. Special treatment, they argue, is arbitrary: there are many deep and valuable human concerns, and religion is only one of these.

This is the deepest division that the gay rights/religious liberty controversy has produced. Religious liberty has been protected since the founding. It has been a basic principle of American government. Now it has been called into question. The challenge is to defend it in terms that can make sense to the growing number of nonreligious Americans.

The liberals are right at the level of high theory, but wrong at the level of legal doctrine. Religion is indeed only one of many good things. However, these can be honored by the law only one at a time.

The American political left has always been concerned with the worst off members of society. Its understanding of who is worst off has shifted over time. It was once concerned with economic redistribution: minimum wage, unionization, a social safety net, and so forth. It was transformed by the struggles of the 1960s over racial equality, the Vietnam war, the sexual revolution and the counterculture. This created the opening for the gay rights movement. It now stood for, as Hunter S. Thompson put it, the "right to be weird."[2] It promised to free us from the traditional white male heterosexual Anglo template. In a way, the old idea of religious liberty was radicalized: each person should be free to find his own way to salvation.

The objection to singling out religion is that it biases this individual quest in favor of certain answers, answers that are not the right ones for everyone. It will, however, be impossible to deliver on the promise of a right to be weird while doing without the older idea of a specifically religious liberty.

"Religion is, by its nature, the highest of human concerns," writes Kathleen Brady. "Nothing can be more important to individuals than their relationship with the divine."[3] Accommodating it may impose heavy costs on nonbelievers, but the value of religion is so great that "there should be few, if any limits on the sacrifices that the political community is willing to make."[4] She proposes that "religious believers should be afforded relief whenever laws substantially burden practices essential to their relationship with the divine unless there is no way to alleviate the burden without endangering the existence, peace, or safety of the state, or basic conditions of public order, or invading the rights of others."[5]

If you share Brady's religious premises, this might make sense. If you don't, then it is dangerous fanaticism.

Given the primacy that Brady gives to religious interests, it is not clear why the nonreligious rights of others should constitute a veto. How could God's commands be overridden by such mundane matters as the state's peace and safety, public order, or rights? At one point she admits this: "If the relationship between persons and the divine is the highest of human concerns, a balancing process that limits free exercise when the interests of the state outweigh infringements of religious liberty makes no sense."[6] But she shrinks from the logical implications of her argument.[7]

Her argument builds on the assertions in James Madison's *Memorial and Remonstrance* that "it is the duty of every man to render to the Creator such homage, and such only, as he believes to be acceptable to him," and that "every man who becomes a member of any particular Civil Society [must] do it with a saving of his allegiance to the Universal Sovereign."[8] Michael McConnell has made this quotation a premise for an argument (never stated by Madison) that religion ought to be a basis for exemptions because it involves a duty to God.[9] "If the scope of religious liberty is defined by religious duty (man must render to God 'such homage . . . as he believes to be acceptable to him'), and if the claims of civil society are subordinate to the claims of religious freedom, it would seem to follow that the dictates of religious faith must take precedence over the laws of the state, even if they are secular and generally applicable."[10] McConnell claims that religion has a unique claim to accommodation, because "no other freedom is a duty to a higher authority."[11] Even those who do not believe in God should understand the value of avoiding "conflicts with what are perceived (even if incorrectly) as divine commands."[12]

Steven D. Smith is impressed by this logic, but takes it further than McConnell, who prudently supports *Sherbert*-style interest balancing.[13] Smith is troubled by courts' willingness to balance religion against other goods. That treats religious scruples as just another intense human desire, to be weighed against other less exalted desires. Smith relies on "Madison's careful demonstration that every person's first obligation (over which the state and civil society have no 'cognizance') is to God—an obligation, Madison stressed, that must be measured by the person's own judgment."[14] Madison thought "that our duties to 'the Creator' are prior to our duties to society."[15] Accommodation is an imperative: "A government that defies what a transcendent authority is thought to command would be in a different and more unsatisfactory position than a government that merely declines to recognize some other sort of potentially meritorious objection."[16] In the conception Smith aims to revive, "the church and its officials were something like the ambassadors of the kingdom of God within the secular domain . . . and they thus enjoyed a sort of diplomatic immunity from secular law."[17] Like McConnell, Smith relies on the first paragraph of Madison's *Memorial and Remonstrance* to show that this conception is reflected (albeit imperfectly) in the American law of religious liberty.[18]

Smith cites with approval Michael Paulsen's argument that religious accommodation is "based on an acknowledgment of a transcendent reality, or at least of the possibility of such a reality."[19] Paulsen is more extreme than Brady, McConnell, or Smith. Another way of putting this point is that he is unusually courageous and clear-sighted about the implications of the notion that religion is more valuable than anything else. He shows where this logic leads, though he doesn't regard it as a *reductio ad absurdum*.

The canonical formulation is that accommodation can be denied only if this is necessary to a compelling state interest. Paulsen correctly observes that the compelling interest formulation "subtly implies ultimate state supremacy, rather than the priority of God."[20] Paulsen thinks (as does Smith) that religious freedom presupposes that God's demands precede, and are superior in obligation to, those of the state. "As a matter of the constitutional text, the problem remains that there is no compelling-interest override written into the Free Exercise Clause; it is all judicial interpretation. How can such an exception be justified as proper constitutional interpretation?"[21]

It would seem, then, that the state must yield to religion in every context. "God's commands—God's will, God's purposes—rightfully trump man's. Freedom of religion, understood as a human legal right, is government's recognition of the priority and superiority of God's true commands over anything the State requires or forbids."[22]

Paulsen understands (what Smith never acknowledges) that this will put the state in an embarrassing position when, say, Abraham thinks that God has commanded him to sacrifice his son Isaac.

So Paulsen adds a proviso: deference "must give way in clear, or extreme, cases—because surely there are some claims individuals make about God's commands that are simply intolerably and irredeemably false."[23] This is not because the state's commands are superior to God's. God forbid. "There are some things that we can and should confidently say God thinks are always and everywhere wrong (or at least we should so presume)."[24] In such a case, "there is *no true command of God to be obeyed*."[25]

He knows he's entered the valley of the shadow of death. "Past a certain point, quickly reached, the business of judging the truth or validity of religious beliefs destroys religious liberty."[26] This business also has other discomforts. Paulsen cannot bring himself to say that Abraham was wrong, and he thinks that the refusal of lifesaving medical care to children by Christian Scientists and Jehovah's Witnesses presents "extraordinarily difficult problems."[27] (In fact, such cases are easy: courts always order the medical treatment.)

The logic of religious liberty, Paulsen thinks, makes inevitable a state role as the arbiter of religious truth. He thus places himself athwart a long tradition that has held that allowing the state to do that inevitably corrupts religion. In the *Memorial and Remonstrance*, Madison went on to argue that the idea "that the Civil Magistrate is a competent Judge of Religious truth . . . is an arrogant pretension falsified by the contradictory opinions of Rulers in all ages."

Madison's rhetorical move invoking the priority of God made sense within a Lockean framework, where religious and secular duties operated in different spheres, so that conflict could easily be avoided. Locke had no use for exemptions from generally applicable laws: if the state is doing its legitimate business, religious objections could have no weight. If religious exemptions are to be justified, it must be on some basis other than Madison's suggestion that religious duties categorically override secular ones. The effort to build a theory of religious liberty on that suggestion is a dead end.

So let's start over.

The increasingly common objection is that it is arbitrary and unfair to privilege religion in the way American law does. Some think there should never be accommodation.[28] The more common view is that accommodation is appropriate, but under a different description; that because it is morally arbitrary and unfair to single out "religion," a different category, such as "conscience," should be used.

A different objection is that the bounds of "religion" are so indeterminate that the term is meaningless. The academic study of religion has tended to conclude that "religion" is a term without a referent. There are, of course, individual systems of belief and practice, such as

Christianity and Buddhism, but they have nothing in common that makes a category of religion a sensible one.

The singling out of religion, I will argue here, is appropriate precisely *because* it doesn't correspond to any real category of morally salient thought or conduct, and thus is flexible enough to capture intuitions about accommodation while keeping the state neutral about theological questions. It is the most workable proxy for whatever genuine value ought to be promoted in accommodation cases. Other, more specific categories are either too sectarian to be politically usable, too underinclusive to substitute for religion, or too vague to be administrable.

"Religion" is an appropriate category of protection because it refers to interests, not otherwise signifiable, urgent enough to be a basis of rights. Perhaps this cluster concept *doesn't* correspond to any real category of morally salient thought or conduct. The case for exemptions will have to be based on personal interests that are commensurable with other interests that may defeat them. Otherwise there is no good answer to Abraham.

First Amendment doctrine has used "neutrality" as one of its master concepts, but it treats religion as a good thing. Religious conscientious objectors are often accommodated. Disestablishment protects religion from manipulation by the state. The law's neutrality is its insistence that religion's goodness be understood at a high enough level of abstraction that (with the exception of a few grandfathered practices, such as "In God We Trust" on the currency) the state takes no position on any live religious dispute. America, the most religiously diverse nation on earth, has been unusually successful in dealing with its diversity.[29]

When law singles out religion for special treatment, we can reasonably ask what purpose it hopes to promote by doing so. The earliest and most obvious answer is that there is a good specific to religion— salvation by Christ is the classic one—and that religion should be singled out in order to promote that good. Of course, when you do that, you can easily end up with a pretty narrow definition of religion. Henry Fielding's Mr. Thwackum declared, "Nor is religion manifold, because there are various sects and heresies in the world. When I mention religion I mean the Christian religion; and not only the Christian religion, but the Protestant religion; and not only the Protestant religion, but the Church of England."[30]

Locke's classic defense of toleration rested in part on the claim that "true and saving Religion consists in the inward perswasion of the Mind, without which nothing can be acceptable to God."[31] Locke thought that the religious divisions that existed "for the most part" concerned "frivolous things . . . that (without any prejudice to Religion or the Salvation of Souls, if not accompanied with Superstition or Hypocrisie) might either be observed or omitted," and that such matters ought not to divide "Christian Brethren, who are all agreed in the Substantial and truly Fundamental part of Religion."[32] Many proponents of religious liberty relied on a similarly latitudinarian theology.

Of course, latitudinarianism—the view that differences in religious doctrine don't matter—is controversial. Many religions reject it and proclaim themselves the only true path to heaven. People with such views have had a variety of reasons for keeping the state from enforcing the true faith: the state is an unreliable source of religious authority; it is likely to alter religious teaching in a pernicious way to suit its own interests; establishment produces undeserved contempt toward religion; the state's legitimate authority does not extend to religious questions.[33]

Theologically intolerant people can therefore embrace a regime of religious toleration. In such a regime, the true religion can flourish. The protection of religion is then a proxy for the protection of the True and Only Religion.

The point can be made more precisely by attempting to specify the good that religion supposedly delivers. There are multiple candidates for that position, including salvation (if you think you need to be saved), harmony with the transcendent origin of universal order (if it exists),[34] responding to the fundamentally imperfect character of human life (if it is imperfect),[35] courage in the face of the heartbreaking aspects of human existence (if that kind of encouragement helps),[36] a transcendent underpinning for the resolution to act morally (if that kind of underpinning helps),[37] contact with that which is awesome and indescribable (if awe is something you feel),[38] and many others. In the cottage industry of proposals to discard the category of religion and substitute something else, these haven't gotten much attention, for the excellent reason that they are theologically loaded. It is not just that they are narrower and more specific than religion. Their goodness is a specifically religious goodness that depends on contestable metaphysical premises. Secular liberal philosophers tend to shy away from such notions. When most people outside the academy deem religion valuable, on the other hand, these are the sorts of considerations they have in mind. There are a lot of religious people out there. When religion is regarded as good, it is usually for religious reasons.

Different religions conceive these goods differently. That has political implications. The fact that there is so much contestation among religions as to which of these goods is most salient is itself a reason for the state to remain vague about this question. Privileging any of them would discriminate among religions. American law's neutrality is neutrality among religions.[39]

One reason for using religion as a proxy for particular ends such as salvation is that if the good the state pursues is described in this vague way, the state need not assess the comparative value of those ends. There is also, of course, disagreement about which religions actually achieve these goods. If the pertinent good is salvation, for instance, then the state should figure out which religion actually delivers it.[40] The broad category of religion evades that task.

Religion then is a proxy for the genuine religious good (if there is one), and part of its value is that we need not agree about what it is a proxy for.

Secular political theorists focus on secular ends. A number of these have been proposed as substitutes for religion, including individual autonomy, a source of meaning inaccessible to other people, psychologically urgent needs (treating religion as analogous to a disability that needs accommodation), comprehensive views, and conscience.[41]

All are underinclusive. Consider conscience, the most widely advocated substitute.[42] Conscience *excludes* some claims that are widely recognized as valid. Many religious claims that are uncontroversially weighty, and which nearly everyone would want to accommodate, are not conscientious. A paradigm case for religious exemption, for most proponents of such exemptions, is the ritual use of peyote by the Native American Church, which the Supreme Court declined to protect in *Employment Division v. Smith*,[43] but which received legislative accommodation shortly thereafter.[44] Yet neither of the claimants in *Smith* was motivated to use peyote by religious conscience. Al Smith was motivated primarily by interest in exploring his Native American racial identity, and Galen Black was merely curious about the Church.[45]

The emphasis on conscience focuses excessively on duty. Many and perhaps most people engage in religious practice out of habit, adherence to custom, a need to cope with misfortune, injustice, temptation, and guilt, curiosity about religious truth, a desire to feel connected to God, or happy religious enthusiasm, rather than a sense of duty prescribed by sacred texts or fear of divine punishment. Core religious practices often have nothing to do with conscience. One illustrative bit of data: when a survey asked Catholics why they attended Mass, the largest group, 37%, pointed to "the feeling of meditating and communicating with God," while only 20% referred to "the need to receive the Sacrament of Holy Communion," and only 6% said "the Church requires that I attend."[46] This experience-based religiosity is increasingly common in the United States across all religious denominations.[47] The most recent Congressional pronouncement on religious liberty, the Religious Land Use and Institutionalized Persons Act of 2000, declares that "the term 'religious exercise' includes any exercise of religion, whether or not compelled by, or central to, a system of religious belief."[48]

Conscience is also underinclusive because it focuses on those cases in which the agent feels impelled by a duty that she is capable of performing without depending on external contingencies. "Conscience" is a poor characterization of the desire of a church to expand its building to be able to hold its growing congregation, as in *City of Boerne v. Flores*.[49] Conscientious resistance to the law was not an option. The reconstruction could not be done without the help of architects and contractors, whom the city could prevent from doing the work merely by withholding the necessary permits. The problem is even more pronounced in *Lyng v. Northwest Indian Cemetery Protective Association*, a widely criticized decision in which Native Americans objected to a proposed logging road that would pass through an ancient worship site sacred to their tribe. The logging road, the Court conceded, would "virtually destroy" the ability of the Native Americans "to practice their religion." Nonetheless, the Court, evidently persuaded that exemptions had to be based on conscience, held that there was no constitutionally cognizable burden, because the logging road had "no tendency to coerce individuals into acting contrary to their religious beliefs."[50] Once more, this result was quickly reversed by Congress.[51]

The secular objection to the use of "religion" as a category is perhaps best captured by Christopher Eisgruber and Lawrence Sager, who argue that "religion does not exhaust the commitments and passions that move human beings in deep and valuable ways."[52] They claim that the state should "treat the deep, religiously inspired concerns of minority religious believers with the same regard as that enjoyed by the deep concerns of citizens generally."[53] They go on to argue that the nonreligious have equally deep concerns. That's true. But "deep" is not an administrable legal category. It is too vague for that. Even if we know what we mean, we can't know it when we see it. We are too opaque to one another, our depths are too personal and idiosyncratic, for us to tell which of one another's commitments and passions really merit respect.[54] Reliance on imperfect proxies is an inescapable part of social life.

The unavailability of a secular analogue for religion is also apparent with respect to an issue that thus far we have not discussed, the disestablishment of religion. American law is clear that the state must be neutral with respect to religious questions. Government "may not aid, foster, or promote one religion or religious theory against another or even against the militant opposite. The First Amendment mandates governmental neutrality between religion and religion, and between religion and nonreligion."[55] What could be the secular analogue to this doctrine?

Two such analogues have been proposed. One is liberal neutralitarianism, which holds that the state should be neutral toward all controversial conceptions of the good life. Its weaknesses are the subject of large literature.[56] The other is John Rawls's claim that the government should be neutral toward all "comprehensive views." A conception is comprehensive, Rawls explains, "when it includes conceptions of what is of value in human life, and ideals of personal character, as well as ideals of friendship and of familial and associational relationships, and much else that is to inform our conduct, and in the limit to our life as a whole."[57] "A conception is fully comprehensive if it covers all recognized values and virtues within one rather precisely articulated system."[58] There cannot be social consensus around such fully comprehensive conceptions.[59] So neutrality toward them, at least in the design of the basic structure of society, is necessary if there is to be the secular good of "civic friendship," in which we the citizens exercise power over one another on the basis of "reasons we might reasonably expect that they, as free and equal citizens, might reasonably also accept."[60]

However, many religious views are not fully comprehensive. Most religious people do not rely on their religious beliefs to structure their lives in this pervasive way. Perhaps in response to this, Rawls also wants to exclude any "partially comprehensive" conception, which comprises "a number of, but by no means all, nonpolitical values and virtues and is rather loosely articulated."[61] This is an odd locution. It is like saying that a person with a speck of dirt on his shoulder is partially buried. Rawls is brought to this incoherent position because he is attempting to capture the moral basis of disestablishment of religion in terms that make no mention of religion. The fact that a philosopher as brilliant as Rawls couldn't do it is powerful evidence that it can't be done.

No single factor justification for singling out religion can succeed. Any single factor justification will be overinclusive and underinclusive. Any invocation of any factor X (whether it is religious or secular) as a justification will logically entail substituting X for religion as a basis for special treatment, making religion disappear as a category of analysis. This substitution will be unsatisfactory. There will be settled intuitions about establishment and accommodation that it will be unable to account for. Any X will be an imperfect substitute for religion, but a theory of religious freedom that focuses on that X will not be able to say why religion, rather than X, should be the object of solicitude.

There are two ways around this difficulty. One is to say that these are not ends that the state can directly aim at, and that religion is a good proxy. This does justify some imprecision in the law. We want to give licenses to safe drivers, but these are not directly detectable, so we use the somewhat overinclusive and underinclusive category of "those who have passed a driving test."[62] But this doesn't work for at least some of the substitutes on offer. The state can aim directly at accommodating conscience, say, or autonomy.

The other way is to say that religion is an adequate (though somewhat overinclusive and underinclusive) proxy for multiple goods, some of which are not ones that can directly be aimed at (at least in the United States). Each of those goods is, at least, more likely to be salient in religious than in nonreligious contexts.[63] The fact that there is so much contestation among religions as to which of these goods is most salient is itself a reason for the state to remain vague about this question. Because religion—or, at least, that subset of it that is likely to come before American courts—captures multiple goods, any substitute that aims at any one of them will be underinclusive.[64] None of these can capture settled intuitions about accommodation. There are *lots* of good reasons for accommodation. Neglecting *any* of them is unfair. Religion is not just a proxy for something else. It is a proxy for many something elses. It is a bundle of proxies.

The fundamental objection to religion as a category is that it is itself underinclusive. That claim is hard to test, because the bounds of the category are so uncertain. The debate among legal scholars about whether religion is special is chronically confused by their failure to grasp a point familiar in the academic study of religion: religion is a label for something that probably has no reality outside the human imagination.

That is not a theological claim! The proposition that the Christian God exists outside the human imagination, for instance, does not entail that religion, encompassing everything connoted by that word, is an entity that exists outside the human imagination. The set of all the various religions, taken together, do not comprise a natural kind. Religion—at least, as a legal category—has no essence. If it has a determinate meaning, it is simply because there is a settled and familiar practice of applying the label of religion in predictable ways.[65]

Jonathan Z. Smith and Talal Asad each claim that the term "religion" denotes an anthropological category, arising out of a particular Western practice of encountering and accounting for foreign belief systems associated with geopolitical entities with which the West was forced to deal.[66] William Cavanaugh argues that the distinction between religion, understood as a distinctively unstable and dangerous set of beliefs, and patriotism, imagined as a stabilizing and valid reason to kill and die, is part of the legitimizing mythology of the modern state.[67] Arising thus out of a specific historical situation, and evolving in unpredictable ways thereafter, "religion" would be surprising if it had any essential denotation.

There are dissenting views. Martin Riesebrodt, for example, argues that all religions serve common functions: they promise to avert misfortune, help their followers manage crises, and bring both temporary blessings and eternal salvation.[68] For legal purposes, it does not matter who is correct. Even if theorists could converge upon a single definition, American law has not relied upon that definition, and the definition may not be suited to the law's purposes.

The question of religious accommodation arises in cases where a law can allow some exceptions. Many laws, such as military conscription, taxes, environmental regulations, and antidiscrimination laws, will accomplish their ends even if there is some deviation from the norm they set forth, so long as that deviation does not become too great. In such cases, special treatment is sometimes appropriate.[69] Religious exemption is the practice of singling out religion as a basis for such special treatment. If there is no such thing as religion, the justification must ultimately depend on some desideratum other than religion. Religion can only be a proxy.

The closest the Supreme Court has come to addressing the question of how to define religion for legal purposes is a pair of draft exemption cases during the Vietnam war. Both involved claimants who conscientiously objected to war, but who would not avow belief in God. The Court responded with a functional definition of religion, holding that the question a court must answer is "whether a given belief that is sincere and meaningful occupies a place in the life of its possessor parallel to that filled by the orthodox belief in God of one who clearly qualifies for the exemption."[70] It explained that the pertinent objection "cannot be based on a 'merely personal' moral code," but it gave no example of the line that it was drawing. These were statutory interpretation cases, only tangentially related to the constitutional issue: two concurring opinions declared that if the statute were read less broadly, it would violate the establishment clause.[71] Since then the Court has offered no further clarification of what it means by religion.

What in fact unites such disparate worldviews as Christianity, Buddhism, and Hinduism is a well-established and well-understood semantic practice of using the term "religion" to signify them and relevantly analogous beliefs and practices. Efforts to distill this practice into a definition have been unavailing. But the common understanding of how to use the word has turned out to be all that is needed. Courts almost never have any difficulty in determining whether something is a religion or not.

The list of reported cases that have had to determine a definition of religion is a remarkably short one. The reference I rely on here, *Words and Phrases*, is one of the standard works of American legal research, a 132-volume set collecting brief annotations of cases from 1658 to the present. Each case discusses the contested definition of a word whose meaning determines rights, duties, obligations, and liabilities of the parties.[72] Some words have received an enormous amount of attention from the courts. Two examples, *Abandonment* and *Abuse of Discretion*, drawn at random from the first volume of this immense compilation, each exceed 100 pages.[73] "Religion," on the other hand, takes up less than five pages.[74] The question of what "religion" means is theoretically intractable but, as a practical matter, barely relevant. We know it when we see it. And when we see it, we treat it as something good.

The category of religion in American law has changed its denotation over time.[75] Its inherent imprecision, and its deployment as a proxy, respond to conditions of religious diversity that appear to be permanent conditions of modernity.

We are in our depths opaque to one another. But we are similar enough to know where the deep places are likely to be.

Those deep places consist, in large part, in goods toward which we are drawn. The valorization of choice itself makes sense only if the objects of choice have independent significance, so that some choices are especially weighty.[76] These choices are the "fundamental religious, moral, and philosophical interests" that, Rawls thought, the parties to any fair social contract "must keep themselves free to honor."[77]

The goods are contestable. Some people reasonably reject them. Many are indifferent to religion. Some have never felt sexual desire. Some even find the demands of morality alienating.[78] The exigency of these goods is nonetheless a general fact about human psychology, at least in American society. Around here, one—not the only!—locus of depth is the nebula of practices and longings that cluster around the loose term "religion." If people were radically idiosyncratic in the needs that they assigned such weight, then the parties to the social contract would have no basis upon which to discern "forms of belief and conduct the protection of which we cannot properly abandon or be persuaded to jeopardize."[79]

We share recognition of the value of these goods, at least at an abstract level. That fact illuminates our individual perspectives on substantive religious beliefs that we find preposterous. *Your* specific religious beliefs and rituals strike me as weird and repellent. I am amazed that anyone can find transcendent meaning in *that*. But I know that religion falls within a field of human activity in which many of us deem our own beliefs and rituals good and worthy of respect, and in which our religious commitments are often unintelligible to one another. I can appreciate the urgency of your demand for a space in which to pursue your idiosyncratic religious needs.

This structure of argument supporting toleration and accommodation is not unique to conscience or religion. Consider sex. *Your* specific desires strike me as weird and repellent. I am amazed that anyone can be turned on by *that*. But I know that sex falls within a field of human activity in which many of us deem our own desires good and worthy of respect, and in which our desires are often unintelligible to one another. That's the argument for gay rights. I can appreciate the urgency of your demand for a space in which to pursue your idiosyncratic needs.

In each of these categories, the case for toleration and accommodation rests on a distinctive interlocking pattern of mutual transparency and opacity. Were there no transparency, we would not have devised these categories, which transcend our own specific orientations toward the good as we apprehend it. Were there no opacity, we would not be impelled to institutionalize our appreciation of the good under such intentionally vague descriptions as "religion" or "sexuality."

8

The racism analogy is misleading

During the controversy over the Indiana RFRA, the *New York Times* ran an editorial with this title: "In Indiana, Using Religion as a Cover for Bigotry."[1] The implicit assumption is that the objection to facilitating same-sex marriage isn't really religion at all, that it is a "cover" for something else. Something nasty.

That allegation wounds conservatives. Justice Anthony Kennedy's majority opinion in the Supreme Court decision recognizing same-sex marriage, *Obergefell v. Hodges*, was careful to declare that "many who deem same-sex marriage to be wrong reach that conclusion based on decent and honorable religious or philosophical premises, and neither they nor their beliefs are disparaged here."[2] The dissenters were not mollified. Chief Justice Roberts argued that Justice Kennedy's opinion portrays all who disagree with it as "bigoted."[3] Justice Scalia read Kennedy as saying that those who oppose same-sex marriage "cannot possibly be supported by anything other than ignorance or bigotry."[4] Justice Alito warned that despite the majority's "reassurances," the analogy to interracial marriage "will be used to vilify Americans who are unwilling to assent to the new orthodoxy." They will "risk being labeled as bigots and treated as such by governments, employers, and schools."[5]

The labeling and vilification are the most influential reason for refusing any religious exemption from antidiscrimination law. "Some views are truly bad enough that they deserve repudiation rather than accommodation," declares John Corvino.[6] Maggie Gallagher observes, "We do not draft legislative accommodations for irrational hatred."[7]

As we've seen, it's a long-settled custom in the United States to accommodate religious (and lately also nonreligious) conscientious objectors when this can be done without undermining the law's purposes. Chapter 4 presumed that principle and inquired whether the wedding vendors can thus be accommodated. But we did not engage with another, equally powerful principle: zero tolerance for racism and similar malign ideologies. Religious accommodation is often made available, but not for religious racists.

There could not and should not have been religious exemptions from the Civil Rights Act of 1964. From this one might infer—many do infer—that views like those of religious racists are not entitled to even the mild, defeasible presumption of accommodation that is generally extended to conscientious objectors.[8] A zero-tolerance rule will defeat proposals for accommodation at the outset.

The racism analogy is a conversation-stopper not only on the left, but also on the right. When people who resist same-sex marriage hear the analogy, Jonathan Rauch observes, they "snap into a defensive crouch and shut down."[9] He thinks we just shouldn't go there. But we are there. The analogy is ubiquitous, and it makes negotiation impossible, makes the very idea of negotiating repugnant.

This chapter will address the analogy, clarify what its claims are, and argue that it should not shut down the possibility of accommodation.

There is a growing consensus on the left that heterosexism is as evil as racism, and that it should be treated with comparable disdain.

Consider the contrast between the invocations at President Barack Obama's two inaugurals. For his first inaugural Obama chose evangelical leader Rick Warren, despite their disagreement about a California referendum banning same-sex marriage in the state. Warren's choice was controversial, but Obama was firm: "We're not going to agree on every single issue, [we need] to create an atmosphere where we can disagree without being disagreeable and then focus on those things that we hold in common as Americans."[10] Four years later, Louie Giglio, a pastor who had led the fight against human trafficking, was selected. A 1994 speech in which he described homosexuality as a "sin in the eyes of God" immediately surfaced. Giglio hadn't even expressed a view about gays' civil rights, as Warren had. It was a purely religious view. The White House came under enormous pressure to revoke the invitation, and he withdrew. The inaugural committee then stated: "We were not aware of Pastor Giglio's past comments at the time of his selection and they don't reflect our desire to celebrate the strength and diversity of our country at this Inaugural."[11] Michael Wear, who was in charge of the administration's evangelical outreach, nearly resigned over the episode. "In 2009, our diversity demanded we accept that there will be voices we disagree with in public spaces. In 2013, diversity required us to expel dissent."[12]

I happen to believe that there is no moral difference between heterosexual and homosexual sex, that Giglio is wrong to think that there is such a moral difference, and that this falsehood has been the cause of enormous harm. It would be a better world if no one believed this stuff.

If you disagree, I will not here try to convince you. I will, however, explain why my opinions about sexuality and morality do not necessarily entail that you must be treated the way Giglio was treated. Or even that you must be denied exemption from antidiscrimination law.

What, precisely, does it mean to say that objections to homosexual conduct are the moral equivalent of racism? It can mean more than one thing. The racism analogy is actually several different analogies. They need to be distinguished before we even know what we are arguing about. Otherwise, discussion tends to slide unconsciously from one to another. One might be comparing (1) their effects, (2) their moral errors, (3) the evil intentions of those who hold them, or (4) their status as views that are appropriately stigmatized. I will argue that even if heterosexism is just like racism on all of these dimensions, there are important differences. Religious heterosexism is (5) generally nonviolent. And (6) unlike in 1964, when the Civil Rights Act was passed, religious claims can be accommodated without defeating the point of the law. Establishing a legitimate place for dissenters, in a gay-friendly legal regime, would actually be helpful in addressing some of the most pressing contemporary gay rights issues, notably the often dire conditions of gay teenagers.

The first comparison focuses solely on effects. There are sometimes patterns of mistreatment based on socially salient traits, such as race. When that mistreatment—of which discrimination is one instance—occurs, it is destructive whatever the discriminator's motives, indeed even if the discriminator's reasons are sound. In a society in which racial segregation has led black people, in aggregate, to have worse educations than whites, it may be rational for employers to rely on that generalization to discriminate. Those individually rational decisions would then perpetuate a self-reinforcing pattern of subordination. That is good reason to prohibit them. Antigay prejudice produces the same kind of cumulative destructive effects as racism, ranging from employment discrimination to homicidal violence. However, that does not tell us whether religious accommodations can be permitted without defeating the purposes of antidiscrimination laws. Aggregate effects won't change much if a few people are permitted to discriminate.

A second analogy is that both treat people unjustly, on the basis of irrelevant characteristics. The soundness of this analogy depends on the premise that there is no valid reason for treating gay sex as inferior to heterosexual sex.

Those who hold traditional views of sexuality think there are such reasons. Justice Alito explains why they reject same-sex marriage: they believe "marriage is essentially the solemnizing of a comprehensive, exclusive, permanent union that is intrinsically ordered to producing new life, even if it does not always do so."[13] Whatever the merits of this notion,[14] it is not about gay people. It is focused on the value of a certain kind of heterosexual union.[15] The existence of gay people is a side issue.[16] The function of marriage, on this view, is to sanctify a human good that gay people happen to be unable to realize: their exclusion does not discriminate against them any more than art museums discriminate against blind people. The idea that homosexual sex is always wrong is harder to justify on nonreligious grounds, but it purports to be a reason why refraining from sex is in the deepest interests of gay people themselves.[17]

They are following the sexual ethic that, they believe, their religion has taught for centuries. They take those teachings seriously. They think that life and morality make no sense without a religious basis. Not all believers think that those traditions condemn as immoral any sexual activity outside heterosexual marriage. Every major religion is divided on that question. But these people honestly do think that.

I think that these ideas are obviously wrong. But that is what I think of an enormous range of beliefs, religious and other. Most Americans agree that some religious beliefs are contemptible lies. They disagree about which ones. This is nothing new. It is the chronic condition of the United States, probably the most religiously diverse nation in the history of the world.

The way we have coped with this diversity is to treat religion—understood at such an abstract level as to ignore all doctrinal differences—as a good, and to accommodate it where this is possible. We address the chronic human problems of suffering, guilt, and death in many different ways, and we treat one another's resolutions of those problems with respect even when they make no sense to us.

Accommodation from generally applicable laws always involves minorities—which means, in the context of religion, people who believe things that we in the majority regard as false. If they were the majority, the legal obligation they question wouldn't be there in the first place. Catholic countries don't ban sacramental wine. Falsity doesn't defeat the case for exemptions.

This brings us to a third analogy, the one that is probably doing most of the work. Racists are evil! And those who oppose gay equality would not claim to believe this garbage if they were not, in the words of *The New York Times*, using religion as a cover for bigotry. The *Times* isn't alone. A majority of the US Commission on Civil Rights declared that proposals for religious accommodation "represent an orchestrated, nationwide effort by extremists to promote bigotry, cloaked in the mantle of 'religious freedom,'" and "are pretextual attempts to justify naked animus against lesbian, gay, bisexual, and transgender people."[18] The same view underlay the declaration of the commissioner, in *Masterpiece Cakeshop*, that "to me it is one of the most despicable pieces of rhetoric that people can use to—to use their religion to hurt others." The Court observed that this disparaged the baker's religion "in at least two distinct ways: by describing it as despicable, and also by characterizing it as merely rhetorical—something insubstantial and even insincere." The Court might also have looked more closely at the phrase "use their religion"—a locution that also appeared in that *New York Times* headline. The implication is that the baker was not really motivated by his religion. He is using religion as a phony excuse for his malicious desire to harm. One uses a tool, and is not used by it.

Not only do such people not deserve accommodation. We don't mind if they are unhappy. Their unhappiness even gives us some satisfaction. It serves them right. Either they have it coming, or their pain could teach them to change their ways, or both.

The word "bigot" elicits an image of pure viciousness, sometimes hiding behind a mask of piety. It is reminiscent of what Coleridge wrote about Shakespeare's Iago, that whatever justifications he offered for his actions were "the motive-hunting of motiveless Malignity." Or Milton's Satan: "Evil, be thou my good."

But it's not true. In the most prominent cases, conservative Christians have been willing to endure huge fines, and sometimes the destruction of their businesses, rather than facilitate what they believe to be sinful conduct. In some of the cases they had previously been friendly with the gay complainants. They're idealists.

That doesn't mean, however, that they're different from racists. Here the analogy works, but it is radically misleading. There are racist idealists, too. Lester Maddox, who thought that segregation was mandated by the Bible, closed his restaurant in 1965 rather than integrate it. (After his resistance made him famous, he was elected governor of Georgia.)

The picture of racists as hate-filled demons isn't fair to them. It also supports a false distinction between racism and the rejection of homosexuality. Both views have been held by many otherwise decent people. That fact does not make the views less destructive and repugnant. But regarding the people themselves as vicious is its own form of vicious stereotype.

Ryan Anderson, resisting the analogy, argues that opposition to interracial marriage "is an outlier from the historic understanding and practice of marriage, founded not on decent and honorable premises but on bigotry."[19] So he infers that the racists had bad intentions. "Given the irrelevance of race to almost any transaction, and given the widespread and flagrant racial animus of the time, no claims of benign motives are plausible."[20] The intolerable character of these views explain why they could not have been accommodated.

An exemption to a law prohibiting racial discrimination in public accommodations could undermine the purpose of that law by sending the message that intentional racism is protected conduct. In sending that message, such an exemption would amplify existing messages that say African Americans count for less, are subhuman, and may be treated as such. In doing so, it increases the odds that people engage in deplorable acts based on notions of white supremacy.[21]

Michael Perry embraces similar reasoning:

The claim that same-sex sexual conduct is immoral does not assert, imply, or presuppose that those who engage in the conduct are morally inferior human beings, any more than the claim that theft is immoral asserts, implies, or presupposes that those who steal are morally inferior human beings. By contrast, "the very point" of laws that criminalized interracial marriage was "to signify and maintain the false and pernicious belief that nonwhites are morally inferior to whites."[22]

This is bad history. Many whites in the deep South accepted racial segregation because that was the natural and familiar order of things, the world they grew up in, or because they sincerely believed an interpretation of Christianity that mandated it. Their daily experience taught them that black people were happy with their lot. (The black people had learned to act contented whenever whites were watching, because any hint of dissent could place one in mortal danger.) Contra Perry, they believed that the racial hierarchy of their society was consistent with the Christian idea of the equality of souls before God. Racism, when it is conscious and pursued as a project, has a different face today, because it no longer consists in insouciant acceptance of the status quo. One must have a positive desire to lower the status of black people, and such desire is almost always accompanied by resentment and hatred. That is conspicuous in the contemporary alt-right movement. It was not ever thus.

Racial segregation rested on an elaborate racist theology. (So did slavery.) The Bible declares that God "separated the sons of Adam," and "hath determined . . . the bounds of their habitation."[23] From these and other verses the racist theologians inferred that it was not His intention that the races mix. Any effort to end racial distinctions defied God's plan and was evil. The most extreme form of that evil was interracial sex and marriage.[24]

Many examples of this racist religion can be offered. A prominent Virginia minister, Rev. James F. Burks of Bayview Baptist Church, declared that "when man . . . disregards the boundary lines God Himself has drawn, man assumes a prerogative that belongs to God alone."[25] The sermon was reprinted in many newspapers and circulated as a pamphlet. Mississippi Senator Theodore G. Bilbo explained that "miscegenation and amalgamation are sins of man in direct defiance with the will of God."[26] Georgia Governor Herman E. Talmadge argued that "God himself segregated the races."[27] The trial judge in *Loving v. Virginia*, the case in which the Supreme Court ultimately struck down laws against interracial marriage, was merely echoing conventional theology when he declared: "Almighty God created the races white, black, yellow, malay and red, and he placed them on separate continents. And, but for the interference with his arrangement, there would be no cause for such marriage. The fact that he separated the races shows that he did not intend for the races to mix."[28] Racist theology became more articulate in response to Martin Luther King Jr.'s invocation of Christianity against segregation. But it wasn't a new idea. "The theology of separate races constituted a kind of cultural religion that permeated the hearts and minds of attorneys and judges throughout the courts of the South for a hundred years after the Civil War."[29]

You may be inclined to dismiss this theology as a rationalization for an unjust social structure. And of course these beliefs would not have been adopted if the underlying racial hierarchies had not already been in place. But all religion has a legitimating function, bestowing an ultimate ontological status on always-precarious social institutions.[30] The fact that a religious belief has social causes does not necessarily mean that it is false or insincere. All beliefs have social causes.

The struggle over racial equality was a struggle of theologies, each often sincerely held. King's triumph was to reshape Christianity so that almost no one any longer takes its racist forms seriously.

One may, of course, plunge into theological controversy and say that there is a crucial disanalogy: one religious belief is sounder than the other. Damon Linker writes that the difference between the two theologies is that strictures against homosexuality are rooted far more deeply in the Judeo-Christian tradition than racism ever was. Yes, slavery is found throughout the Scriptures and comes in for criticism only, at best, by implication. But race-based slavery—and the racism that made it possible and continues to infect ideas and institutions throughout the West to this day—receives no explicit endorsement from the Bible.

Which isn't to say that those seeking to justify race-based slavery or racism couldn't, and didn't, twist biblical passages to make them provide such justification.[31]

If, however, the Establishment Clause means anything, it means that the state is not to adjudicate such controversies.[32] If the state started rejecting claims because of their bad theological bona fides, that would be the end of religious freedom.

You might regard this racist biblical exegesis as so daffy no one could possibly believe it. But that's not only true of racist theology. It is the problem of religious diversity. Nothing is more manifestly implausible than other people's religions.

The recognition that many racists were sincere believers disrupts settled narratives on both right and left. It makes it impossible for conservatives to say that because *we* are nice people, it follows that we are nothing at all like the racists. It makes it impossible for gay rights advocates to say that because you believe horrible things, it follows that you are horrible people.

I once showed John Rawls, the late Harvard philosopher who is the patron saint of modern liberals, the following passage by the conservative Christian theorist David Smolin:

> The problem, from a Christian perspective, is not that the non-Christian cannot sufficiently understand Christian doctrines, but rather that the non-Christian will not accept them. The barrier to becoming Christian is primarily ethical and stems from the sinful human nature, which refuses to submit to God.[33]

Rawls remarked that this was the attitude that most irritated him: the notion that if people disagree with us they must be evil.

The Left does it too. *The problem is not that the conservative Christian cannot sufficiently understand the value of same-sex relationships, but rather that the Christian will not accept them. The barrier to recognizing the value of same-sex relationships is primarily ethical* . . . Here, once more, the gay rights/religion controversy is an example of deeper currents in political polarization. Increasingly, across multiple political issues, honest disagreement is taken as evidence of bad character. That tendency is particularly salient here.

Racism is often regarded as if it were uniquely evil, sharply distinct from all the other misperceptions that lead people to mistreat one another. Heterosexism is then alleged to be similarly extraordinary. But there's nothing unique here. Our understandings of other human beings are routinely delusional. We constantly rely on stereotypes and snap judgments. And we often do this sincerely, trying our best to do what is right.

Justice Kennedy writes:

Prejudice, we are beginning to understand, rises not from malice or hostile animus alone. It may result as well from insensitivity caused by simple want of careful, rational reflection or from some instinctive mechanism to guard against people who appear to be different in some respects from ourselves.[34]

Prejudice "can stem from indifference or insecurity as well as from malicious ill will."[35] These passages were repeatedly quoted with approval by the Obama Administration in its amicus briefs in the Supreme Court same-sex marriage cases.[36] Here prejudice begins to be indistinguishable from ordinary error.

Iris Murdoch argues that the chief enemy of morality is "personal fantasy: the tissue of self-aggrandizing and consoling wishes and dreams which prevents one from seeing what is there outside one."[37] Liberalism is the enemy of this kind of fantasy. It demands sympathetic identification with the other. (As in its own way does liberalism's Siamese twin, capitalism, which requires that one know one's market.[38]) The gay rights movement's principal enemy is the once-ubiquitous bizarre fantasy of what gay people must be like.

The polarization of American politics rests on similar abuses of fantasy.

Sometimes, of course, our misjudgments are reprehensible. They originate in culpable self-indulgence and intellectual laziness. That's Kennedy's point. We have an obligation to reflect on our insensitivity and try to overcome it.

A prime example is the conservative condemnation of transgender people. "Bathroom bills" require them to use the sex-segregated toilet of their genetic sex, placing them at risk of physical assault on the basis of imaginary fears. This book is written in a forgiving mood, but this is the movement on the Religious Right that is hardest to forgive. Although conservative Christians continue to make unreasonable demands that gay people be celibate, they no longer seem to want them to leave the planet. Many of them remain unreconciled to the very existence of transgender people.

Some racists accept their culture's racism so unquestioningly that their moral culpability is uncertain. Others guiltily weave an elaborate tissue of self-justifying rationalizations. Some are motivated by pure malignity. Similarly with heterosexism. It is hard for people who do not know us to tell whether we are wicked, culpably negligent, or invincibly ignorant. We often don't see the truth about ourselves.[39]

If you need an analogy, a better one than the racism move is with the anti-vaxxers, who foolishly think that they are protecting their children by refusing to vaccinate them. They are a public health menace. But their ignorant notions are not an insincere pretext for hurting children. They are otherwise decent people who happen to hold badly wrongheaded beliefs.

There has been a lot of philosophical work on the Problem of Evil. It isn't noticed often enough that its close sibling is the Problem of Stupid. It can be hard to tell them apart.

A final analogy is that just like racists, heterosexists are disgusting. This is not an argument so much as a visceral reason for denying their claims. It regards their views as so repellent as to be the object of a kind of taboo. This kind of reaction can be seen in the inaugural committee's comment on Giglio: one 1994 statement that homosexuality is sinful rendered him unfit to give Obama's invocation in 2012.

A similar taboo has developed for racism. It was not always the case that "racist" was one of the worst things one could call a person. That ethic was deliberately constructed. It has done a lot of good. Pervasive prejudice has to be combated with equally strong cultural forces.

Liberal theorists are uncomfortable with the invocation of such primitive impulses, but they appear to be an ineradicable part of humanity's moral vocabulary.[40] Ideas of purity had been powerfully deployed on behalf of racism. The Left captured purity and turned it against the enemy. Racism itself has come to be stigmatized as contaminating. A similar cultural reversal has been directed at "homophobia."[41] As with racism, the stigmatization of gays is so deeply rooted in American culture that it is probably necessary to rely on this kind of countertaboo in order to respond to it. In each case, the aim is to induce citizens to regard the relevant prejudice as itself ritually unclean.

That's why it is such a conversation stopper to ask, "Would you exempt religiously based discrimination against interracial couples?" The reaction is instantaneous. Yuck. That would be gross, even if there were only one such discriminator in the world.[42] But disgust is an unreliable basis for political action.[43] The question raises a deep problem if there is some principle that covers both cases and demands that both be treated similarly. Legislation is not thus constrained: one can accommodate selectively.

The Left's sense of contamination goes beyond discrimination. It can extend even to those who comply with the law, if they think the wrong thoughts. A Canadian jeweler willingly custom-made a pair of engagement rings for a same-sex couple. When they discovered that the jeweler had publicly posted a sign saying, "The sanctity of marriage is under attack. Let's keep marriage between a man and a woman," the couple demanded their money back. After being inundated with hateful emails, phone calls, and threats, the jeweler gave in.[44] It appears that he would be wrong whether he discriminated or not.

The racism analogy is malign and destructive insofar as it leads Americans to regard their fellow citizens as hateful demons. Demons are, of course, mythical creatures, and the very notion of them raises logical puzzles: how could any being with free will be unchangeably evil? But, Samuel Fleischacker observes, when we designate others as demons, we license whatever mistreatment is necessary to defend ourselves against them, and so "become ourselves as close as human beings can to being demons."[45]

This kind of crude Manicheanism has its political uses. But when it reaches the point that large numbers of citizens look at one another as irredeemable fiends, it has gotten out of hand. We are going to have to live together.

In many ways, then, the analogy to racism is sound. Heterosexism is harmful, it's based on error, some (but not all) of its proponents have bad motives, and it's appropriately treated with disgust. The analogy is, however, misleading to the extent that it ignores the fact that even some racists were foolish rather than evil. There are also important disanalogies.

In 1964, when the Civil Rights Act was enacted, religious objections to integration were so common among Southern whites that any accommodation would inevitably have defeated the aims of the statute. Most of them would have pounced upon the opportunity.[46] That's why it was so obvious that those claims—even if they were sincere and made by good-willed people with innocently mistaken views—had to be rejected. Racism remains a powerful force in American culture and politics, so that a zero-tolerance response is appropriate.[47]

I have argued that it is unlikely that there will be a flood of exemption claims, even in the parts of the country that are most opposed to same-sex marriage. Your judgment of likelihood may reasonably differ from mine. And such slippery-slope concerns could be a sound basis for opposing any exemptions. But notice how this response shifts the conversation.

The same kind of uncertain guess must be made whenever religious accommodations are proposed. One must always ask whether there will be so many claims that the law's purpose will be thwarted—whether the exemption of the Catholic Mass from the 1919 Volstead Act's prohibition of alcohol would lead huge numbers to convert to Catholicism just so they can imbibe (it didn't), or whether exempting all pacifists would hamstring the military draft (at the end of the Vietnam war, it did). It is no longer about evil people, or contamination by bigotry. It does not rule out accommodations as a matter of principle.

I suspect that many gay people misperceive the situation for the following reason. Discrimination and violence—open, unapologetic, hateful—have been part of their daily experience since adolescence. If you're subjected to enough of that stuff, you're going to see the danger of it everywhere. It's hard to get your mind around the fact that the vicious monster who abused you is now in hospice care.

I published an earlier version of this book's argument in a law review article,[48] which elicited an angry response from Shannon Gilreath and Arley Ward. That response deserves to be addressed in detail. They answered the preceding paragraph (which first appeared in that article) by pointing out that the monster is still pretty vicious:

> Gay youth are disproportionately homeless—put out or driven out by religiously-motivated cruelty. Also, "28% of homosexual youth were dropping out of secondary school because of discomfort and fear." Gay youth are disproportionately addicted to alcohol and drugs. And gay youth have a suicide rate nearly five times that of their straight counterparts. . . . The most recently-available FBI hate crime statistics show that 20% of all hate crimes committed in the United States are perpetrated on gay people. This, despite the fact that we account for around 4% of the overall population. Within this class of already heinous, bias-motivated crimes, we also fare horribly when it comes to the most vicious crimes against the person. Gay men are the victims of 40% of all bias-related murders. That equals two in every five. Lesbians comprise 66% of rapes. And this despite the fact that we know FBI statistics are dramatically underreported.[49]

All this is true. I was wrong to write that "the gay rights movement has won."[50] They are right to call me out for it. Like many gay rights advocates, I was too focused on the then-recent marriage victory.

But I stand by my next sentences: "It will not be stopped by a few exemptions. It should be magnanimous in victory."[51] The victory is not complete, but it is major. Denying exemptions is not necessary in order to address the atrocities Gilreath and Ward enumerate. Those atrocities will not be prevented by shutting down a few Christian bakeries and florists.

Gilreath and Ward write that any exemption from antidiscrimination law would make gay people into "a legal underclass that can be deprived of all manner of services and accommodations under the imprimatur of the state."[52] Antidiscrimination law in most states is an exception to the normal rule of contract at will. All citizens thus are already in this "underclass," unless the deprivation is based on a forbidden category of discrimination. Merchants can even turn away African Americans, so long as they don't do so on the basis of race. They can, for example, demand identification and then reject anyone, black or white, who was born in August.

Gilreath dismisses the idea that market incentives will do any good: "But any system of subordination exists and subsists by rendering the inferior dependent upon the superior. In a tortured paradox, subordinated people are asked to depend upon the people who subordinate them to protect them from subordination."[53] Those same market forces protect everyone, not just gay people.

Gilreath and Ward go on:

"Thugs who randomly attack gay people on city streets," Koppelman writes, "are not motivated by moral objections to [gay people's] conduct." I would like to know exactly which thugs he asked. When religious ethos brands gays as untouchable, unnatural, and abominable, the fact that they can be harmed with impunity should be no surprise.[54]

The logic is depressingly familiar: some members of group X hurt me, therefore every member of X is malevolent and dangerous. Violence against gays is "more often than not born of religious prejudice."[55] Measures to accommodate the occasional baker or florist "are really proposals for the institutionalization of violence against Gays, with impunity for it in law."[56] Religion is the enemy and must be fought at every turn. This kind of thinking happens a lot. Many Americans are profoundly ignorant of Islam. After the September 11, 2001 attacks, they were ripe for paranoid libels, culminating in the incomparable Trump's declaration that "Islam hates us."

The notion that all religious conservatives yearn to beat up gay people has been an effective rhetorical trope, but it unfairly stereotypes those it purports to describe—much like the vicious old notion of gay men as misogynistic, amoral sociopaths. (It also overstates the role of religion, and understates the role of masculine gender anxiety, in the violence that does take place.[57]) Among people who believe that homosexual conduct is intrinsically wrong, the vast majority repudiate violence, and many even support antidiscrimination protection for gays. In Alabama, for example, a majority oppose same-sex marriage but 58% support a discrimination law.[58]

Violence was integral to the system that religious racists sought to defend. Consider again Senator Bilbo, whose theology we quoted earlier. He understood what it took to deny black citizens the franchise: "White people will be justified in going to any extreme to keep the nigger from voting. You and I know what's the best way to keep the nigger from voting. You do it the night before the election. I don't have to tell you any more than that. Red-blooded men know what I mean."[59] He vigorously opposed a proposed federal prohibition of lynching: "Upon your garments and the garments of those who are responsible for this measure will be the blood of the raped and outraged daughters of Dixie, as well as the blood of the perpetrators of these crimes that the red-blooded Anglo-Saxon white southern men will not tolerate."[60] (Yet even he wasn't self-consciously evil. He was unusual among Mississippi politicians in avoiding racist appeals for most of his career, although he went far in the other direction in his last years, when there was a real possibility that civil rights legislation would be enacted. He declared to a black newspaper editor in a 1947 deathbed interview: "I am honestly against the social intermingling of negroes and whites. But, I hold nothing personal against negroes as a race. God made them as they are and they should be proud of that God-given heritage as I am of mine."[61] Morally judging even Bilbo is a complex matter.)

Bilbo rejected, as a matter of principle, a politics based on mutual respect. The condition of his soul has no political relevance. He urged his followers to physically attack black people who asserted a right to such respect. There is no place in a free society for such views.

The conservative Christian wedding vendors, on the other hand, just want to be left alone. It is possible to live with them. They can even be helpful against the worst abuses that gay people suffer.

Homelessness is one of the cruelties that Gilreath and Ward enumerate. It is worse than discrimination. The most pressing gay rights issue today is the toxic environment that many gay teenagers face.[62] They reveal their sexuality to their families at younger ages than they once did, and those families are often utterly unequipped to understand them. Their parents often throw them out of the house, or make their lives so difficult that they run away. At least 20% of homeless youth identify as LGBT, even though that group is 3 to 5% of the general population. On the most conservative estimate, there are more than 100,000 of them in the United States.[63] They are vulnerable to depression, substance abuse, and crime. Lacking marketable skills, they are likely to engage in "survival sex," exchanging sex for money, food, clothing, shelter, or drugs.[64]

What do Gilreath and Ward propose to do about that? How will shutting down wedding vendors help?

Legal coercion is the wrong tool for the job. Family conflict is the source of most youth homelessness, gay or straight. Parents need to be persuaded to change their treatment of their LGBT children. Who are they likely to listen to? Not Gilreath, or Ward, or me.

On the other hand, consider Russell Moore, president of the Southern Baptist Convention's Ethics & Religious Liberty Commission. He promotes the religious ideas that Gilreath and Ward blame for violence and homelessness. He calls on those attracted to persons of the same sex "to cease such sexual activity in obedience to Christ."[65] Homosexual conduct is categorically wrong: "There are no circumstances in which a man and a man or a woman and a woman can be morally involved in a sexual union."[66] He opposes any antidiscrimination protection for gay people,[67] explaining that while he doesn't want them "treated spitefully or unfairly," any legal protection "aids and abets the cultural forces that would render historic Christian beliefs on sexuality (and even marriage) suspect and eventually out of bounds."[68] If you are waiting for these views to disappear, you will wait a long time.

Moore also acknowledges, however, that "gay and lesbian homelessness is an issue that the Christian church ought to care about."[69] He is admirably emphatic about this issue.

> I had someone tell me not long ago, who works with homeless teenagers, about how many homeless gay and lesbian and transgender teenagers he comes across who are thrown out on the street by Christian parents. Brothers and sisters that ought to be a scandal to us. The scripture does not call us to throw our children out on the streets.[70]

And:

> We have a situation in American culture where gay and lesbian people have often been treated really really badly. That's one of the reasons why we've spent a lot of time trying to work specifically with parents of gay and lesbian kids to say, "How do you respond when your child announces, 'I'm gay or I'm lesbian'?" And the answer to that is not rejection, the answer to that is not shunning, the answer to that is certainly not putting someone out of the house. The answer to that is loving your child and bearing with your child and if you disagree with your child, you disagree with your child.[71]

He has also repudiated "ex-gay" therapy as the fraud that it is.[72] He is not alone.

There are movements within conservative Christianity to support LGBT youth and their families without abandoning their traditional sexual ethics. They get almost no support from gay rights organizations. Opportunities for collaboration are being neglected. Both sides have an interest in making those communities better places for gay youth to live, and the young people themselves often are looking for ways to reconcile their sexuality with their religious beliefs. On the rare occasions that staff from conservative religious schools have met with LGBT advocates to learn one another's perspectives and concerns, the schools have responded by reaching out more actively to their LGBT students. The Council on Christian Colleges and Universities has sponsored programming on how member schools can be more supportive of LGBT students. They can do this without unqualified acceptance of gay sexuality.[73]

Moore denounced Trump's racism and nativism during the 2016 election, and struggled unsuccessfully to persuade his fellow evangelicals that they would betray their principles if they supported him. His opposition to Trump almost cost him his job.

Is Moore really the enemy?

When Churchill was asked whether, in helping Stalin to resist Hitler's invasion, he was compromising his anticommunist principles, he responded: "Not at all. I have only one purpose; the destruction of Hitler, and my life is much simplified thereby. If Hitler invaded Hell, I would make at least a favorable reference to the Devil in the House of

Commons."[74] Our purpose should be preventing parents from making their gay children homeless. Our life should be much simplified thereby.

It is pernicious to say or imply that gay people are intrinsically defective and irredeemable; that because of their unchosen desires, they deserve eternal punishment. Can one live with people who think and say that? We already do. That's what Calvinists think and say about everyone. Only the unmerited grace of God saves (some of) us. They inflict dignitary harm on the entire human race. We can live with it.

Both gay people and religious conservatives seek space in society wherein they can live out their beliefs, values, and identities. As with the old religious differences that begot the Establishment Clause of the First Amendment, each side's most basic commitments entail that the other is in error about moral fundamentals, that the other's entire way of life is predicated on that error and ought not to exist.

I feel that way about my conservative friends who believe that no one should ever engage in homosexual sex. They are gravely and tragically wrong. It is deplorable that they believe what they believe. It would be a better world if no one held these particular religious views. They should be ashamed of themselves and repent that they ever believed these things. It is good that their view is (slowly!) disappearing. "Their children's children shall say they have lied."[75]

But of course they feel the same way about me. So what are we supposed to do?

Disagreement about moral fundamentals is nothing new. It is the chronic human condition. The point of freedom of speech and religion is not to end these conflicts, but to redirect them to nonviolent channels. Their nonviolence does not mean that they will be pleasant.

Here's the last analogy with racism. It's an awful, hurtful idea, and it's distressing to encounter it. So is heterosexism. That analogy, however, points in the direction of toleration. We tolerate racist speech.

There is one harm that the state mustn't protect you from: the specific offense of discovering that some of your fellow citizens despise what you hold sacred. The harm here is of the same kind as the harm caused by blasphemous or heretical speech.

Free speech welcomes what many people will find painful: the open collision of moral views. When John Stuart Mill's classic defense of free speech balances liberty against harm, Jeremy Waldron has observed, that balancing cannot count as harm the moral distress of having your most cherished views denounced, or of contemplating ways of life antithetical to your own.[76] A core value of free speech is that it will and must induce such distress. Mill, and liberalism more generally, places great value on "ethical confrontation—the open clash between earnestly held ideals and opinions about the nature and basis of the good life."[77] Moral distress, "far from being a legitimate ground for interference ... is a positive and healthy sign that the processes of ethical confrontation that Mill called for are actually taking place."[78] Part of the reason for protecting illiberal ideas is that they promise to induce that distress.[79] This valorization of moral distress is not peculiar to Mill. It is a central part of the free speech tradition.[80]

The gay rights movement was permitted, by free speech law, to disseminate views that were almost universally regarded as so offensive to religious sensibilities as to be intolerable.[81] Freedom of speech permitted gay people to escape that societal institution of solitary confinement familiarly called "the closet." The movement was allowed with impunity to provoke enormous moral distress in its adversaries.

Robert Frost famously said, "A liberal is a man too broadminded to take his own side in a quarrel."[82] But liberalism is in fact a demanding creed.[83]

Often there's no joy in discovering what others really think of the gods we worship. It is more comfortable to fantasize that everyone basically agrees with us about fundamentals. The suppression of blasphemy and heresy thus encourages a kind of solipsism.[84] If we are going to have transparency, if we are to escape the solitary confinement of our own minds,[85] then we are going to have to learn to live with moral confrontation.

America tolerates racism. It lets racist citizens think for themselves and pursue their ideals. They can even cause dignitary harm by preaching their loathsome views. Americans have managed to resist Communism and Naziism without the state hectoring us about them.[86] The enemy is heterosexism. It is not the occasional merchant who dissents from antidiscrimination laws. We can work to eliminate his ideas without eliminating him.

9

There are many ways to compromise

Some political deals are what Avishai Margalit calls "rotten compromises," such as "an agreement to establish or maintain an inhuman regime."[1] A rotten compromise is "a compromise one should avoid under any circumstances."[2] Compromising the gay rights/religious liberty question is not that.

Margalit observes that even when a compromise isn't rotten, there can still be substantial obstacles. One of these, familiar to him as an Israeli, is the idea of the holy: any compromise is sacrilege. Claims then become absolute. "The politics of the holy may include cessation of violence but never cessation of the expectation of violence."[3] There is also a tendency to overstate the pain of our own compromises without attention to the stakes for the other. "We tend to regard our own concessions as real sacrifices and minimize the concessions of the other side."[4] One can see all of these in the gay rights/religion controversy: each side attributes the worst possible motives to the other, assigns a kind of sacred status to its own interests, and regards the other's as trivial.

Compromise has its dangers. "Ideals may tell us something important about what we would like to be," Margalit writes. "But compromises tell us who we are."[5] A refusal to compromise, when one was possible, also tells us who we are.

This book has focused on public accommodation laws. For that reason, I haven't discussed the most important and encouraging compromise that has occurred to date. In a deal between the gay community and the Church of Jesus Christ of Latter-Day Saints, tirelessly facilitated by Professor Robin Fretwell Wilson, the Utah legislature banned discrimination on the basis of sexual orientation in employment or housing. The law does not apply to employers of fewer than 15 employees. Churches, the Boy Scouts, and religious nonprofits and their affiliates are completely exempt. But the statute does not cover public accommodations at all. That one evidently was too tough for the legislature to take on.

There have, however, been specific compromises proposed, and in some cases enacted. This chapter critically evaluates them. I mentioned my own in chapter 4, and develop it further here. Assessing it demands comparison with others that are on offer, so I begin with them. Even the most problematic of them, such as the Mississippi statute, has elements that would be worth considering if coupled with antidiscrimination protection for gay people—protection that, to say it again, does not exist in most states.

I'll begin with those that require no change at all in present law.

The religiously scrupulous could choose to work for businesses that will serve as buffers between them and the public, in order to insulate them from work that they are unwilling to do.[6] A wedding vendor is always free to merge their company with some larger enterprise, some of whose employees had no objection to participating in same-sex weddings. Any business can accommodate religious objectors by giving tasks involving same-sex marriages only to the employees who have no religious objections. Customers never even have to know about the arrangement.[7]

A business can also refrain from holding itself out to the public, and rely entirely on private social networks. No public website, no phone book listing. Word of mouth, perhaps within megachurches, for example, might be able to generate a large enough customer base for a business to remain in operation. It can provide services without being a public accommodation. Given the high failure rate of small businesses, however, it would be foolish not to want as large a customer base as possible.[8]

The remedy to which religious conservatives have been most drawn is a state-level mini-RFRA, such as was contemplated in Arizona, Indiana, and many other states. It is what the fighting has been about. Such laws may appear to be an attractive compromise, because they call on courts directly to balance religious liberty against the interest in protecting gay people from discrimination.

These have been overrated as a defense. Wedding vendors' claims have been rejected by courts in New Mexico, New York, Colorado,

Oregon, and Washington State.[9] The trouble is the vagueness of the RFRA standard: it's hard to predict how a court will apply it in any particular case. Each side of the controversy thus has some basis for focusing on its worst case scenario.[10]

It's hard to compromise when we don't know what we are agreeing to. Lawyers distinguish between rules and standards. A rule is clear and easy to apply: there's no doubt about how you're obligated to respond to a red traffic light. Standards, on the other hand, such as the injunction to drive with a reasonable degree of care, involve more discretion and unpredictability in the application. Rules are cruder, but one can be much more confident about how they will be applied.[11] RFRA enacts a standard, not a rule. When we look for a compromise here, only rules will do.

That is the deepest problem with any proposed judicial resolution. All, whether they are based on religious liberty, free speech, or a statutory RFRA, involve the application of contestable standards. The principles with which judges work do not yield bright lines, but rather general considerations that must be worked out on a case by case basis. This is a job for legislatures, not for courts.

The vagueness of mini-RFRAs may explain why conservative interest has shifted to more specific statutes. The most comprehensive of these is Mississippi's 2016 Protecting Freedom of Conscience from Government Discrimination Act. It holds that businesses and individuals may not be subjected to any adverse action for actions reflecting their beliefs that "(a) Marriage is or should be recognized as the union of one man and one woman; (b) Sexual relations are properly reserved to such a marriage; and (c) Male (man) or female (woman) refer to an individual's immutable biological sex as objectively determined by anatomy and genetics at time of birth."[12] Similar legislation is being considered in a number of other states.

The statute mentions nearly every issue that frightens conservative Christians. Its proponents view it in entirely defensive terms. "Because the Supreme Court has already essentially validated this view that same-sex couples can marry, this is the balancing act to say, 'Well, people with religious beliefs also still have rights,'" declared Forest Thigpen, president of the Mississippi Center for Public Policy.[13] The beliefs in question are protected against adverse tax, benefit, and employment treatment, fines, and the denial of occupational licenses. The statute provides a defense against private suits. The law protects religious organizations' decisions regarding employment, housing, the placement of children in foster or adoptive homes, or the solemnization of marriage; parents' decisions to raise their children in accordance with one or more of the enumerated beliefs, and businesses providing wedding services. Doctors and mental health counselors may decline services on the basis of those beliefs so long as it does not interfere with "visitation, recognition of a designated representative for health care decision-making, or emergency medical treatment necessary to cure an illness or injury as required by law." Businesses providing wedding services are likewise protected. Any entity may establish sex-specific standards for locker rooms or restrooms. County clerks and judges may decline to license or celebrate marriages, provided the official gives prior notice and "any legally valid marriage is not impeded or delayed as a result of any recusal."

The provisos for visitation and avoiding delay indicate that the law attempts, in its own way, to offer a compromise. It protects what it takes to be the most urgent interests of gay couples. But it does so weakly: it does not say what happens if every clerk in a single office has the same objection.

Most religious accommodation statutes exempt specified conduct. This one singles out particular beliefs and then exempts a huge range of conduct associated with those beliefs. It thus authorizes a broad license to deny services in any circumstance in which the provision of those services might be taken to connote approval of same-sex marriage. A restaurant could eject a couple in the middle of their meal when it realizes that they are gay.

The law's license to discriminate is so broad as to essentially wipe out any antidiscrimination protection, since any defendant in a discrimination suit could offer it as a defense. This doesn't have much effect today, since Mississippi has no statewide antidiscrimination protection for gay people. One city, Jackson, offers such protection, and its law loses much of its effect as a result of the statute.

When the law was challenged, the district court concluded that the law violates the Equal Protection Clause of the Fourteenth Amendment, because it authorizes "arbitrary discrimination against lesbian, gay, transgender, and unmarried persons." It also violates the Establishment Clause: "The state has put its thumb on the scale to favor some religious beliefs over others." The injunction was reversed on technical grounds unrelated to the merits, and so the constitutional question remains unresolved.[14] (The law also provoked a protest campaign that distributed stickers to businesses announcing, "We Don't Discriminate. If You're Buying, We're Selling."[15])

This clumsy and one-sided statute won't solve our problem.

There have been other statutes designed to help conservative Christians.[16] They tend to be reactive, in response to various perceived threats. For example, in response to the nonfunding of the Christian Legal Society, a Kansas law forbade state colleges from discriminating against student groups that impose religious conditions on their members.[17]

Many proposals protect religious entities from losing contracts or grants on grounds of discrimination. In some communities, only a few organizations provide social services, and if they are allowed to discriminate, benefits to LGBT people could be cut off altogether.[18]

Some proposals target wedding services, nullifying antidiscrimination laws as applied to them. Some cover only businesses that reflect artistic or creative expression. Some allow foster care or adoption agencies to discriminate when their religion so dictates. A few permit religiously motivated denial of health care or mental health counseling.

A group of law professors—Robin Fretwell Wilson, Thomas C. Berg, Carl H. Esbeck, Richard W. Garnett, and Edward McGlynn Gaffney Jr.—has proposed a model statute. They have refined it over a period of years in response to objections.

The model statute declares that "no individual, sole proprietor, or small business shall be required to . . . provide goods or services that assist or promote the solemnization or celebration of any marriage, or provide counseling or other services that directly facilitate the perpetuation of any marriage" if doing so would cause those providers "to violate their sincerely held religious beliefs." A "small business" is defined as an entity "(A) that provides services which are primarily performed by an owner of the business; or (B) that has five or fewer employees; or (C) in the case of a legal entity that offers housing for rent, that owns five or fewer units of housing." It also provides that landlords who own "five or fewer units of housing" need not "provide housing to any married couple." The statute further provides that it would not apply if "a party to the marriage is unable to obtain [similar goods or services] without substantial hardship."[19]

Flynn worries about the breadth of the model statute's language:

> Although framed in terms of marriage and sexual orientation, the exemptions' reach extends far beyond both: they excuse compliance from fair housing laws, healthcare, education, adoption, employment, government contracts, licensing, grants, tax-exempt status, and anywhere else that public accommodations laws apply. In addition, they permit sincerely-held religious objections based on any protected classification, including race, sex, sexual orientation, and religion.[20]

She fears that the statute will be invoked a lot.[21] Elizabeth Sepper observes that the term "facilitate" "arguably sweeps in businesses and individuals that might be expected to acknowledge a couple's married status or treat same-sex couples equally to opposite-sex couples at any time in their married lives."[22]

The "substantial hardship" proviso is vague, and it is uncertain whether it can be refined into a rule clear enough to guide people prospectively. Critics have concluded that this drafting problem makes the proposal unworkable.[23] As drafted, it would be a reliable safe harbor for religious dissenters in urban areas where search costs are low. These cases have thus far arisen only in such areas. A great deal turns on how many claims for exemption arise.

Another intractable difficulty is that a drafter must decide whether an accommodation would apply to religious objections to the facilitation of other marriages, such as interracial marriages. There is no good answer to that question: either we declare that heterosexism isn't as bad as racism, a result repugnant to gay rights advocates, or we license discrimination against interracial couples, a result repugnant to almost everyone. Which is the least bad will be determined by politics. But keep in mind that the problem is largely theoretical: in recent years, there has been one reported case of a person refusing to facilitate interracial unions, which elicited nearly unanimous condemnation.[24]

The closest one can come to a resolution under present law is for a business to exercise its free speech rights in a way that makes it unlikely that gay couples will ever show up. The principal defect of this approach is that it opens up opportunities for abuse. That is what leads me to conclude that businesses should be permitted to refuse to facilitate same-sex weddings if they publicly make their objections clear.

In the wedding photographer case, the New Mexico Supreme Court declared that "businesses retain their First Amendment rights to express their religious or political beliefs. They may, for example, post a disclaimer on their website or in their studio advertising that they oppose same-sex marriage but that they comply with applicable antidiscrimination laws."[25] That will persuade most gay customers to look elsewhere, with no formal change in antidiscrimination law. The New Mexico court does not notice that this accommodation is in tension with the antidiscrimination laws of some states, which would treat this kind of disclaimer as creating an actionable hostile environment. I've argued elsewhere that this application of hostile environment law raises such severe free speech problems that state courts should avoid construing their statutes in this way.[26] The New Mexico court essentially did that: it evidently supposes, and in effect announces, that such disclaimers are now permissible in that state.

Can the disclaimers explicitly ask gay couples to stay away? Consider a model statement suggested by Russell Nieli:

> We are required by the Sexual Orientation and Gender Identity (SOGI) provision of New York State's anti-discrimination statute to make our wedding facilities available to anyone who seeks to use them, including gay and lesbian couples who want to marry under New York's same-sex marriage law. We believe strongly in the democratic process and the rule of law. For this reason, we will obey the state law governing our business. However, we obey this law only under the gravest protest, as we believe it violates our deepest moral and religious convictions. It does so needlessly and with apparent intent to polarize our country and inflame an already overheated cultural war.
>
> We are Christians, and we believe that marriage is exclusively a relationship between one man and one woman. It should not, in our

view, be construed as a relationship between people of the same sex or relationships involving three or more people.

We realize, however, that there are many people today who do not agree with us on these matters, and who hold their opposing views just as strongly as we hold ours. We respect the views of such people. We only ask that such people respect our own views in the same way that we respect theirs, and that, in the interest of tolerance and religious pluralism, they join us in seeking repeal of a law which requires us to violate our conscience. Those people who do not believe that marriage need be restricted to its traditional form and who seek a venue to celebrate non-traditional marriages have access to many other catering halls in this area that would be more than happy to accommodate their wishes.

Please do not ask us to violate our religious beliefs. We all must work together to accommodate our sincerely held differences in these matters. Our continued existence as a free, vibrant, tolerant and loving people surely depends upon it.[27]

The last four sentences of Nieli's announcement are addressed directly and specifically to same-sex couples, rather than being an announcement to the world of the owner's views. They clearly indicate that such couples are not welcome, and so are a "constructive refusal to serve"—an action that is not expressly discriminatory, but that offers service on such harsh terms that it might as well be. They are not protected by freedom of speech: discrimination is illegal, and free speech does not protect threats to engage in illegal conduct.[28] They are also unnecessary. The preceding sentences make the owner's views clear.

The question whether any sign is a constructive refusal to serve is a contextual one, and so does not lend itself to a formulaic solution. The New Mexico court, however, offers a constitutionally protected template, much briefer than Nieli's—"We oppose same-sex marriage but we comply with applicable antidiscrimination laws."

Such an announcement is protected by the First Amendment. But it leaves open the possibility that wedding vendors could thus make themselves targets for abusive and malicious lawsuits.

That is what happened after the Supreme Court's decision in *Masterpiece Cakeshop*.[29] The baker, Jack Phillips, had paid a steep price for his intransigence. He stopped baking wedding cakes altogether, sacrificing about 40% of his business. He had to lay off half his employees. He received hateful phone calls and emails, including multiple death threats. Rocks were thrown through the bakery's windows. He was forced to install security cameras. His wife was afraid to set foot in the bakery.

One Denver attorney, Autumn Scardina, made it her mission to penalize him even further. In September 2017, Phillips received an email asking for a custom cake "to celebrate" Satan's "birthday." The cake was to have "red and black icing" and include "an upside down cross, under the head of Lucifer." The customer described the cake as "religious in theme" and reminded Phillips that "religion is a protected class." Phillips declined, and a few days later received a phone call asking for a similar cake, with an image of Satan smoking marijuana. "Scardina" appeared on the caller ID screen. On the day the Supreme Court issued its decision, an email from "a member of the Church of Satan" included the following request:

> I'm thinking a three-tiered white cake. Cheesecake frosting. And
> the topper should be a large figure of Satan, licking a 9" black Dildo.
> I would like the dildo to be an actual working model, that can be
> turned on before we unveil the cake. I can provide it for you if you
> don't have the means to procure one yourself.

A few weeks later, two visitors to the cake shop requested a custom cake with a pentagram, a symbol commonly linked to witchcraft. When Phillips asked for the customers' names, one answered "Autumn Marie." Phillips believes that was Scardina. He refused all these requests, which he was entitled to do, since he would not have baked these cakes for anyone. There was no discrimination.

Finally, Scardina cleverly requested a cake that was blue outside and pink inside, and then explained that the cake's purpose was to celebrate her transition from male to female. This was a trap, and Phillips fell for it. He obviously would have had no problem creating a cake with those colors if it reflected a mere aesthetic preference. But he would not bake the exact same cake for a transgender woman. The Civil Rights Commission found him liable.

Phillips sued the state, claiming that "Colorado has been on a crusade to crush [him] because its officials despise what he believes and how he practices his faith."[30] He picked the wrong target. The crusade was coming, not from the state, but from Scardina.

As a matter of Colorado law, the Commission made the right call. Phillips will sell the exact same cake to most people, but not to Scardina. It is true that the same object will have different significations in different contexts, but as I showed in chapter 5, any exception based on that premise will destroy all of antidiscrimination law.

The district court refused to dismiss Phillips's complaint against the Commission, relying on the Supreme Court's confused finding that it was inappropriately discriminatory to allow some refusals to bake cakes and not others. It concluded that "this disparate treatment reveals . . . hostility towards Phillips."[31] The most basic reason for the disparate treatment—the statute, like all laws, prohibits some but not all human conduct; some refusals are discriminatory and some are not—eluded the court. The Commission then decided not to take a chance on what the Supreme Court, with Anthony Kennedy replaced by Brett Kavanaugh, would do with the case.[32] It agreed with Phillips to terminate both proceedings.

Scardina then filed her own lawsuit, as she had a right to do.[33] She is not bound by what the Commission has done. Plaintiffs do not lose their right to sue because they are acting out of spite toward the defendants. As this is written, the suit is pending.

In this sorry controversy, charges often fly around of malicious desires to hurt others. Here, however, the charge seems justified. Scardina evidently was on a campaign to destroy Phillips, and figured out a way to entrap him. She came up with a cake design with no explicit message for Phillips to reject, but which had a significance that would repel him and induce him to refuse. Phillips's legal claim made no sense, but he had a strong moral claim not to be targeted in this way.

One might defend Scardina by observing that it has not been unusual for civil rights groups to use testers to determine whether real estate brokers discriminated against blacks. This kind of entrapment is a necessary remedy to massive housing discrimination, a problem that persists to this day.[34] But Phillips was unlikely ever to discriminate against even a transgender person unless confronted with the unlikely scenario that Scardina crafted.

Scardina wanted to punish him for his religious views. That is not a desire the law should honor. But if religious objectors reveal their compunctions publicly, those are the only kind of civil rights suits that are likely to be filed.

That brings us to my own proposal, to exempt wedding vendors from antidiscrimination law on condition that they give prior notice of their objections to facilitating same-sex marriages. Recall that when we surveyed the injuries of discrimination in chapter 4, we concluded that the most important one in the wedding vendor context is the uncertainty about when one will next encounter discrimination—an exhausting source of stress that poisons all one's commercial interactions. Prior notice is a way to prevent that. In the absence of such a notice, customers will know that the nondiscrimination norm is in operation and can be relied upon.

One standard way, in all religious exemption cases, of preventing a stampede of requests is to require that exemptions be accompanied by an alternative burden that makes the claim somewhat costly to the claimant: alternative compulsory service for conscientious objectors from the draft, and so forth. That also filters out insincere claims. One of the principal worries of gay rights advocates is that if any accommodation is permitted, there will be so many that there will be no protection at all. A disclosure requirement makes that unlikely.

Those who feel they must do what their religion demands, even at great personal cost, have the strongest religious liberty claims. A prior-notice requirement is a good way to pick those people out. Open avowal would have protected Willock from the unpleasant surprise she got in response to her email: she would never have contacted Elane Photography in the first place. The specific, personal insult to which she was subjected would not have happened.

There are also practical problems with the various proposals that would exempt wedding vendors without any requirement of prior notice. The costs of no notice are not merely unfair surprise. An exemption that can be invoked on an ad hoc basis would eviscerate the law, because it would be available as a defense in any case at all.[35] Any responsible lawyer would at least ask the client about religious scruples, and some will try to elicit positive answers.

This proposal has elicited the objection that it compels speech. Steven D. Smith writes in another context: "A vendor who does not want to celebrate a same-sex marriage contrary to his convictions may at the same time have no desire affirmatively and publicly to proclaim to all the world that same-sex marriage is sinful. He may wish to bear his witness in quieter ways—with a 'still, small voice,' perhaps."[36] But this amounts to a desire to be able to keep customers in doubt about whether they will be rejected. As a general matter, it is not an impermissible speech compulsion when property owners and product manufacturers are required to warn of hidden dangers. Here the harms in question are not just that of direct injury, but also the corrosive effect of uncertainty. Presumably whenever a vendor does turn away a same-sex couple, that fact will become known. It is not unreasonable to demand that that harm be prevented from happening in the first place, rather than merely reported after the fact.

Recall that John Locke's response to religious diversity was to argue that it need not produce conflict so long as there were clear boundaries of property. A congregation could do what it liked within its own building. Those who regarded its activities as heretical were free to assemble in a different building of their own. In the spirit of Locke, we should look for clear boundaries here, where people with radically different views of what makes a good life can go about their lives without encroaching on one another. Public notice lets the world know where those boundaries are.

What I propose here would of course have been no help against Scardina, because the refusal in her case had nothing to do with same-sex weddings. Here a simple legislative response is available. In some jurisdictions, a defense of entrapment is available in criminal cases in which a police officer induced a normally law-abiding person to commit a crime. A similar defense could be crafted for civil cases like Scardina's, where (unlike the housing discrimination cases) absent the contrived lawsuit, the likelihood that the defendant would have unlawfully discriminated is remote.

There remains the prospect of illegal harassment. Professor Douglas Laycock was once open to a prior-notice requirement if the LGBT community wanted that. But he now thinks that "any such merchant would risk boycotts, defamatory reviews, and, simultaneously, repeated confrontational demands for service from gay couples. The merchant would also risk vandalism and worse." He concludes that such merchants' "only hope in much of the country is to lie low as much as possible and to invoke any exemption rights as quietly and diplomatically as possible."[37]

Any legal regime can be thwarted by illegal violence. A liberal society aims at a world in which people with radically differing views can live together in peace, and in which the disclosure of one's difference is safe. The state alone cannot guarantee that. But the state can create its legal preconditions: rules that if obeyed, will create safe space for everyone. They clearly signal what everyone is entitled to. A disclosure regime can do that. A regime in which gay people face unforeseeable discrimination cannot. It is also doubtful that any exemption can be asserted without the world finding out that this has happened. America does have a problem of censorship-by-mob, but that goes beyond this particular issue.

A comparable problem arose when gay people began coming out of the closet. Doing so was rare, because the consequences were severe: people lost jobs, friends, even family relationships. The numbers increased to the point where it was no longer remarkable. Attitudes toward gay people changed as gay people themselves became more familiar.[38] Law needs to authorize conservative Christians to come out of the closet as well. Like gay people in the bad old days, they are the objects of vicious stereotypes that are unlikely to survive contact with the actual people.

This book has confined its focus to the wedding vendor cases. The tension between gay rights and religious liberty has also manifested in other areas. I described some of them at the end of chapter 2. Our discussion thus far should provide a template for them. In each case, the interests in question are not absolute, and decent compromises are possible.

The basic idea, in the public accommodations context, is to keep the two groups separate, each able to live the lives they want without infringing on the other. That basic approach should be followed elsewhere. In some of them, such as accreditation of religious

universities or licensing of counselors who are unwilling to facilitate same-sex marriages, the answer is easy: let them work in their
corner of their professions, leaving the services to be provided by
others. But this solution only works if they are not entirely blocking
access to the good that their profession distributes. The worst thing
about the American practice of religious accommodation is that we
do not always make sure that this doesn't happen. In Europe, conscientious objections for health providers are limited in order to
guarantee medical access for patients. In the United Kingdom, for
example, doctors with conscientious objection to abortion must
refer patients to another provider without such compunctions.[39]
That raises complicity issues of its own, but there are other ways to
guarantee access.

In America, Catholic hospitals are permitted to endanger their
patients' lives by refusing necessary medical treatments that are inconsistent with Catholic doctrine. That privilege extends even to
hospitals that are no longer Catholic, but which once were, and were
sold with a contractual proviso that they would continue to ob-
serve Catholic moral constraints—what Elizabeth Sepper has called
"zombie Catholic Hospitals."[40] Exemptions should be restricted to the
strongest objectors. Here an accommodation is extended, and access
to medical treatment is restricted, even when there is no objector to
accommodate.

The basic aim should be to accommodate religion in ways that do not
inflict harm on discrete and identifiable third parties. Whether or not this
is required by the establishment clause,[41] it is sound political practice.

This approach has its limitations. There are some areas in which it
won't work. Businesses that employ nonadherents of the owner's religion, such as Hobby Lobby, are an obvious instance. Some conservative writers have argued that in order to avoid complicity, religious
employers ought not to provide benefits to same-sex spouses.[42]

Economic analysis shows that when benefits are provided, they are
a substitute for wages.[43] If employers are permitted to selectively deny
benefits to gay employees because they do not want to facilitate same-
sex marriages, the gay employee will get less compensation, on an ongoing basis, than the heterosexual employee.

The most prominent religious accommodation for employers that has been under discussion was in the federal Employment Non-Discrimination Act passed by the Senate in November 2013, which would have prohibited employment discrimination based on sexual orientation. It absolutely exempted from the law's coverage any "religious corporation, association, educational institution, or society."[44] A religiously affiliated hospital thus may fire a nurse when it discovers that he is gay. This would have licensed an enormous amount of raw discrimination, unrelated to the requirements of any religion. The last version of the proposal dropped this provision.[45]

The most recent federal proposal to bar LGBT discrimination, the Equality Act, which passed the House of Representatives in May 2019, expressly exempts the statute from RFRA.[46] It is not clear that religious nonprofits would have the right to discriminate on the basis of anything other than religious affiliation. They could not, for example, require any employees to conform to a moral requirement not to engage in sexual intercourse outside of heterosexual marriage, because such a requirement would likely be deemed to be discrimination on the basis of sexual orientation. That goes too far in the other direction. A rival bill, the Fairness For All Act, does a better job of striking a reasonable balance.[47]

As a general matter, employment discrimination against LGBT people should be prohibited. Religious schools, which the Equality Act would cover, present a different case. Justice William Brennan, one of the Court's most liberal justices, explained:

> Religious organizations have an interest in autonomy in ordering their internal affairs, so that they may be free to "select their own leaders, define their own doctrines, resolve their own disputes, and run their own institutions. Religion includes important communal elements for most believers. They exercise their religion through religious organizations, and these organizations must be protected."[48]

Private schools are incubators for cultural dissent. Teachers teach by example. A school's mission is jeopardized if the school is required to employ teachers who openly defy its teachings. The world of private schools is another sector of the economy that is fragmented and competitive. Similarly with married student housing in religious colleges. Religious conservatives need safe spaces as much as anyone else does. They should be entitled to discriminate within their own enclaves.

The scholars' model state statute is similarly overbroad.[49] It excuses any "organization operated for charitable or educational purposes which is supervised or controlled by or in connection with a religious organization" from treating any marriage as valid if this would violate religious beliefs, and says that small businesses need not "provide benefits to any spouse of an employee."[50] These provisions permit employers to selectively deny family benefits to gay employees. "Religious dissenters can live their own values," Laycock writes, "but not if they occupy choke points that empower them to prevent same-sex couples from living *their* own values. If dissenters want complete moral autonomy on this issue, they must refrain from occupying such a choke point."[51] Employer-provided health insurance is precisely such a choke point.[52] "The First Amendment," the Supreme Court has said, "gives no one the right to insist that in pursuit of their own [religious] interests others must conform their conduct to his own religious necessities."[53]

The statute's accommodation of employers is limited to those with "five or fewer employees." Such employers are generally not required to provide benefits of any kind. It may thus be argued that the accommodation subtracts nothing from the rights of their employees.[54]

For such employers, however, the real burden of an antidiscrimination law (and many such laws do apply to small employers)[55] is that it puts them to the choice of either providing insurance to their employees on a nondiscriminatory basis or not providing insurance at all (and so sending them to the Obamacare exchanges, where they will get insurance of the same quality the employer would have provided). The model statute creates a third option: providing substandard insurance on a discriminatory basis. The married gay employee will have higher out-of-pocket costs than the married heterosexual employee (because the former must purchase separate insurance for their spouse). Why is that option better than the alternatives? How is religion burdened if the employer is put in a position where he must pay his employees cash instead of discriminatory in-kind benefits?

Rod Dreher writes that the conflict between gay rights and religious liberty will become most intense "when they start trying to tell us how to run our own religious institutions—churches, schools, hospitals, and the like—and trying to close them or otherwise destroy them for refusing to accept LGBT ideology."[56] He is right to worry.

As I said, I'm a gay rights advocate. I would very much like to banish to the margins of society the notion that homosexual sex is inferior to heterosexual sex. I want gay people to suffer no disadvantage or humiliation whatsoever because there are other people who believe that nonsense. But I also believe that the margins of society should be a safe place, where those who do not conform to majoritarian norms, and whose views I regard as disastrously misguided, can live their lives in peace and security.

I take as my model the boxer Sugar Ray Robinson.

My father, George Koppelman, grew up near New York City. He told me the following story. A friend of his entered the city's amateur boxing competition, the Golden Gloves. He unexpectedly found himself matched against Robinson.

Robinson is regarded by many sportswriters as the greatest fighter of all time. He held the welterweight title from 1946 to 1951 and the middleweight championship five times between 1951 and 1960. During his amateur career, in which he won Golden Gloves titles in 1939 and 1940, he was undefeated, 85–0, with 69 knockouts, 40 of them in the first round.

My father's friend (I don't remember his name) was terrified, and evidently it showed. As they touched gloves before the fight began, Robinson leaned toward him and whispered, "Don't worry. I'm not going to hurt you. I'm just going to win."

Robinson easily beat him on points and never hit him very hard.

The gay rights movement should emulate Robinson. We shouldn't want to hurt them. We should just want to win.

Law cannot and should not try to eradicate the idea that homosexual conduct is inherently worthless and harmful. It is too deeply ingrained in religious views that large numbers of Americans hold. It involves theological questions that are none of the state's business.

Diversity of opinion, about matters that matter a lot, is an inevitable consequence of a free society. It is possible to have cold respect among people who regard one another's views as repulsive, grave moral errors. We can live peacefully together in mutual contempt.

But this understates what we can achieve together. A free society begets thoughts we hate. But a free society is inspiring. The challenge of modern politics is to tell a story of who Americans are in which each faction can recognize itself and see a home for itself.

Part of America's promise has always been to be a place where diversity can flourish. We all ought to be proud of this common identity: we are a society that as much as possible, makes room for the enormous range of human variation. That is one message of the rainbow flag. Religious conservatives should find that there is a place here for them too.

Acknowledgments

For helpful comments on earlier drafts, thanks to Stephanie Barclay, Tom Berg, Mary Anne Case, Fred Gedicks, Shannon Gilreath, John Inazu, Doug Laycock, Joan Lefford, Steven Lubet, Ira Lupu, Linda McClain, Shannon Minter, Doug NeJaime, Martha Nussbaum, Destiny Peery, Jonathan Rauch, Elizabeth Sepper, Steven D. Smith, and Nelson Tebbe. The manuscript was also improved by extensive discussions with students in my winter 2018–2019 class in Discrimination, Religion, and Bigotry, and audiences at the 2019 Annual Law and Religion Roundtable, the James Madison Program in American Ideals and Institutions, Princeton University, the Program on Church, State & Society at Notre Dame Law School, and the Philosophy Department at University College, Dublin, where Peter Stone and Karim Sadek provided useful commentary. A modified form of chapter 8 was given as the 2019 Annual Law and Religion Lecture at Brigham Young University. Thanks also to Tom Gaylord and Deepa Ramakrishnan German for research assistance.

My practice of using chapter titles, read in sequence, to summarize the book gratefully emulates Deirdre McCloskey, *Bourgeois Dignity: Why Economics Can't Explain the Modern World* (2010).

I also have benefited from the friendship of many conservative Christian scholars and advocates with whom I remain in radical disagreement about sexual ethics. Respectful conversation, with smart people whom I regard as fundamentally mistaken, has made me less ignorant and confused. I wish I could share that experience with more of my friends on the left.

Notes

Introduction

1. I use this term, somewhat clumsily, to refer to those who, on the basis of their Christian beliefs, think that marriage is inherently heterosexual and that sexual activity with a person of the same sex is morally wrong. The term is clumsy because those specific ideas are rejected by some Christians who hold conservative religious or political views. I use it because there appears to be no better term available to refer to this group.

2. Rob Suls, Deep Divides Between, Within Parties on Public Debates About LGBT Issues, Pew Research Center, Oct. 4, 2016; Pew Research Center, Where the Public Stands on Religious Liberty vs. Nondiscrimination, Sept. 28, 2016. For a more recent survey with similar results, see Daniel Greenberg et al., Fifty Years After Stonewall: Widespread Support for LGBT Issues—Findings from American Values Atlas 2018, PRRI, Mar. 26, 2019.

3. I use the term "gay rights" to encompass the rights of lesbian, gay male, bisexual, and transgender persons.

4. Shannon Gilreath and Arley Ward, Same-Sex Marriage, Religious Accommodation, and the Race Analogy, 41 Vt. L. Rev. 237, 277–78 (2016).

5. Steven D. Smith, Pagans and Christians in the City: Culture Wars from the Tiber to the Potomac 7 (2018).

6. Steven D. Smith, What Masterpiece Cakeshop Is Really About, Public Discourse, Oct. 24, 2017.

7. Maggie Gallagher, Why Accommodate? Reflections on the Gay Marriage Culture Wars, 5 Nw. J. L. & Soc. Pol'y 260, 269 (2010).

8. Jenna Portnoy, Va. House Vote Hints at a Generational Divide on Gay Rights, Wash. Post, Feb. 18, 2016.

9. Rod Dreher, Does Faith = Hate?, Am. Conservative, Oct. 9, 2013.

10. David French, Liberty Gained and Power Lost, The Dispatch, Jan. 10, 2020.

11. Jonathan Rauch, Gay Rights, Religious Liberty, and Nondiscrimination: Can a Train Wreck Be Avoided?, 2017 U. Ill. L. Rev. 1195, 1196.

12. "The situations we encounter differ from each other in subtle ways that no panoply of principles could ever manage to capture. Principles deal in samenesses, and there just aren't enough samenesses to go around." Jonathan Dancy, Ethics Without Principles 2 (2004).

13. Robin Fretwell Wilson, The Nonsense About Bathrooms: How Purported Concerns over Safety Block LGBT Nondiscrimination Laws and Obscure Real Religious Liberty Concerns, 20 Lewis & Clark L. Rev. 1373, 1379–83 (2017).

14. Douglas Laycock, Liberty and Justice For All, in Religious Freedom, LGBT Rights, and the Prospects for Common Ground 25 (William Eskridge, Jr. and Robin Fretwell Wilson, eds. 2018).

15. See Frank Newport, Religion Big Factor for Americans Against Same-Sex Marriage, Gallup, Dec. 5, 2012 (Americans who oppose same-sex marriage are most likely to explain their position on the basis of religious beliefs or interpretation of biblical passages).

16. In 2017, 33% of Americans thought that homosexual sex is not morally acceptable, compared with 53% in 2001. Jeffrey M. Jones, Americans Hold Record Liberal Views on Most Moral Issues, Gallup, May 11, 2017.

17. Hillary Clinton, What Happened (2017).

18. See, e.g., Andrew Koppelman, Antidiscrimination Law and Social Equality 146–76 (1996); Andrew Koppelman, Judging the Case Against Same-Sex Marriage, 2014 U. of Illinois L. Rev. 431; Why Scalia Should Have Voted to Overturn DOMA, 108 Nw. U. L. Rev. Colloquy 131 (2013); Sexual Disorientation, 100 Geo. L.J. 1083 (2012); DOMA, Romer, and Rationality, 58 Drake L. Rev. 923 (2010); Defending the Sex Discrimination Argument for Lesbian and Gay Rights: A Reply to Edward Stein, 49 U.C.L.A. L. Rev. 519 (2001), reprinted in 1 The Dukeminier Awards: Best Sexual Orientation Law Review Articles of 2001 49 (2001); Dumb and DOMA: Why the Defense of Marriage Act is Unconstitutional, 83 Iowa L. Rev. 1 (1997); Is Marriage Inherently Heterosexual?, 42 Am. J. of Jurisprudence 51 (1997); Why Discrimination Against Lesbians and Gay Men Is Sex Discrimination, 69 N.Y.U. L. Rev. 197 (1994); Note, The Miscegenation Analogy: Sodomy Law as Sex Discrimination, 98 Yale L.J. 145 (1988). I coauthored amicus briefs in Lawrence v. Texas, the Supreme Court case that invalidated laws against homosexual sex, and Hollingsworth v. Perry and Obergefell v. Hodges, both of which considered a right to same-sex marriage. See Brief of Amicus Curiae Constitutional Law Professors Bruce A. Ackerman et al., Lawrence and Garner v. Texas, No. 02-102, 2003 WL 136139; Brief of Amici Curiae William N. Eskridge Jr., et al., Hollingsworth v. Perry, No. 12-144, 2013 WL 840011; Brief of Amicus Curiae Stephen Clark et al., Obergefell v. Hodges, No. 14-556,

2015 WL 1048436. The argument that I developed in 1994, that antigay discrimination is a form of sex discrimination, was adopted by two federal courts of appeals. *Zarda v. Altitude Express*, Inc., 883 F.3d 100 (2d Cir. 2018); *Hively v. Ivy Tech Cmty.* Coll. of Ind., 853 F.3d 339 (7th Cir. 2017). I coauthored a Supreme Court amicus defending that result. Brief of Amici Curiae William N. Eskridge Jr. and Andrew Koppelman, *Bostock v. Clayton County*, Georgia, No. 17-1628, 2019 WL 2915046.

19. U.S. Commission on Civil Rights, Peaceful Coexistence: Reconciling Nondiscrimination Principles with Civil Liberties 160–61 (September 2016) (statement of Commissioners Achtenberg, Castro, Kladney, Narasaki and Yaki).

20. Ryan T. Anderson & Robert P. George, Freedom to Marry & Dissent, Rightly Understood, Real Clear Policy, May 4, 2014.

21. See J. G. Kosciw et al., The 2017 National School Climate Survey: The Experiences of Lesbian, Gay, Bisexual, Transgender, and Queer Youth in Our Nation's Schools (GLSEN 2018).

22. Shannon Price Minter, Belief and Belonging: Reconciling Legal Protections for Religious Liberty and LGBT youth, in Religious Freedom, LGBT Rights, and the Prospects for Common Ground 38 (William Eskridge, Jr. and Robin Fretwell Wilson, eds. 2018).

23. I document the history of this idea in detail in Andrew Koppelman, Corruption of Religion and the Establishment Clause, 50 Wm. & Mary L. Rev. 1831 (2009).

24. This point has been made by others. Robin Fretwell Wilson, A Marriage of Necessity: Same-sex Marriage and Religious Liberty Protections, 64 Case W. L. Rev. 1161 (2014); Douglas Laycock and Thomas C. Berg, Protecting Religious Liberty and Same-Sex Marriage, 99 Va. L. Rev. Online 1 (2013); Alan Brownstein, Gays, Jews, and Other Strangers in a Strange Land: The Case for Reciprocal Accommodations of Religious Liberty and the Right of Same-Sex Couples to Marry, 45 U.S.F. L. Rev. 389 (2010).

25. Jean-Jacques Rousseau, On The Social Contract 131 (Roger D. Masters ed., Judith R. Masters trans., 1978) (1762).

26. These pitfalls are avoided in Nelson Tebbe, Religious Freedom in an Egalitarian Age (2017), but as will become clear, I would not articulate the pertinent interests as he does. See chapters 4 and 7. For further critique, see Andrew Koppelman, Tebbe and Reflective Equilibrium, 31 J. Civ. R. & Econ. Dev. 125 (2018). My analysis more closely resembles Frank S. Ravitch, Freedom's Edge: Religious Freedom, Sexual Freedom, and the Future of America (2016), but our books engage different issues.

27. See Koppelman, Antidiscrimination Law and Social Equality, 1–114.

28. Joseph Raz, The Morality of Freedom 166 (1986).
29. Ibid., 180.

Chapter 1

1. US Commission on Civil Rights, Peaceful Coexistence: Reconciling Nondiscrimination Principles with Civil Liberties 29 (Sep. 2016) (statement of Chairman Martin R. Castro).
2. Edmund Fawcett, Liberalism: The Life of an Idea (2d ed. 2018).
3. John Milton, Areopagitica (1644), in Complete Poems and Major Prose 739 (Merritt Y. Hughes ed. 1957).
4. Ibid. at 728.
5. Ibid. at 742.
6. John Locke, A Letter Concerning Toleration 26 (1689; James H. Tully ed. 1983).
7. Ibid.
8. Ibid. at 27.
9. Ibid. at 38.
10. Ibid. at 37.
11. *People v. Philips*, N.Y. Ct. of Gen Sessions (1813), in Michael W. McConnell et al., Religion and the Constitution 94 (4th ed. 2016).
12. *Reynolds v. U.S.*, 98 U.S. (8 Otto.) 145, 161–62 (1878).
13. *Sherbert v. Verner*, 374 U.S. 398 (1963).
14. Stephen Siegel, The Origin of the Compelling State Interest Test and Strict Scrutiny, 48 Am. J. Leg. Hist. 355 (2006).
15. Richard H. Fallon Jr., Strict Judicial Scrutiny, 54 UCLA L. Rev. 1267, 1271, 1312 (2007).
16. Compare *Jimmy Swaggart Ministries v. Bd. of Equalization of Cal.*, 493 U.S. 378 (1990) (denying religious organization exemption from state taxes on sales of Bibles and other religious literature); *Hernandez v. Comm'r*, 490 U.S. 680 (1989) (denying taxpayers exemption from limit on tax deduction for donations to their church); *Lyng v. NW. Indian Cemetery Prot. Ass'n*, 485 U.S. 439 (1988) (denying Native American claimants relief from government construction of road on government property deemed sacred by claimants); *O'Lone v. Estate of Shabazz*, 482 U.S. 342 (1987) (denying Muslim prison inmates exemption necessary for them to meet in weekly congregational service); *Bowen v. Roy*, 476 U.S. 693 (1986) (denying federal welfare benefits applicant exemption from requirement that he obtain and furnish a social security number for his daughter); *Goldman*

v. Weinberger, 475 U.S. 503 (1986) (denying orthodox Jewish military officer exemption from uniform requirement that would preclude him from wearing yarmulke); *Tony & Susan Alamo Found. v. Sec'y of Labor*, 471 U.S. 290 (1985) (denying religious organization exemption from minimum wage and reporting provisions of Fair Labor Standards Act); *United States v. Lee*, 455 U.S. 252 (1982) (denying Amish employer exemption from requirement that he pay social security taxes on employees); *Gillette v. United States*, 401 U.S. 437 (1971) (denying claimant who religiously objected to "unjust" war rather than all wars exemption from draft), with *Frazee v. Ill. Dep't of Emp't Sec.*, 489 U.S. 829 (1989) (granting unemployment compensation benefits to appellant who refused to work on Sundays at a temporary retail position due to his sincerely held religious beliefs even though he was not a member of a recognized religion); *Hobbie v. Unemp't Appeals Comm'n of Fla.*, 480 U.S. 136 (1987) (granting unemployment compensation benefits to appellant who refused to work on her Sabbath); *Thomas v. Review Bd. of Ind. Emp't Sec. Div.*, 450 U.S. 707 (1981) (granting unemployment compensation benefits to appellant who terminated his job because his religious beliefs forbade him from participating in the production of war materials); *Sherbert v. Verner*, 374 U.S. 398 (1963) (granting persons resigning or dismissed from employment for religiously motivated refusals to work on certain days or at certain duties held exempt from "availability for work" condition for receipt of unemployment benefits); *Wisconsin v. Yoder*, 406 U.S. 205 (1972) (granting Amish parents exemption from state law requiring school attendance to age sixteen).

17. See Amy Adamczyk, John Wibraniec, and Roger Finke, Religious Regulation and the Courts: Documenting the Effects of Smith and RFRA, 46 J. Church & State 237, 250 tbl. 1 (2004).

18. James E. Ryan, Note, Smith and the Religious Freedom Restoration Act: An Iconoclastic Assessment, 78 Va. L. Rev. 1407, 1416–17 (1992). Other studies drawing from different samples have converged on the conclusion that most religious liberty claims lose. Gregory C. Sisk and Michael Heise, Muslims and Religious Liberty in the Era of 9/11: Empirical Evidence from the Federal Courts, 98 Ia. L. Rev. 231 (2012); Adam Winkler, Fatal in Theory and Strict in Fact: An Empirical Analysis of Strict Scrutiny in the Federal Courts, 59 Vand. L. Rev. 793 (2006); Gregory C. Sisk, How Traditional and Minority Religions Fare in the Courts: Empirical Evidence from Religious Liberty Cases, 76 U. Colo. L. Rev. 1021 (2005); Gregory C. Sisk, Michael E. Heise, and Andrew P. Morriss, Searching for the Soul

of Judicial Decision-Making: An Empirical Study of Religious Freedom Decisions, 65 Ohio St. L.J. 491 (2004); Thomas C. Berg, The New Attacks on Religious Freedom Legislation, and Why They Are Wrong, 21 Cardozo L. Rev. 415 (1999).

19. The classic citation is Ronald Dworkin, Rights as Trumps, in Theories of Rights 153 (Jeremy Waldron ed. 1984).

20. See Thomas C. Berg, Minority Religions and the Religion Clauses, 82 Wash. U. L. Q. 919, 968–70 (2004).

21. See, e.g., Gonzalez v. O Centro Espirita Beneficiente Uniao Do Vegetal, 546 U.S. 418, 430–31 (2006) (holding that Government must show not only that it has a compelling interest in applying a law to the particular religious claimant, and not merely that its interest is compelling in the abstract).

22. *Employment Division v. Smith*, 494 U.S. 872, 879 (1990), quoting Reynolds v. United States, 98 U.S. 145, 166–67 (1879).

23. Ibid. at 888.

24. Ibid. at 889 n.5.

25. 42 U.S.C. §§2000bb–1(a), (b).

26. *City of Boerne v. Flores*, 521 U.S. 507 (1997).

27. The number of filed claims plunged after *Smith*, from 310 decided in the nine-and-a-quarter years before the decision to thirty-eight in the three-and-a-half years after it. Under RFRA, success rates rose to 45.2% and the number of filed claims in that three-year period rose to 114, perhaps in response to the strong legislative signal that courts should take religious impact very seriously. See Adamczyk et al., Religious Regulation and the Courts, 250 tbl. 1.

28. Douglas Laycock, Sex, Atheism, and the Free Exercise of Religion, 88 Detroit-Mercy L. Rev. 407, 412–13 (2011).

29. State Religious Freedom Restoration Acts, National Conference of State Legislatures, May 4, 2017.

30. Adam Winkler, Fatal in Theory and Strict in Fact: An Empirical Analysis of Strict Scrutiny in the Federal Courts, 59 Vand. L. Rev. 793, 860, 861 (2006) (surveying fifty-four statutory and four constitutional cases between 1990 and 2003 that applied strict scrutiny to government denial of a religious exemption).

31. See Christopher C. Lund, Religious Liberty After Gonzales: A Look at State RFRAs, 55 S.D. L. Rev. 466 (2010).

32. See Andrew Koppelman, The Story of Welsh v. United States: Elliott Welsh's Two Religious Tests, in First Amendment Stories 293 (Richard Garnett and Andrew Koppelman, eds., 2012).

33. Eugene Volokh, A Common-Law Model for Religious Exemptions, 46 UCLA L. Rev. 1465 (1999).

34. Gonzales v. O Centro Espirita Beneficente Uniao do Vegetal, 546 U.S. 418, 432 (2006).

35. Ibid. at 439.

36. Christopher C. Lund, Keeping Hobby Lobby in Perspective, in The Rise of Corporate Religious Liberty 285 (Micah Schwartzman et al. eds. 2016).

37. *Holt v. Hobbs*, 135 S. Ct. 853 (2015).

38. David M. Shapiro, Lenient in Theory, Dumb in Fact: Prison, Speech, and Scrutiny, 84 Geo. Wash. L. Rev. 972 (2016).

Chapter 2

1. William Saletan, The Photographer's Story, Slate, Mar. 7, 2014.

2. Petition for writ of certiorari, *Elane Photography v. Willock*, 7.

3. *Elane Photography v. Willock*, 309 P.3d 53 (2013), cert. denied, 572 US 1046 (2014).

4. Jordan Lorence, Supreme Court Turns Down Elane Photography Case, National Review Online, Apr. 7, 2014.

5. Todd Starnes, Do Gay Rights Trump Religious Rights? Supreme Court won't Hear Wedding Photographers' Case, Fox News, Apr. 7, 2013.

6. Tom Strode, Supreme Court Declines Photographers' Appeal, Baptist Press, Apr. 7, 2014.

7. Quoted in Ryan T. Anderson, Clashing Claims, National Rev., Aug. 23, 2013.

8. Warren Richey, For Those on Front Lines of Religious Liberty Battle, a Very Human Cost, Christian Science Monitor, July 16, 2016.

9. Legis. Counsel of the Colo. Gen. Assemb., An Analysis of 1992 Ballot Proposals, Gen. Assemb. 58-369, at 9–10 (1992).

10. See 85% Think Christian Photographer Has Right to Turn Down Same-Sex Wedding Job, Rasmussen Reports, July 12, 2013 (responses to "Suppose a Christian wedding photographer has deeply held religious beliefs opposing same-sex marriage. If asked to work a same-sex wedding ceremony, should that wedding photographer have the right to say no?"). Three years later, Americans were evenly split on the question, with few on either side expressing any sympathy for the other point of view. Rob Suls, Deep divides between, within parties on public debates about LGBT issues, Pew Research Center, Oct. 4, 2016; Pew Research Center, Where the Public Stands on Religious Liberty vs. Nondiscrimination, Sept. 28, 2016.

11. Quoted in Lila Shapiro, Leading Gay Marriage Opponent On Losing The Battle: "I Have A Lot More Freedom Now," Huffington Post, Mar. 2, 2014.

12. Here is the language:

> No individual or religious entity shall be required by any governmental entity to do any of the following, if it would be contrary to the sincerely held religious beliefs of the individual or religious entity regarding sex or gender: (a) Provide any services, accommodations, advantages, facilities, goods, or privileges; provide counseling, adoption, foster care and other social services; or provide employment or employment benefits, related to, or related to the celebration of, any marriage, domestic partnership, civil union or similar arrangement; (b) solemnize any marriage, domestic partnership.

Quoted in Michael McGough, Kansas Goes Off the Deep End with an Anti-Gay Bill, L.A. Times, Feb. 15, 2014; see kslegislature.org/li/b2013_14/measures/documents/hb2453_01_0000.pdf.

13. Katy Steinmetz, Kansas Bill Allowing Businesses to Snub Gay Couples Is "Dead," Time, Feb. 18, 2014.

14. Arizona S.B. 1062, 51st, Leg., 2d sess.

15. See Christopher C. Lund, Religious Liberty after Gonzales: A Look at State RFRAs, 55 S.D. L. Rev. 466 (2010).

16. A License to Discriminate, N.Y. Times, Feb. 25, 2014, A24.

17. Quoted in Nagourney, Arizona Bill Allowing Refusal of Service to Gays Stirred Alarm in the G.O.P.

18. Fernanda Santos, Arizona Governor Vetoes Bill on Refusal of Service to Gays, N.Y. Times, Feb. 26, 2014; Fernanda Santos, Governor of Arizona is Pressed to Veto Bill, N.Y. Times, Feb. 24, 2014.

19. Adam Nagourney, Arizona Bill Allowing Refusal of Service to Gays Stirred Alarm in the G.O.P., N.Y. Times, Feb. 27, 2014.

20. Warren Richey, In Mississippi Gay Rights Battle, Both Sides Feel They Are Losing, Christian Science Monitor, July 14, 2016.

21. S. 2681, 2014.

22. For both versions, see Miss. Legis. 2014 Regular Sess., S. 2681, http://billstatus.ls.state.ms.us/2014/pdf/history/SB/SB2681.xml.

23. Mark Joseph Stern, Mississippi Passed Its Anti-Gay Segregation Bill. Will It Be Struck Down?, Slate, Apr. 4, 2014. See also Mississippi Governor Phil Bryant Signs Anti-Gay Bill, Politico, Apr. 4, 2014.

24. Letter of Ira C. Lupu and Robert W. Tuttle to Speaker Philip Gunn et al., Mar. 10, 2014.

25. It provided, in pertinent part:

Notwithstanding any other provision of law, if doing so would violate a person's deeply held religious beliefs, a person acting in a nongovernmental capacity may not be:

(a) Penalized by the state or a political subdivision of this state for declining to solemnize, celebrate, participate in, facilitate, or support any same-sex marriage ceremony or its arrangements, same-sex civil union ceremony or its arrangements, or same-sex domestic partnership ceremony or its arrangements; or

(b) Subject to a civil action for declining to solemnize, celebrate, participate in, facilitate, or support any same-sex marriage ceremony or its arrangements, same-sex civil union ceremony or its arrangements, or same-sex domestic partnership ceremony or its arrangements.

Oregon Family Council, Protect Religious Freedom Initiative, Nov. 21, 2013.

26. Zack Ford, Oregon Conservatives Suddenly Drop Arizona-Style "License To Discriminate" Initiative, ThinkProgress, May 12, 2014; Anna Staver, Family Council Drops Initiative Targeting Gay Weddings, Statesman Journal, May 12, 2014.

The Oregon Family Council's proposed title was "Protects persons choosing non-participation in same-sex ceremonies based on conscience or religious belief from penalization." The title approved by the state Supreme Court was " 'Religious belief' exceptions to anti-discrimination laws for refusing services, other, for same-sex ceremonies, 'arrangements.' " Ford, Oregon Conservatives Suddenly Drop Arizona-Style "License To Discriminate" Initiative.

27. Bill Would Let Michigan Doctors, EMTs Refuse to Treat Gay Patients, CBS News, Dec. 11, 2014.

28. Matt Hennie, Anti-Gay Bill Suffers Near Fatal Blow in State House, Project Q, Mar. 26, 2015.

29. Jim Galloway, Agreement on Both Sides: "Religious Liberty" Bill Would Gut Local Anti-Discrimination Ordinances, AJC.com, Mar. 26, 2015.

30. Matt Hennie, State's Ex Top Lawyer Rips "Religious Freedom" Bills, Project Q, Feb. 24, 2015.

31. Here it is: The Text of Indiana's "Religious Freedom" Law, IndyStar, Mar. 27, 2015. The Indiana Constitution already contained religious liberty protections, but their scope was ambiguous. Douglas Laycock, Letter to Indiana Senate Judiciary Committee, in Religious Liberty, v. 3: Religious

Freedom Restoration Acts, Same-sex Marriage Legislation, and the Culture Wars 606 (2018).

32. It was sometimes claimed that this was a difference from the federal RFRA, but this was not accurate, since under a different provision of federal law corporations are "persons." See Kristine Guerra and Tim Evans, How Indiana's RFRA Differs from Federal Version, Indianapolis Star, Apr. 2, 2015; Why Law Professor Douglas Laycock Supports Same-Sex Marriage and Indiana's Religious Freedom Law, Religion & Politics, Apr. 1, 2015, in Religious Liberty, v. 3, 620.

33. House Amendment 3, https://iga.in.gov/legislative/2015/bills/senate/101#document-b58a93e0.

34. House Amendment 5, https://iga.in.gov/legislative/2015/bills/senate/101#document-6aa19d1f.

35. House Amendment 6, https://iga.in.gov/legislative/2015/bills/senate/101#document-246dc292. This amendment provided that such a sign "must be posted and maintained in a conspicuous place that is visible to customers of the person's business before customers enter the premises of the business," must "state that the person believes a governmental entity substantially burdens the person's exercise of religion by requiring the person's business to serve individuals who are members of certain groups," and must "specifically identify the certain groups or classes of individuals" thus excluded. Similar information must be posted on any web site maintained by the business.

36. Robbie Couch, Indiana's Anti-Gay Law Prompts Thousands of Businesses to Stand Up For Diversity, Huffington Post, Mar. 30, 2015.

37. Adam Wren, The Week Mike Pence's 2016 Dreams Crumbled, Politico, Apr. 1, 2015.

38. Ben Kepes, Salesforce.com Makes A Stand Against Bigotry, Forbes, Mar. 26, 2015.

39. Wren, The Week Mike Pence's 2016 Dreams Crumbled.

40. https://twitter.com/hillaryclinton/status/581267449523343360?lang=en.

41. RFRA: Michiana Business Wouldn't Cater a Gay Wedding, ABC57, Apr. 1, 2015.

42. Conor Friedersdorf, Should Mom-and-Pops That Forgo Gay Weddings Be Destroyed? The Attack on Memories Pizza and Its Implications, Atlantic, Apr. 3, 2015. The pizzeria eventually reopened, and some months later a gay couple took great satisfaction in buying two pizzas there and serving it at their wedding ceremony. Billy Hallowell, Gay Couple Ordered Two Large Pies From Memories Pizza: What They Did Next Is Getting a Lot of Attention, The Blaze, Sept. 29, 2015. The pizzeria owner

was untroubled when he learned the truth about the order. "We weren't catering to their wedding," he said. "They were picking [pizzas] up." Billy Hallowell, Christian Owner of Memories Pizza Responds to Claim That His Shop "Catered" a Gay Wedding, The Blaze, Oct. 1, 2015.

43. Monica Davey and Mitch Smith, Indiana Governor, Feeling Backlash From Law's Opponents, Promises a "Fix," N.Y. Times, Mar. 31, 2015.

44. See Monica Davey, Campbell Robertson, and Richard Perez-Pena, Indiana and Arkansas Revise Rights Bills, Seeking to Remove Divisive Parts, N.Y. Times, Apr. 2, 2015. The amendment provides that the law does not:

(1) authorize a provider to refuse to offer or provide services, facilities, use of public accommodations, goods, employment, or housing to any member or members of the general public on the basis of race, color, religion, ancestry, age, national origin, disability, sex, sexual orientation, gender identity, or United States military service;

(2) establish a defense to a civil action or criminal prosecution for refusal by a provider to offer or provide services, facilities, use of public accommodations, goods, employment, or housing to any member or members of the general public on the basis of race, color, religion, ancestry, age, national origin, disability, sex, sexual orientation, gender identity, or United States military service; or

(3) negate any rights available under the Constitution of the State of Indiana.

http://www.indianahouserepublicans.com/clientuploads/PDF/RFRA/CC005005_MS.pdf.

45. Kristine Guerra and Tim Evans, RFRA Revision Does Not Widely Extend Discrimination Protections for LGBT, Experts Say, Indianapolis Star, Apr. 3, 2015.

46. David Edwards, Oklahoma Dem Amendment: Christian Businesses Must Post Notice of Anti-Gay Discrimination, Rawstory, Mar. 12, 2015.

47. Nelson Tebbe, Micah Schwartzman, and Richard Schragger, Why Arkansas Is Worse Than Indiana, Balkinization, Apr. 1, 2015.

48. Jena McGregor, Wal-Mart CEO Speaks Out Against "Religious Freedom" Bill in Arkansas, Wash. Post, Apr. 1, 2015; Hiroko Tabuchi and Michael Barbaro, Walmart Emerges as Unlikely Social Force, N.Y. Times, Apr. 1, 2015.

49. Campbell Robertson and Timothy Williams, Arkansas Governor Asks Lawmakers to Recall Religious Exception Bill, N.Y. Times, Apr. 1, 2015.

50. Howard Friedman, Arkansas Quickly Enacts Narrower Version of RFRA Than Originally Passed, Religion Clause Blog, Apr. 2, 2015.

51. See Monica Davey, Campbell Robertson, and Richard Perez-Pena, Indiana and Arkansas Revise Rights Bills, Seeking to Remove Divisive Parts, N.Y. Times, Apr. 2, 2015.

52. Nelson Tebbe, Micah Schwartzman, and Richard Schragger, Why Arkansas Is Worse Than Indiana, Balkinization, Apr. 1, 2015.

53. *Bob Jones University v. United States*, 461 U.S. 574, 592 (1983).

54. See, e.g., Jonathan Turley, An Unholy Union: Same-Sex Marriage and the Use of Governmental Programs to Penalize Religious Groups With Unpopular Practices, in Same-Sex Marriage and Religious Liberty: Emerging Conflicts 59 (Douglas Laycock et al. eds., 2008); Douglas W. Kmiec, Same-Sex Marriage and the Coming Antidiscrimination Campaigns Against Religion, in ibid. at 103.

55. Douglas Laycock, Afterword, in ibid. at 193, quoted in Andrew Koppelman, Gay Rights, Religious Accommodations, and the Purposes of Antidiscrimination Law, 88 S. Cal. L. Rev. 619, 624 (2015). A vehement and thorough critic of the Bob Jones doctrine found hardly any examples of its actually being used by the IRS to deny an exemption. Johnny Rex Buckles, Reforming the Public Policy Doctrine, 53 U. Kan. L. Rev. 397, 404–407 (2005). As Kmiec acknowledges, the IRS has never extended Bob Jones to any discrimination other than race. Kmiec at 110.

56. John Inazu, Confident Pluralism: Surviving and Thriving through Deep Difference 79 (2016).

57. Rod Dreher, What Hill Do We Die On, Then?, Am. Conservative, Sept. 4, 2015.

58. Christopher McCrudden, Marriage Registrars, Same-Sex Relationships, and Religious Discrimination in the European Court of Human Rights, in The Conscience Wars: Rethinking the Balance between Religion, Identity, and Equality 414 (Susanna Mancini & Michel Rosenfeld eds. 2018); John M. Finnis, Equality and Religious Liberty: Oppressing Conscientious Diversity in England, in Religious Freedom and Gay Rights: Emerging Conflicts in the United States and Europe 21 (Timothy Samuel Shah et al. eds., 2016).

59. A Google News search in major US newspapers of "religio! AND discriminat!" produced 1252 results in 2011, 1472 in 2012, 1597 in 2013, 1962 in 2014, 3122 in 2015, 2604 in 2016, and 2851 in 2017. The search "religio! AND bigot!" yielded 386 in 2013, 433 in 2014, 877 in 2015, 1051 in 2016, 892 in 2017. The search "religio! AND bigot! AND (gay OR homosexual)" produced 175 in 2013, 169 in 2014, 297 in 2015, 229 in 2016, and 134 in 2017.

60. John Corvino, Ryan Anderson, and Sherif Girgis, Debating Religious Liberty and Discrimination 113–14 (2017).

61. Tom Gjelten, Christian Colleges Are Tangled In Their Own LGBT Policies, NPR Morning Edition, Mar. 27, 2018. In Canada, it has already happened: a proposed Christian law school was denied accreditation because of its policy prohibiting students and faculty from "engaging in sexual intimacy that violates the sacredness of marriage between a man and a woman." Elizabeth Redden, A Win for LGBTQ Rights, or a Loss for Religious Freedom?, Inside Higher Ed., June 18, 2018.

62. Harry Bruinius, Would California Bill Infringe on Religious Liberty of Christian Colleges?, Christian Science Monitor, July 1, 2016.

63. See Susan J. Stabile, Religious Convictions About Homosexuality and the Training of Counseling Professionals: How Should We Treat Religious-Based Opposition to Counseling About Same-Sex Relationship?, in Law, Religion and Health in the United States 263 (Holly Fernandez Lynch et al. eds. 2017).

64. Steven D. Smith, Die and Let Live? The Asymmetry of Accommodation, in Religious Freedom and Gay Rights: Emerging Conflicts in the United States and Europe 190 (Timothy Samuel Shah et al. eds. 2016).

Chapter 3

1. Michael Wear, Why Did Obama Win More White Evangelical Votes Than Clinton? He Asked for Fhem, Wash. Post, Nov. 22, 2016.

2. Amy Chozick, Hillary Clinton's Expectations, and Her Ultimate Campaign Missteps, N.Y. Times, Nov. 9, 2016.

3. Stephen Mansfield, Choosing Donald Trump: God, Anger, Hope, and Why Christian Conservatives Supported Him 119 (2017).

4. Mansfield, Choosing Donald Trump, 122; Michael McGough, Hillary Clinton Tweaks Her "Safe, Legal and Rare" Abortion Mantra, L. A. Times, Feb. 9, 2016.

5. Mansfield, Choosing Donald Trump, 121.

6. Faith and the 2016 Campaign, Pew Forum, Jan. 27, 2016.

7. Mansfield, Choosing Donald Trump, 118–19.

8. Q&A: Barack Obama, Christianity Today, Jan. 23, 2008.

9. Ruth Graham, Why Hillary Clinton Bombed With White Evangelical Voters, Slate, Dec. 15, 2016.

10. The distinction between the two understandings of rhetoric is already clear in Plato, Phaedrus (circa 370 B.C.).

11. Michael Wear, Reclaiming Hope: Lessons Learned in the Obama White House About the Future of Faith in America 162 (2018).

12. Matthew 25:34-40, New International Version.

13. Jeremy Weber, Billy Graham Center Explains Survey on Evangelical Trump Voters, Christianity Today, Oct. 18, 2018.,

14. Emma Green, White Evangelicals Believe They Face More Discrimination Than Muslims, Atlantic, Mar. 10, 2017.

15. John Fea, Believe Me: The Evangelical Road to Donald Trump (2018).

16. Quoted in Andrew Whitehead et al., Make America Christian Again: Christian Nationalism and Voting for Donald Trump in the 2016 Presidential Election, 79 Soc. of Rel. 147, 151 (2018).

17. Liberty University speech, Jan. 18, 2016, quoted in Michael Wear, Why Did Obama Win More White Evangelical Votes Than Clinton? He Asked for Them, Wash. Post, Nov. 22, 2016.

18. Bob Fredericks, Trump Asked CIA Why They Spared Family When Killing Terrorist Target, N.Y. Post, Apr. 6, 2018.

19. Michelle Boorstein and Julie Zauzmer, White Evangelical Christians Fail to Condemn Family Separations at US Border, Independent, June 20, 2018.

20. See Michelle F. Margolis, From Politics to the Pews: How Partisanship and the Political Environment Shape Religious Identity (2018).

21. David French, The True Sin of American Evangelicals in the Age of Trump, National Review, Mar. 13, 2018.

22. Carol Kuruvilla, New Study Reveals White Evangelicals' Troubling Beliefs On Race And Immigration, Huffington Post, Nov. 5, 2018.

23. Myriam Renaud, Myths Debunked: Why Did White Evangelical Christians Vote for Trump?, Martin Marty Center for the Public Understanding of Religion, Jan. 19, 2017.

24. Wear, Reclaiming Hope, 235.

25. Pew Forum on Religion and Public Life, How the Faithful Voted: A Preliminary 2016 Analysis, Nov. 9, 2016.

26. Margolis, From Politics to the Pews, 24-27.

27. Michael Lipka, A Closer Look at America's Rapidly Growing Religious "Nones," Pew Research Center, May 13, 2015.

28. In U.S., Decline of Christianity Continues at Rapid Pace, Pew Research Center, Oct. 17, 2019.

29. Barry A. Kosmin and Ariela Keysar, American Religious Identification Survey 2008, Summary Report (2009); Barry A. Kosmin and Ariela Keysar, Religion in a Free Market (2006).

30. Pew Research Center, U.S. Public Becoming Less Religious 15 (Nov. 3, 2015). This is a sharp decline from a 2007 survey, which reported that 70% believed in God.

31. Pew Forum on Religion and Public Life, "Nones" on the Rise: One-in-Five Adults Have No Religious Affiliation 22 (2012).

32. Michael Hout and Claude S. Fischer, Why More Americans Have No Religious Preference: Politics and Generations, 67 Am. Sociological Rev. 165 (2002); see also Robert D. Putnam and David E. Campbell, American Grace: How Religion Divides and Unites Us 120-32 (2010).

33. Becka A. Alper, Why America's "Nones" Don't Identify with a Religion, Pew Research Center, Aug. 8, 2018. See also Amelia Thomson-DeVeaux and Daniel Cox, The Christian Right Is Helping Drive Liberals Away From Religion, Five Thirty Eight, Sept. 18, 2019.

34. Margolis, From Politics to the Pews, 20–24.

35. Putnam and Campbell, American Grace, at 129, 123, 106.

36. Ibid. at 81.

37. Ibid. at 129; see also 393.

38. Pew Research Social and Demographic Trends, A Survey of LGBT Americans: Attitudes, Experiences and Values in Changing Times, June 13, 2013, ch. 6.

39. Pew Research Center, Religious Landscape Study, Views About Homosexuality, 2014; Daniel Cox and Robert P. Jones, America's Changing Religious Identity, PRRI, Sept. 6, 2017.

40. Greenberg Quinlan Rosner Research, Inside the GOP: Report on Focus Groups with Evangelical, Tea Party, and Moderate Republicans, Oct. 3, 2013.

41. Alexis de Tocqueville, Democracy in America 300 (1835–40; George Lawrence trans., J. P. Mayer ed. 1969).

42. Kosmin and Keysar, American Religious Identification Survey 2008; Pew Research Center, America's Changing Religious Landscape, May 12, 2015; In U.S., Decline of Christianity Continues at Rapid Pace, Pew Research Center, Oct. 17, 2019.

43. Among evangelicals, the proportion saying so has risen from 34% in September 2014 to 41% in June 2016. Pew Research Center, Evangelicals increasingly say it's becoming harder for them in America, July 14, 2016.

44. Robert P. Jones et al., How Immigration and Concerns About Cultural Changes are Shaping the 2016 Election, PRRI/Brookings, June 23, 2016.

45. Putnam and Campbell, American Grace, at 370, 414–18. A less detailed 2018 survey by a different organization found similar patterns: 46% of Americans supported a right to refuse, compared with 48% who rejected

such a right. That survey found a shift from a year earlier, where it had found only 41% supporting a right to refuse and 53% rejecting such a right. Republicans supporting a right to refuse had risen from 67% in 2017 to 73% in 2018; Democrats hardly changed at all (27% vs. 24%). Alex Vandermaas-Peeler et al., Wedding Cakes, Same-Sex Marriage, and the Future of LGBT Rights in America, PRRI, Aug. 2, 2018.

46. David Brion Davis, The Problem of Slavery in Western Culture (1966).

47. John Compton, Evangelical Origins of the Living Constitution (2014).

48. A. James Reichley, Religion in American Public Life 219-42 (1985).

49. Thus Rev. Jerry Falwell in 1965: "Believing the Bible as I do, I would find it impossible to stop preaching the pure saving gospel of Jesus Christ and begin doing anything else—including the fighting of communism, or participating in the civil rights reform. . . . Preachers are not called to be politicians, but to be soul winners." Quoted in Richard John Neuhaus, The Naked Public Square: Religion and Democracy in America 10 (1986).

50. Robert Wuthnow, The Restructuring of American Religion 218-22 (1988).

51. Sarah Barringer Gordon, The Spirit of the Law: Religious Voices and the Constitution in Modern America (2010).

52. Charles Taylor, A Secular Age (2007). For a short summary of this important but long book, see my review, Naked Strong Evaluation, 56 Dissent 105 (Winter 2009).

53. Sam Harris, Letter to a Christian Nation 18-19 (2006).

54. Orlando Patterson, Slavery and Social Death 78 (1982).

55. Letter to a Christian Nation, 54.

56. The historical ignorance of the contemporary "new atheist" movement is ruthlessly anatomized in John Gray, Seven Types of Atheism (2018).

57. Catechism of the Catholic Church, § 2404, quoting Gaudium et Spes §69 (1965).

58. Gaudium et Spes §69.

59. Emily Ekins, Religious Religious Trump Voters: How Faith Moderates Attitudes about Immigration, Race, and Identity, Democracy Fund Voter Study Group, Sept. 2018.

60. Elspeth Reeve, How to Tell Paul Ryan Wants to Be Veep: He's Rejected His Former Idol Ayn Rand, Atlantic Wire, Apr. 26, 2012.

61. Atlas Shrugged 961 (1957; Signet 1996).

62. Letter to the Editor, N.Y. Times, Nov. 3, 1957, quoted in Harriet Rubin, Ayn Rand's Literature of Capitalism, N.Y. Times, Sept. 15, 2007. I elaborate on the defects of Rand's philosophy in Involving Orcs (review of Lisa Duggan, Mean Girl: Ayn Rand and the Culture of Greed), New Rambler (Dec. 2019).

Chapter 4

1. Quoted in Kendall Thomas, Beyond the Privacy Principle, 92 Colum. L. Rev. 1431, 1463 (1992). A physician reported that injuries suffered by the victims of homophobic violence that he had treated were so "vicious" as to make clear that "the intent is to kill and maim":

> Weapons include knives, guns, brass knuckles, tire irons, baseball bats, broken bottles, metal chains, and metal pipes. Injuries include severe lacerations requiring extensive plastic surgery; head injuries, at times requiring surgery; puncture wounds of the chest, requiring insertion of chest tubes; removal of the spleen for traumatic rupture; multiple fractures of the extremities, jaws, ribs, and facial bones; severe eye injuries, in two cases resulting in permanent loss of vision; as well as severe psychological trauma the level of which would be difficult to measure.

   Id., 1466. Other illustrations may be found in id., 1462-70. This article is old, but what it describes has not changed. On recent trends, see Tim Fitzsimons, Anti-LGBTQ hate crimes rose 3 percent in '17, FBI finds, NBC News, Nov. 14, 2018. Reports are regularly released by the National Coalition of Anti-Violence Programs at https://avp.org/resources/reports/.

2. Gordon W. Allport, The Nature of Prejudice 49 (1954).

3. Ibid. at 57.

4. Ibid. at 59.

5. Ibid. at 14.

6. See Andrew Koppelman, Why Gay Legal History Matters, 113 Harv. L. Rev. 2035 (2000).

7. Brief of amici Lambda Legal Defense and Education Fund et al., Masterpiece Cakeshop v. Colorado, 9.

8. For a comprehensive review of the evidence, see Jennifer C. Pizer, Brad Sears, Christy Mallory, and Nan D. Hunter, Evidence of Persistent and Pervasive Workplace Discrimination against LGBT People: The Need for Federal Legislation Prohibition Discrimination and Providing for Equal Employment Benefits, 45 Loyola L. Rev. 715 (2012). For evidence that discrimination in public accommodations is as common with sexual orientation as it is with race and sex, see Christy Mallory and Brad Sears, Refusing to Serve LGBT People: An Empirical Assessment of Complaints Filed under State Public Accommodations Non-Discrimination Laws, 8 J. Rsch in Gender Stud. 109 (2018). See also the scholarship cited in the report accompanying the Employment Non-Discrimination Act of 2013, S. Rep. 113-105 (2013), at 14–19.

9. Preserve Freedom, Reject Coercion (Dec. 2016).
10. Ryan T. Anderson, Sexual Orientation and Gender Identity (SOGI) Laws Threaten Freedom, Heritage Found. Backgrounder, Nov. 30, 2015, 2, 6. Anderson draws the second quotation from Hans Bader, Employment Non-Discrimination Act Makes as Little Sense as Chemotherapy for a Cold, Competitive Enterprise Institute Open Market, June 13, 2012.

   My views on this question are misunderstood by Anderson and Girgis. They don't answer the massive evidence of discrimination cited by their interlocutor Corvino. John Corvino, Ryan Anderson, and Sherif Girgis, Debating Religious Liberty and Discrimination 74–77 (2017). Instead they rely on one statement of mine. In making an earlier case for religious exemptions, I wrote:

   > Hardly any of these cases have occurred: a handful in a country of 300 million people. In all of them, the people who objected to the law at issue were asked directly to facilitate same-sex relationships by providing wedding, adoption or artificial insemination services, counseling, or rental of bedrooms. There have been no claims of a right to simply refuse to deal with gay people.

   Ibid. at 187, quoting Andrew Koppelman, Gay Rights, Religious Accommodations, and the Purposes of Antidiscrimination Law, 88 S. Cal. L. Rev. 619, 643 (2015). From this they infer that "the strongest case for enacting [antidiscrimination protection for gay people]— denials of housing, or employment, or medical care—are mercifully rare to vanishing." A few sentences earlier in the same article, though, I wrote: "Discrimination is, of course, part of the daily experience of every openly gay person in the United States." I also argued that "Discrimination against gay people causes similar economic harm" to that caused by discrimination against African Americans before the Civil Rights Act of 1964. My quoted passage refers to religious objections to discrimination laws, not to the underlying discrimination. Its claim is that—as with any other case for religious accommodation—objectors can be accommodated without defeating the law's purpose, not that the law isn't necessary.
11. Robin Fretwell Wilson, The Nonsense About Bathrooms: How Purported Concerns over Safety Block LGBT Nondiscrimination Laws and Obscure Real Religious Liberty Concerns, 20 Lewis & Clark L. Rev. 1373, 1379–83 (2017).
12. One concern can be set aside at the outset. Some worry that any exception diminishes the authority of the law. John Corvino offers what he calls the "Swiss cheese" objection: "poking the law full of holes undermines both its

efficacy and authority." Debating Religious Liberty and Discrimination, 216. Frederick Schauer has shown, however, that "there is no logical distinction between exceptions and what they are exceptions to, their occurrence resulting from the often fortuitous circumstance that the language available to circumscribe a legal rule or principle is broader than the regulatory goals the rule or principle is designed to further." Frederick Schauer, Exceptions, 58 U. Chi. L. Rev. 871, 872 (1991). The question of whether to exempt Quakers from military service, for example, arises only because the idea of military service does not, in the English language, automatically exclude religious pacifists. The only question is what shape the law should take, given the many competing legitimate interests that must be accommodated. John Finnis is right that many laws state general propositions that, were they not qualified by exceptions, "would be manifestly unjust, intolerable, and contrary to many accepted public policies." John M. Finnis, Equality and Religious Liberty: Oppressing Conscientious Diversity in England, in Religious Freedom and Gay Rights: Emerging Conflicts in the United States and Europe 31 (Timothy Samuel Shah et al. eds., 2016). Imagine a law of homicide without an exception for self-defense.

13. John Locke, A Letter Concerning Toleration 46 (James H. Tully, ed. 1983) (1689).

14. Ibid., 29.

15. See, e.g., Murray Rothbard, For a New Liberty: The Libertarian Manifesto 206 (rev. ed. 1978); Ayn Rand, The Virtue of Selfishness: A New Concept of Egoism 126–34 (1964); Robert Bork, Civil Rights—A Challenge, 149 New Republic, Aug. 31, 1963, at 22; Milton Friedman, Capitalism and Freedom 108–15 (1962).

16. Given the tendency of some ethnic groups to violently dominate others, such conditions exist in many parts of the world. See Tarunaibh Khaitan, A Theory of Discrimination Law (2015).

17. See Andrew Koppelman, Justice for Large Earlobes! A comment on Richard Arneson's "What is Wrongful Discrimination?", 43 San Diego L. Rev. 809 (2006).

18. Andrew Koppelman, The Tough Luck Constitution and the Assault on Health Care Reform (2013); Andrew Koppelman with Tobias Barrington Wolff, A Right to Discriminate? How the Case of Boy Scouts of America v. James Dale Warped the Law of Free Association (2009); Koppelman, Antidiscrimination Law and Social Equality; Andrew Koppelman, Feminism and Libertarianism: A Response to Richard Epstein, 1999 U. of Chicago Legal

Forum 115; Andrew Koppelman, Richard Epstein's Imperfect Understanding of Antidiscrimination Law, Law and Liberty Forum, Jan. 12, 2016.

19. I once discovered at a libertarian conference, in response to a request for a show of hands, that I was the only one at the table who was entirely confident that the Civil Rights Act of 1964 was not unconstitutional.

20. US Commission on Civil Rights, Peaceful Coexistence: Reconciling Nondiscrimination Principles with Civil Liberties (Sep. 2016).

21. Findings and Recommendations, in ibid., 25.

22. Ibid. at 40 (statement of Commissioners Achtenberg, Castro, Kladney, and Yaki).

23. Ibid. at 29 (statement of Chairman Martin R. Castro).

24. Ibid. at 41 (statement of Commissioner Karen K. Narasaki).

25. Andrew Koppelman, Antidiscrimination Law and Social Equality 181–90 (1996).

26. James J. Heckman and J. Hoult Verkerke, Racial Disparity and Employment Discrimination Law: An Economic Perspective, 8 Yale L. & Pol'y Rev. 276, 281 (1990).

27. Ibid.

28. Ibid.

29. Ibid.

30. Robin Fretwell Wilson, Bathrooms and Bakers: How Sharing the Public Square Is the Key to a Truce in the Culture Wars, in Religious Freedom, LGBT Rights, and the Prospects for Common Ground 415–16 (William Eskridge Jr. and Robin Fretwell Wilson, eds. 2018). This may be a departure from preexisting common law rules; see Joseph William Singer, No Right to Exclude: Public Accommodations and Private Property, 90 Nw. U. L. Rev. 1283 (1996); but it is now the law in most places. See, e.g., *Feldt v. Marriott Corp.*, 322 A.2d 913, 915 (D.C. 1974).

31. See Rick Perlstein, Before the Storm: Barry Goldwater and the Unmaking of the American Consensus 363–64 (2001); see also at 462 (quoting Goldwater speech, coauthored by William Rehnquist, declaring that "the freedom to associate means the same thing as the freedom not to associate").

32. More generally, property rights are created by the law for reasons and should not be defined in a way inconsistent with those reasons. See Thomas Nagel and Liam Murphy, The Myth of Ownership (2002); Jeremy Waldron, The Right to Private Property (1989).

33. Barry M. Goldwater, Job Protection for Gays, Wash. Post, July 13, 1994.

34. See generally Richard Epstein, Forbidden Grounds: The Case Against Employment Discrimination Laws (1992).

35. Ibid. at 28–58.

36. See Samuel Issacharoff, Contractual Liberties in Discriminatory Markets, 70 Tex. L. Rev. 1219, 1242–43 (1992) (book review); Symposium, Forbidden Grounds: The Case Against Employment Discrimination Laws, 31 San Diego L. Rev. 1 (1994)(critiques by Ian Ayres, Drew Days, Evan Tsen Lee, Jerry L. Mashaw, and Richard H. McAdams); see also John J. Donohue III, Is Title VII Efficient?, 134 U. Pa. L. Rev. 1411, 1415–19 (1986) (similarly responding to neoclassical economic attacks on antidiscrimination law).

37. Joseph Fishkin, The Anti-Bottleneck Principle in Employment Discrimination Law, 91 Wash. U. L. Rev. 1429, 1444–52 (2014).

38. Mark Joseph Stern, Anti-Gay Segregation May Soon Be Coming to Oregon, Slate, Feb. 4, 2014.

39. Elizabeth Sepper, Gays in the Moralized Marketplace, 7 Ala. C.R. & C.L. L. Rev. 129, 150 (2015).

40. 42 U.S.C. §3603(b).

41. Quoted in Bruce Ackerman, We the People 3: The Civil Rights Revolution 142 (2014).

42. Brief of amici curiae law and economics scholars Richard Epstein et al., Masterpiece Cakeshop v. Colorado, 12, citations omitted.

43. Brief of amici Lambda Legal Defense and Education Fund et al., Masterpiece Cakeshop v. Colorado, 18–19.

44. Nathan B. Oman, Doux Commerce, Religion, and the Limits of Antidiscrimination Law, 92 Ind. L. J. 693, 723 (2017).

45. This was suggested as an ameliorative modification by Elizabeth Sepper, who however is not necessarily endorsing any accommodations whatever.

46. Justin McCarthy, U.S. Support for Gay Marriage Edges to New High, Gallup, May 15, 2017.

47. Justin McCarthy, Americans' Support for Gay Marriage Remains High, at 61%, Gallup, May 19, 2016. A 2018 survey found 79% support. Daniel Greenberg, et al., Fifty Years After Stonewall: Widespread Support for LGBT Issues—Findings from American Values Atlas 2018, PRRI, Mar. 26, 2019.

48. Daniel Greenberg et al., Americans Show Broad Support for LGBT Nondiscrimination Protections, PRRI, Mar. 12, 2019.

49. Alex Vandermaas-Peeler, et al., PRRI, Emerging Consensus on LGBT Issues: Findings From the 2017 American Values Atlas (May 1, 2018). In 2018, the national number had inched up to 71%; Alabama's, 59%. Greenberg, et al., Fifty Years After Stonewall.

50. Quinnipiac University Poll, U.S. Voters Still Say 2-1 Trump Committed Crime, Quinnipiac University National Poll Finds; But Voters Oppose Impeachment 2-1, May 2, 2019.

51. Robert P. Jones et al., Beyond Same-sex Marriage: Attitudes on LGBT Nondiscrimination Laws and Religious Exemptions from 2015 American Values Atlas, PRRI (Feb. 18, 2016).

52. Robert P. Jones et al., Majority of Americans Oppose Laws Requiring Transgender Individuals to Use Bathroom Corresponding to Sex at Birth Rather than Gender Identity, PRRI (Aug. 25, 2016).

53. Jeffrey M. Jones, Americans Hold Record Liberal Views on Most Moral Issues, Gallup, May 11, 2017.

54. One may object that attitudinal shifts can be unpredictable. Before the rise of Trump, few would have predicted that a candidate with such openly racist views could succeed, or could trigger a resurgence of racism. But Trump is in fact the result of a long term shift in attitudes: among whites, especially less educated whites, racial resentment has steadily increased for the past 40 years, and is increasingly concentrated among Republican voters. Analysis of the voter data concludes that such resentment was the strongest influence on Republican primary voters who supported him: "Trump's embrace of the birther myth, his forwarding of tweets from white supremacists, his attacks on Mexican and Muslim immigrants, and his claims of massive voter fraud in African American communities directly targeted white racial and ethnic fears." Alan Abramowitz, The Great Alignment: Race, Party Transformation, and the Rise of Donald Trump 140 (2018); see also John Sides et al., Identity Crisis: The 2016 Presidential Campaign and the Battle for the Meaning of America 69–96 (2018). That same appeal helped him in the general election. A few decades earlier no Republican could have prevailed with such views.

55. I elaborate on this purpose of antidiscrimination law in Antidiscrimination Law and Social Equality (1996).

56. Ibid., 92–99.

57. Douglas NeJaime and Reva B. Siegel, Conscience Wars: Complicity-Based Conscience Claims in Religion and Politics, 124 Yale L.J. 2516 (2015).

58. Ibid., 2563.

59. Ibid., 2543.

60. Robert Post, The Politics of Religion: Democracy and The Conscience Wars, in The Conscience Wars: Rethinking the Balance between Religion, Identity, and Equality 473, 483–84 (Susanna Mancini and Michel Rosenfeld eds. 2018).

61. Ibid., 483.

62. Louise Melling, Religious Refusals and Reproductive Rights: Claims of Conscience as Discrimination and Shaming, in The Conscience Wars: Rethinking the Balance between Religion, Identity, and Equality 375, 391 (Susanna Mancini and Michel Rosenfeld eds. 2018).

63. Melissa Murray, Loving's Legacy: Decriminalization and the Regulation of Sex and Sexuality, 86 Fordham L. Rev. 2671, 2699 (2018); the point is developed in Melissa Murray, Consequential Sex: #MeToo, Masterpiece Cakeshop, and Private Sexual Regulation, 113 Nw. U. L. Rev. 825 (2019).

64. "Although we differ from the witness and his brethren, in our religious creed, yet we have no reason to question the purity of their motives, or to impeach their good conduct as citizens." People v. Philips, N.Y. Ct. of Gen Sessions (1813), in Michael W. McConnell et al., Religion and the Constitution 99 (4th ed. 2016).

65. Ernest J. Weinrib, The Idea of Private Law (1995).

66. See Andrew Koppelman, Justice for Large Earlobes! A comment on Richard Arneson's "What is Wrongful Discrimination?", 43 San Diego L. Rev. 809 (2006).

67. See Patrick Shin, Is There a Unitary Concept of Discrimination?, in Philosophical Foundations of Discrimination Law 163 (Deborah Hellman and Sophia Moreau, eds., 2013).

68. See Koppelman, Antidiscrimination Law and Social Equality 76–92. Iris Marion Young pointed this out long ago:

> If one focuses on discrimination as the primary wrong groups suffer, then the more profound wrongs of exploitation, marginalization, powerlessness, cultural imperialism, and violence that we still suffer go undiscussed and unaddressed. One misses how the weight of society's institutions and people's assumptions, habits, and behavior toward others are directed at reproducing the material and ideological conditions that make life easier for, provide greater real opportunities to, and establish the priority of the point of view of white heterosexual men.

Justice and the Politics of Difference 196–97 (1990). The classic statement of this critique is Alan David Freeman, Legitimizing Racial Discrimination Through Antidiscrimination Law: A Critical Review of Supreme Court Doctrine, 62 Minn. L. Rev. 1049 (1978).

69. Taylor Flynn, Clarion Call or False Alarm: Why Proposed Exemptions to Equal Marriage Statutes Return Us to a Religious Understanding of the Public Marketplace, 5 Nw. J. L. & Soc. Pol'y 236, 240–41 (2010).

70. Ira C. Lupu and Robert W. Tuttle, Same-Sex Family Equality And Religious Freedom, 5 Nw. J. L. & Soc. Pol'y 274, 290 (2010). Accord

Chai R. Feldblum, Moral Conflict and Conflicting Liberties, in Same-Sex Marriage and Religious Liberty: Emerging Conflicts 123, 153 (Douglas Laycock et al. eds., 2008).

71. See, e.g., Ilan H. Meyer, Prejudice, Social Stress, and Mental Health in Lesbian, Gay and Bisexual Populations: Conceptual Issues and Research Evidence, 129 Psych. Bulletin 674 (2003); Vickie M. Mays, Mental Health Correlates of Perceived Discrimination Among Lesbian, Gay, and Bisexual Adults in the United States, 91 Am. J. Pub. Health 1869 (2001).

72. S.Rep. No. 872, 88th Cong., 2d Sess., 16, quoted in *Heart of Atlanta Motel v. United States*, 379 U.S. 241, 291–92 (1964) (Goldberg, J., concurring).

73. Ackerman, We the People 3, 138.

74. Ibid., 139.

75. Joseph William Singer, We Don't Serve Your Kind Here: Public Accommodations and the Mark of Sodom, 95 B.U. L. Rev. 929, 938 (2015), emphasis in original.

76. American Psychological Ass'n, Stress in America: The Impact of Discrimination 8 (2016).

77. Timothy T. Brown et al., Discrimination Hurts: The Effect of Discrimination on the Development of Chronic Pain, 204 Soc. Sci. & Med. 1, 2 (2018). Other evidence of the individualized harm of discrimination, with evidence particularly pertinent to gay people, is compiled in Brief of Amici Ilan H. Meyer et al., Masterpiece Cakeshop v. Colorado.

78. See Kenneth L. Karst, Threats and Meanings: How the Facts Govern First Amendment Doctrine, 58 Stan. L. Rev. 1337, 1339–46 (2006).

79. *Elane Photography v. Willock*, 309 P.3d 53, 59 (2013), cert. denied, 572 US 1046 (2014).

80. This language is adapted from Russell Nieli's proposal, discussed in chapter 9.

81. Flynn, Clarion Call or False Alarm, 254.

82. Ibid. at 257.

83. Insult is the primary injury detected in Julia Raifman et al., Association of State Laws Permitting Denial of Services to Same-Sex Couples With Mental Distress in Sexual Minority Adults: A Difference-in-Difference-in-Differences Analysis, 75 JAMA Psychiatry 671 (2018). The study claims that religious exemptions from antidiscrimination laws cause an increase in mental distress, but the authors do not understand how the laws they study actually operate. For example, they assume that Utah and North Carolina laws allowing clerks and magistrates to recuse themselves from same-sex marriages will lead to "directly experiencing

a refused marriage license," but those laws require that substitute clerks and magistrates be available. The states that constitute their control group include two with antidiscrimination protection for gay people and four without such protection, so most of those states also permit the denial of services. The authors acknowledge that the effect they detect may be the result of "media coverage," which may "affect the salience of these laws." The salience of antigay views is not something that the law can control.

84. Flynn, Clarion Call or False Alarm, 242.
85. Singer, We Don't Serve Your Kind Here, 939.
86. Ibid., 940.
87. Sepper, Gays in the Moralized Marketplace, 157–58.
88. Ira C. Lupu, Moving Targets: Obergefell, Hobby Lobby, and the Future of LGBT Rights, 7 Ala. Civ. Rts. & Civ. Lib. L. Rev. 1, 68–69 (2015).
89. Charles L. Black Jr., The Lawfulness of the Segregation Decisions, 69 Yale L.J. 421 (1960).
90. I draw here on an analogous point about the establishment clause developed in Steven D. Smith, Symbols, Perceptions, and Doctrinal Illusions: Establishment Neutrality and the "No Endorsement" Test, 86 Mich. L. Rev. 266 (1987).
91. Michael W. McConnell, It's Not About the Cake: Against "Altaring" the Public Marketplace, in Religious Freedom, LGBT Rights, and the Prospects for Common Ground 379 (William Eskridge Jr. and Robin Fretwell Wilson, eds. 2018).
92. Warren Richey, Behind Legal Fight Over Religious Liberty, a Question of Conscience, Christian Science Monitor, July 13, 2016.
93. Lupu, Moving Targets, 68.
94. Ackerman, We the People 3, 151.
95. Ibid., 130.
96. Singer, We Don't Serve Your Kind Here, 940.
97. Oman, Doux Commerce, 703.
98. See Deirdre McCloskey, The Bourgeois Virtues: Ethics for an Age of Commerce (2006).
99. Oman, Doux Commerce, 712.
100. Exemption-with-notice is a peculiar form of property right, but property rights ought to be open to reformulation when human needs so require. "Property rights serve human values. They are recognized to that end, and are limited by it." State v. Shack, 277 A.2d 369, 372 (N.J. 1971), quoted in Singer, We Don't Serve Your Kind Here, 940.

Chapter 5

1. The constitutional issue was raised, on similar facts, in the *US case of Lexington Fayette Urban County Human Rights Commission v. Hands on Originals, Inc.*, 2017 WL 2211381 (Ky. App.). The court resolved the question on statutory grounds and did not reach the constitutional issue.

2. *West Virginia St. Bd. of Ed. v. Barnette*, 319 U.S. 624, 642 (1943).

3. *Wooley v. Maynard*, 430 U.S. 705, 715 (1977).

4. Andrew Koppelman with Tobias Barrington Wolff, A Right to Discriminate? How the Case of Boy Scouts of America v. James Dale Warped the Law of Free Association 25–42 (2009).

5. It also means that he may not be required to publicly display a message with which he disagrees. *Wooley v. Maynard*. That strand of the doctrine is not relevant here.

6. Brief of Amicus Christian Legal Society, et. al., *Masterpiece Cakeshop v. Colorado*, 20.

7. Brief amici curiae of Cato Institute, Eugene Volokh, and Dale Carpenter in support of petition for certiorari, *Elane Photography v. Willock*, 2012 WL 5990629, 7.

8. Ibid. at 3. Or, at least, to photographers who make aesthetic choices. Huguenin's attorneys wrote: "She is not a passive surveillance camera, but a professional artist and storyteller speaking through the images that she captures, edits, and arranges in a book." Reply Brief for Petitioner, *Elane Photography v. Willock*, 8.

9. Brief of amicus Am. Unity Fund and Profs. Dale Carpenter & Eugene Volokh, *Masterpiece Cakeshop v. Colorado*, 2017 WL 4918194, 6.

10. Ibid., 8.

11. Ibid., 3, quoting *United States v. O'Brien*, 391 U.S. 367, 376 (1968). See also Brush & Nib Studio, *LC v. City of Phoenix*, 2019 WL 4400328 (Az.), *23 (upholding right of calligraphers to refuse to create custom invitations for same-sex wedding and distinguishing bakers and florists on this ground); Brief of Amici Curiae Cato Institute and Professors Dale Carpenter and Eugene Volokh in Support of Brush & Nib Studio, LC, et al., 2019 WL 174521.

12. *Telescope Media v. Lucero*, 936 F.3d 740, 748–49 (8th Cir. 2019).

13. Robert Post, An Analysis of DOJ's Brief in *Masterpiece Cakeshop*, Take Care Blog, Oct. 18, 2017, https://takecareblog.com/blog/an-analysis-of-doj-s-brief-in-masterpiece-cakeshop.

14. As, after the oral argument, I thought it might. Baking Chaos: *Masterpiece Cakeshop* Argument Misses the Mark, The American Prospect online, Dec. 6, 2017.

15. Leslie Kendrick and Micah Schwartzman, The Etiquette of Animus, 132 Harv. L. Rev. 133, 138–45 (2018); Bernard Bell, A Lemon Cake: Ascribing Religious Motivations in Administrative Adjudications—A Comment on Masterpiece Cakeshop (Part II), Yale J. on Reg: Notice & Comment (June 20, 2018), http://yalejreg.com/nc/a-lemon-cake-ascribing-religious-motivation-in-administrative-adjudications-a-comment-on-masterpiece-cakeshop-part-ii. To begin with the most basic problem, the claim of bias was not raised at any point in the lower court proceedings, and so was not preserved for appeal. It was inappropriate to reverse on this basis. The Court seems to have been reaching for some way to get rid of the case without reaching the merits.

16. The Court also relied on another argument, that the treatment of Phillips and of William Jack, discussed earlier, "could reasonably be interpreted as being inconsistent as to the question of whether speech is involved." Masterpiece Cakeshop, Ltd. v. Colorado Civil Rights Com'n, 138 S.Ct. 1719, 1730 (2018). But the Court did not explain what was inconsistent, and Colorado had offered a consistent rule, which the Court did not discuss: that the baker who would not sell to Jack would not have sold those cakes to anyone—an argument unavailable to Phillips.

17. Quoted in Masterpiece Cakeshop, 138 S.Ct. at 1735 (Gorsuch, J., concurring).

18. Ibid. at 1743 n.2 (Thomas, J., concurring in part and concurring in the judgment). A similar argument is offered in Francis J. Beckwith, Now, I'm Liberal, but to a Degree: An Essay on Debating Religious Liberty and Discrimination, 67 Clev. St. L. Rev. 141, 170–71 (2019).

19. United States v. O'Brien, 391 U.S. 367, 376 (1968).

20. Ibid.

21. 530 U.S. 640 (2000).

22. Ibid. at 653.

23. Andrew Koppelman with Tobias Barrington Wolff, A Right to Discriminate? How the Case of Boy Scouts of America v. James Dale Warped the Law of Free Association (2009).

24. See Newman v. Piggie Park Enters., Inc., 256 F. Supp. 941, 944 (D.S.C. 1966), rev'd, 377 F.2d 433 (4th Cir. 1967), aff'd per curiam, 390 U.S. 400 (1968).

25. See chapter 8.

26. Masterpiece Cakeshop, 138 S.Ct. at 1746 (Thomas, J., concurring in part and concurring in the judgment).

27. Ibid., quoting Heart of Atlanta Motel v. United States, 379 U.S. 241, 291–92 (1964) (Goldberg, J., concurring), who in turn was quoting the Senate

Commerce Committee report on the Civil Rights Act of 1964, S.Rep. No. 872, 88th Cong., 2d Sess., 16.

28. *Masterpiece Cakeshop*, 138 S.Ct. at 1746 (Thomas, J., concurring in part and concurring in the judgment).

29. Ibid. at 1735-36 (Gorsuch, J., concurring).

30. Ibid. at 1746 (Thomas, J., concurring in part and concurring in the judgment).

31. Ibid. at 1733 n.* (Kagan, J., concurring).

32. Congregation of the Doctrine of the Faith, Some Considerations Concerning the Response to Legislative Proposals on the Non-Discrimination of Homosexual Persons (July 22, 1992).

33. *Masterpiece Cakeshop*, 138 S.Ct. at 1730.

34. Ibid., 1736 (Gorsuch, J., concurring). A federal district court later refused to dismiss Phillips's claim of malicious prosecution, discussed in chapter 9, in part on the basis of this argument.

35. Jim Oleske, Justice Gorsuch, Kippahs, and False Analogies in Masterpiece Cakeshop, Take Care Blog, June 19, 2018.

36. Brief of Colo. Civil Rights Comm'n, *Masterpiece Cakeshop*, 15.

37. Ibid., 17.

Chapter 6

1. 134 S.Ct. 2751 (2014).

2. See Timothy Stoltzfus Jost, Health Care at Risk: A Critique of the Consumer-Driven Movement 59–61 (2007).

3. See my The Tough Luck Constitution and the Assault on Health Care Reform 25–31 (2013).

4. Ibid.

5. 42 U.S.C. § 300gg-13(a)(4) (2012).

6. Coverage of Certain Preventive Services Under the Affordable Care Act, 78 Fed. Reg. 79,870, 39,872 (July 2, 2013).

7. Denise Grady, Overhaul Will Lower the Costs of Being a Woman, N.Y. Times, Mar. 29, 2010; Turning to Fairness: Insurance Discrimination Against Women Today and the Affordable Care Act, National Women's Law Center, Mar. 16, 2012.

8. Inst. of Med., Clinical Preventive Services for Women: Closing the Gaps 19–20 (2011) ("IOM Rep."); see also Rachel Benson Gold, The Need for and Cost of Mandating Private Insurance Coverage of Contraception, in Guttmacher Rep. on Pub. Pol'y, Aug. 1998, at 5; James Trussell et al.,

Erratum to "Cost Effectiveness of Contraceptives in the United States," 80 Contraception 229, 229 (2009).

9. See 78 Fed. Reg. at 39,872; IOM Rep. at 105. When I investigated in 2014, the cost of an IUD, the most reliable and cost-effective form of contraception, was very high. The providers now no longer reveal the prices on their websites. Compare Cost Comparison Chart, ParaGard, http:// www.paragard.com/ how-do-i-get-it/Payment.aspx (visited Jan. 24, 2014) (product cost of $754), with http://www.paragard.com/what-it-costs.aspx (last visited Oct. 27, 2017); compare If Mirena Isn't Covered, Mirena, http://www.mirena-us.com/how-to-get-mirena/if-mirena-isnt-covered.php (visited Jan. 24, 2014) (product cost of $927.18); https://www.mirena-us.com/if-mirena-isnt-covered/ (last visited Oct. 27, 2017).

10. See Melissa S. Kearney and Phillip B. Levine, Subsidized Contraception, Fertility, and Sexual Behavior, 91 Rev. of Econ. & Stat. 137 (2009) (decreasing the cost of contraceptives leads to a higher usage rate which, in turn, decreases the rate of unintended pregnancies).

11. A 2007 study found that 52% of women (compared with only 39% of men) failed to fill a prescription, missed a recommended test or treatment, or did not schedule a necessary specialist appointment because of cost. Sheila D. Rustgi et al., Women at Risk: Why Many Women Are Forgoing Needed Health Care, The Commonwealth Fund, May 2009, at 3.

12. IOM Rep. at 102–103.

13. Ibid.; see also 78 Fed. Reg. at 39,872.

14. IOM Rep. at 103–104; see also 78 Fed. Reg. at 39,872.

15. 77 Fed. Reg. 8725, 8727 (Feb. 15, 2012).

16. See Caroline Mala Corbin, The Contraception Mandate, 107 Nw. U. L. Rev. Colloquy 151 (2002).

17. Michael Wear, Reclaiming Hope: Lessons Learned in the Obama White House About the Future of Faith in America 135 (2018).

18. Ibid., 129.

19. See Robert Pear, Birth Control Rule Altered to Allay Religious Objections, N.Y. Times, Feb. 1, 2013.

20. The number is higher now.

21. Douglas Laycock, Religious Liberty, Health Care, and the Culture Wars, in Law, Religion, and Health in the United States 21 (Holly Fernandez Lynch et al. eds. 2017).

22. I emphasized the good news immediately after the decision in Andrew Koppelman, The Hobby Lobby Decision Was a Victory for Women's Rights, New Republic Online, June 30, 2014.

23. E.g., Newland v. Sebelius, 881 F. Supp. 2d 1287, 1297 (D. Colo. 2012).

24. *Monaghan v. Sebelius*, 931 F.Supp.2d 794, 809 (E.D.Mich. 2013).
25. Frederick Mark Gedicks and Andrew Koppelman, Invisible Women: Why an Exemption for Hobby Lobby Would Violate the Establishment Clause, 67 Vanderbilt L. Rev. En Banc 51 (2014).
26. 45 C.F.R. § 147.131(a)–(b) (2013).
27. Ibid. at 2781, quoting Brief for HHS in 13–354, at 15. The Court also noted that "drawing the line between the 'creation of an entirely new program' and the modification of an existing program (which RFRA surely allows) would be fraught with problems." The same judges had, however, drawn exactly that line in making the Affordable Care Act's Medicaid expansion optional for the states, thereby depriving millions of people of health insurance. See Andrew Koppelman, The Tough Luck Constitution and the Assault on Health Care Reform 122–29 (2013).
28. Hobby Lobby, 134 S. Ct. at 2781.
29. Frederick Mark Gedicks and Rebecca G. Van Tassell, Of Burdens and Baselines: Hobby Lobby's Puzzling Footnote 37, in The Rise of Corporate Religious Liberty 323 (Micah Schwartzman et al. eds. 2016).
30. I've argued elsewhere that a law that does this violates the Establishment Clause. Gedicks and Koppelman, Invisible Women; see also Frederick Mark Gedicks and Rebecca Van Tassell, RFRA Exemptions from the Contraception Mandate: An Unconstitutional Accommodation of Religion, 49 Harv. C.R.–C.L. L. Rev. 343 (2015).
31. EEOC v. R.G. & G.R. Harris Funeral Homes, Inc., 201 F. Supp. 3d 837, 841-42 (E.D. Mich. 2016); Franciscan Alliance, Inc. v. Burwell, 227 F. Supp. 3d 660, 693 (N.D. Tex. 2016). For analysis of these cases, see Adam K. Hersh, Daniel in the Lion's Den: A Structural Reconsideration of Religious Exemptions from Nondiscrimination Laws Since *Obergefell*, 70 Stan. L. Rev. 265, 278-82 (2018). Other federal judges have also credited the idea that the theoretical possibility of an entire new spending program could count as a less restrictive means, and thus demand a religious exemption. Eternal Word Television Network, Inc. v. Secretary of U.S. Dept. of Health and Human Services, 818 F.3d 1122, 1190 (11th Cir. 2016) (Tjoflat, J., dissenting); Grace Schools v. Burwell, 801 F.3d 788, 822-23 (7th Cir. 2015) (Manion, J., dissenting); Brandt v. Burwell, F.Supp.3d 462, 489 (W.D. Pa. 2014).
32. See, e.g., Transcript of Oral Argument, at 40, 84, 86, *Burwell v. Hobby Lobby Stores, Inc.*, 134 S.Ct. 2751 (2014) (Nos. 13-354 & -356) (suggestions of counsel at oral argument that women could obtain the coverage denied by Hobby Lobby from a new government program or Title X).
33. *Holt v. Hobbs*, 135 S. Ct. 853, 868 (2015) (Sotomayor, J., concurring) (quoting *U.S. v. Wilgus*, 638 F.3d 1274, 1289 (10th Cir. 2011).

34. Ira C. Lupu, Moving Targets: Obergefell, Hobby Lobby, and the Future of LGBT Rights, 7 Alabama Civ. Rights & Civ. Liberties L. Rev. 1, 35 (2015).

35. Ibid., 37–38.

36. Simon Lazarus, Stripping the Gears of National Government: Justice Stevens's Stand Against Judicial Subversion of Progressive Laws and Lawmaking, 106 Nw. U. L. Rev. 769 (2012).

37. 42 U.S.C. § 2000bb(a)(5) ("The compelling interest test as set forth in prior Federal court rulings is a workable test for striking sensible balances between religious liberty and competing prior governmental interests."); § 2000bb(b)(1) (The purpose of RFRA is "to restore the compelling interest test as set forth in *Sherbert v. Verner*, 374 U.S. 398 (1963) and *Wisconsin v. Yoder*, 406 U.S. 205 (1972)"); see *Gonzales v. O Centro Espirita Beneficente Uniao do Vegetal*, 546 U.S. 418, 424 (2006) (RFRA "adopted a statutory rule comparable to the constitutional rule rejected in Smith").

38. See, e.g., 103 Cong. Rec. H2356 (daily ed., May 11, 1993), archived at http://perma.cc/B63K-AS4Z (describing one purpose of original RFRA bill H.R. 1306 as "to restore the compelling interest test as set forth in Federal court cases before Employment Division of Oregon v. Smith"); 103 Cong. Rec. S14352 (daily ed., Oct. 26, 1993) (remarks of Sen. Kennedy, D-Mass.), archived at http://perma.cc/C5EW-6J7U ("The amendment we will offer today is intended to make it clear that the pre-Smith law is applied under the RFRA in determining whether Government action burden [*sic*] under the freedom of religion must meet the test."); 103 Cong. Rec. S14468 (daily ed., Oct. 27, 1933) (remarks of Sen. Feingold, D-Wis.), archived at http://perma.cc/C5EW-6J7U ("For nearly 20 years the compelling interest standard has proved to be sufficiently flexible to strike an appropriate balance between the free exercise of religion and the functions of Government"); see also H.R. Rep. No. 103-88, 103rd Cong (1993) ("The [compelling-interest] test generally should not be construed more stringently or more leniently than it was prior to Smith."); S. Rep. No. 103-111, 103rd Cong. 9 (1993) (same).

39. *Burwell v. Hobby Lobby*, 134 S.Ct. 2751, 2772 (2014).

40. In the years immediately following *Hobby Lobby*, there was no significant increase in the rate at which claims for religious accommodation prevailed. Stephanie H. Barclay and Mark L. Rienzi, Constitutional Anomalies or As-Applied Challenges? A Defense of Religious Exemptions, 59 B.C. L. Rev. 1595 (2018). But the most problematic moves in the Court's opinion, the demand that the state anticipate accommodations not raised by the claimant and the possibility that those imagined alternatives will include entire new spending programs, are not relevant in most RFRA cases,

and in any case are somewhat undercut by the reservations expressed in Kennedy's concurrence. Now that Kennedy is no longer on the Court, those dangerous possibilities are very much with us, and they are an obstacle to compromise.

41. Thomas Jefferson, Notes on the State of Virginia, in Writings 285 (Merrill D. Peterson ed., 1984).

Chapter 7

1. The argument offered in this chapter draws upon Andrew Koppelman, How Could Religious Liberty Be a Human Right?, 16 Int. J. Const. Law 985 (2018).

2. Hunter S. Thompson, Better Than Sex: Confessions of a Political Junkie 142 (1994).

3. Kathleen Brady, The Distinctiveness of Religion in American Law: Rethinking Religion Clause Jurisprudence 287 (2015).

4. Ibid., 269.

5. Ibid., 304.

6. Ibid., 236.

7. For further critique of Brady, see my review, 97 J. of Religion 548 (2017).

8. James Madison, Memorial and Remonstrance Against Religious Assessments (1785), in 2 The Writings of James Madison 184–85 (1901). Brady quotes it at 80.

9. When he presents his argument for religious accommodation, he frequently begins by quoting this passage from Madison. See Michael W. McConnell, The Origins and Historical Understanding of Free Exercise of Religion, 103 Harv. L. Rev. 1409, 1453, 1497 (1990); Michael W. McConnell, The Problem of Singling Out Religion, 50 DePaul L. Rev. 1, 29 (2000); Michael W. McConnell, Why is Religious Liberty the "First Freedom"?, 21 Cardozo L. Rev. 1243, 1246–47 (2000).

10. McConnell, The Origins and Historical Understanding, at 1453.

11. McConnell, The Problem of Singling Out Religion, at 30; see also Michael W. McConnell, Free Exercise Revisionism and the Smith Decision, 57 U. Chi. L. Rev. 1109, 1151–52 (1990).

12. McConnell, The Problem of Singling Out Religion, at 30.

13. On Sherbert, see chapter 1.

14. Steven D. Smith, Pagans and Christians in the City: Culture Wars from the Tiber to the Potomac 326 (2018).

15. Ibid., 312–13.

16. Ibid., 322.

17. Steven D. Smith, Freedom of Religion or Freedom of the Church?, in Legal Responses to Religious Practices in the United States 267, 268 (Austin Sarat ed., 2012).

18. Ibid. at 273–74.

19. Smith, Pagans and Christians, 314–15, citing Michael Stokes Paulsen, The Priority of God: A Theory of Religious Liberty, 39 Pepperdine L. Rev. 1159 (2013).

20. Paulsen, The Priority of God, 1210.

21. Ibid., 1207.

22. Ibid. at 1160. Paulsen claims that this is the original linguistic meaning of the First Amendment, but he does not cite (and I am not aware of) any writer at the time of the framing who read it as he does. (At the time, the amendment was not understood to mandate any judicial accommodations. See Philip A. Hamburger, A Constitutional Right of Religious Exemption: An Historical Perspective, 60 Geo. Wash. L. Rev. 915 (1992).) Instead, Paulsen imagines a small menu of possible regimes (which omits the one we actually have, see Andrew Koppelman, Defending American Religious Neutrality (2013)), picks from these the one he finds most consistent with religious accommodation, and works out its logical implications.

23. Paulsen, The Priority of God, 1160–61.

24. Ibid. at 1214.

25. Ibid., emphasis in original.

26. Ibid. at 1212.

27. Ibid. at 1208 n.144.

28. See, e.g., Brian Barry, Culture and Equality: An Egalitarian Critique of Multiculturalism (2001).

29. Koppelman, Defending American Religious Neutrality, passim.

30. Henry Fielding, The History of Tom Jones, A Foundling 82 (Modern Library ed. 1940) (1749).

31. John Locke, A Letter Concerning Toleration 27 (1689; James H. Tully ed. 1983).

32. Ibid., 36.

33. See my Corruption of Religion and the Establishment Clause, 50 Wm. & Mary L. Rev. 1831 (2009).

34. John M. Finnis, Natural Law and Natural Rights 89–90 (1980).

35. Keith E. Yandell, Philosophy of Religion: A Contemporary Introduction 17–34 (1999).

36. Paul Tillich, The Courage to Be (1952).

37. Immanuel Kant, Critique of Practical Reason (1788); Religion Within the Limits of Reason Alone (1794).

38. Rudolf Otto, The Idea of the Holy (2d ed. 1950).

39. See generally Koppelman, Defending American Religious Neutrality.

40. See Larry Alexander, Good God, Garvey! The Inevitability and Impossibility of a Religious Justification of Free Exercise Exemptions, 47 Drake L. Rev. 35 (1998).

41. Koppelman, Defending American Religious Neutrality, 120–65.

42. See, e.g., Brian Leiter, Why Tolerate Religion? 15–25 (2013); Martha Nussbaum, Liberty of Conscience: In Defense of America's Tradition of Religious Equality (2008); Kwame Anthony Appiah, The Ethics of Identity 98 (2005); William Galston, The Practice of Liberal Pluralism 45–69 (2005); Amy Gutmann, Identity in Democracy 151–91 (2003); Michael J. Sandel, Democracy's Discontent: America in Search of a Public Philosophy 65–71 (1996); Rogers M. Smith, "Equal" Treatment? A Liberal Separationist View, in Equal Treatment of Religion in a Pluralistic Society 179, 190–94 (Steven V. Monsma and J. Christopher Soper eds., 1998); Ira C. Lupu, The Trouble With Accommodation, 60 Geo. Wash. L. Rev. 743, 775 (1992); Rodney K. Smith, Conscience, Coercion and the Establishment of Religion: The Beginning of an End to the Wanderings of a Wayward Judiciary?, 43 Case W. Res. L. Rev. 917, 926–29, 961 (1993); Rodney K. Smith, Converting the Religious Equality Amendment into a Statute with a Little "Conscience," 1996 BYU L. Rev. 645, 663–66.

43. 494 U.S. 872 (1990). This result was reversed, with respect to federal law, by statute, which the Court has followed. See Gonzales v. O Centro Espirita Beneficente Uniao do Vegetal, 546 U.S. 418 (2006).

44. Christopher L. Eisgruber and Lawrence G. Sager, Religious Freedom and the Constitution 243 (2007).

45. See Garrett Epps, To an Unknown God: The Hidden History of Employment Division v. Smith, 30 Ariz. St. L. Rev. 953, 959–65, 978–85 (1998).

46. That was more than thirty years ago. Joseph Gremillion and Jim Castelli, The Emerging Parish: The Notre Dame Study of Catholic Life Since Vatican II 132 (1987). Since then, American religiosity has become even less duty-centered. For an argument that this feeling of connection is central to modern American Catholic practice, see Andrew Greeley, The Catholic Imagination (2001).

47. See Alan Wolfe, The Transformation of American Religion: How We Actually Live Our Faith (2003); Robert Wuthnow, America and the Challenges of Religious Diversity (2005).

48. 42 U.S.C. § 2000cc-5(7)(A).

49. 521 U.S. 507 (1997).

50. 485 U.S. 439, 451, 450 (1988).

51. Eisgruber and Sager, Religious Freedom and the Constitution 243–44.

52. Christopher L. Eisgruber and Lawrence G. Sager, The Vulnerability of Conscience: The Constitutional Basis for Protecting Religious Conduct, 61 U. Chi. L. Rev. 1245, 1245 n. ++ (1994). They use "deep" repeatedly to describe the claims that should be treated equally with religious ones. Eisgruber and Sager, Religious Freedom and the Constitution, at 87, 89, 95, 101, 197, 241, 246, 252.

53. The Vulnerability of Conscience at 1285.

54. Michael Sandel is right that liberalism presupposes this opacity. Liberalism and the Limits of Justice 172 (1982).

55. *Epperson v. Arkansas*, 393 U.S. 97, 103–104 (1968).

56. See, e.g., George Sher, Beyond Neutrality: Perfectionism and Politics (1997); Robert P. George, Making Men Moral: Civil Liberties and Public Morality (1993).

57. John Rawls, Political Liberalism 13 (expanded ed. 1996).

58. Ibid.

59. Ibid., 61.

60. John Rawls, "The Idea of Public Reason Revisited," in Collected Papers 579 (Samuel Freeman, ed., 1999).

61. Political Liberalism, 13.

62. This routine feature of law is overlooked in Brian Leiter's claim that religion could legitimately be singled out for special protection only because of "features that all and only religious beliefs have, either as a matter of (conceptual or other) necessity or as a contingent matter of fact," or that would not merit such principled toleration if other beliefs have those same features. Why Tolerate Religion?, 27. He is correct that no such features exist. He acknowledges the indispensability of legal proxies (94–99), but does not examine the impact of that concession on his thesis that singling out religion is unfair. For further critique of Leiter, see Andrew Koppelman, How Shall I Praise Thee? Brian Leiter on Respect for Religion, 47 San Diego L. Rev. 961 (2010).

63. Koppelman, Defending American Religious Neutrality, 120–24.

64. Ibid., 124–65.

65. See Koppelman, Defending American Religious Neutrality 6–8, 43–45.

66. Jonathan Z. Smith, Religion, Religions, Religious, in Critical Terms for Religious Studies 269 (Mark C. Taylor ed. 1998); Talal Asad, Genealogies

of Religion: Discipline and Reasons of Power in Christianity and Islam (1993).

67. William T. Cavanaugh, The Myth of Religious Violence: Secular Ideology and the Roots of Modern Conflict 192 (2009).

68. Martin Riesebrodt, The Promise of Salvation: A Theory of Religion (2010).

69. Andrew Koppelman, Secular Purpose, 88 Va. L. Rev. 87, 157–58 n.257 (2002).

70. *United States v. Seeger*, 380 U.S. 163, 166 (1965).

71. Ibid. at 188–93 (Douglas, J., concurring); *Welsh v. United States*, 398 U.S. 333, 344–67 (1970) (Harlan, J., concurring in the result).

72. See Words and Phrases, in West's Encyclopedia of American Law (2d ed. 2008).

73. Abandonment, 1 Words and Phrases 37–147 (2007); Abuse of Discretion, 323–462 and, in the 2008 supplement, 8–25.

74. Religion, 36C Words and Phrases 153–57 (2002 and supp. 2008).

75. Defending American Religious Neutrality, 26–45.

76. Charles Taylor, The Ethics of Authenticity 31–41 (1991).

77. John Rawls, A Theory of Justice 206/181 rev. (1971; revised ed. 1999).

78. Bernard Williams, Ethics and the Limits of Philosophy (1986).

79. Political Liberalism, 311–12.

Chapter 8

1. In Indiana, Using Religion as a Cover for Bigotry, N.Y. Times, Mar. 31, 2015.

2. *Obergefell v. Hodges*, 135 S. Ct. 2584, 2602 (2015).

3. Ibid. at 2626 (Roberts, C.J., dissenting).

4. Ibid. at 2630 (Scalia, J., dissenting).

5. Ibid. at 2642–43 (Alito, J., dissenting).

6. John Corvino, Ryan Anderson, and Sherif Girgis, Debating Religious Liberty and Discrimination 212 (2017).

7. Maggie Gallagher, Why Accommodate? Reflections on the Gay Marriage Culture Wars, 5 Nw. J.L. & Soc. Pol'y 260, 263 (2010).

8. The crucial question of what counts as "views like those of religious racists" has not been theorized by anyone, so far as I can tell.

9. Jonathan Rauch, Opposing Gay Marriage Doesn't Make You a Crypto-Racist, Daily Beast, Apr. 24, 2014.

10. Quoted in Michael Wear, Reclaiming Hope: Lessons Learned in the Obama White House About the Future of Faith in America 179 (2018).

11. Ibid., 187.

12. Ibid., 188.

13. *United States v. Windsor*, 133 S. Ct. 2675, 2718 (2013) (Alito, J., dissenting).

14. For critique, see Andrew Koppelman, More Intuition than Argument (review of Sherif Girgis, Ryan T. Anderson, and Robert P. George, What is Marriage? Man and Woman: A Defense (2012)), 140 Commonweal, May 3, 2013; Andrew Koppelman, Judging the Case Against Same-Sex Marriage, 2014 U. of Illinois L. Rev. 431.

15. See, e.g., Rod Dreher, Sex After Christianity, American Conservative, Apr. 11, 2013.

16. See Girgis et al., What Is Marriage?, at 10–12, 86–93.

17. See Andrew Koppelman, Is Marriage Inherently Heterosexual?, 42 Am. J. of Jurisprudence 51 (1997).

18. US Commission on Civil Rights, Peaceful Coexistence: Reconciling Nondiscrimination Principles with Civil Liberties 160–61 (Sep. 2016) (statement of Commissioners Achtenberg, Castro, Kladney, Narasaki and Yaki).

19. Ryan T. Anderson, Disagreement Is Not Always Discrimination: On Masterpiece Cakeshop and the Analogy to Interracial Marriage, 16 Geo. J. L. & Pub. Pol'y 123, 125 (2018).

20. Ibid., 131.

21. Ibid., 136.

22. Michael J. Perry, Obergefell v. Hodges: An Imagined Opinion, Concurring in the Judgment (June 27, 2015) (Legal Studies Research Paper Series No. 15-356, Emory University School of Law), https://papers.ssrn.com/sol3/papers.cfm?abstract_id=2624022 (quoting John Corvino, Homosexuality and the PIB Argument, 115 ETHICS 501, 509 (2005)).

23. Deuteronomy 32:8, Acts 17:26, King James Version.

24. See generally Fay Botham, Almighty God Created the Races: Christianity, Interracial Marriage, and American Law (2013).

25. See Jane Dailey, Sex, Segregation, and the Sacred After Brown, 91 J. Am. Hist. 119, 121 (2004); see also Jane Dailey, The Theology of Massive Resistance, in Massive Resistance 151 (Clive Webb, ed., 2005).

26. Dailey, Sex, Segregation, at 125 (quoting Theodore G. Bilbo, Take Your Choice: Separation or Mongrelization 109 (1947)).

27. Quoted in Dailey, Sex, Segregation, at 129.

28. Quoted in *Loving v. Virginia*, 388 U.S. 1, 3 (1967).

29. Botham, Almighty God Created the Races, 156.

30. Peter L. Berger, The Sacred Canopy: Elements of a Sociological Theory of Religion (1967).
31. Damon Linker, Is Opposing Gay Marriage the Same as Being a Racist?, The Week, Feb. 13, 2014. In fairness to Linker, he may be expressing no theological view, and simply offering reasons why religious heterosexism is less likely to disappear than religious racism.
32. This point is well developed in Carlos A. Ball, The First Amendment and LGBT Equality: A Contentious History 271–73 (2017).
33. David M. Smolin, Regulating Religious and Cultural Conflict in Postmodern America: A Response to Professor Perry, 76 Iowa L. Rev. 1067, 1086 n.87 (1991).
34. Bd. of Trs. of the Univ. of Ala. v. Garrett, 531 U.S. 356, 374 (2001) (Kennedy, J., concurring).
35. Ibid.
36. See Briefs of Amicus United States in United States v. Windsor, Hollingsworth v. Perry, and Obergefell v. Hodges. Selective sympathy and indifference may indeed constitute an equal protection violation, see Andrew Koppelman, Antidiscrimination Law and Social Equality 28–31, 40–43 (1996), but it does not necessarily show that the actor is a bad person.
37. Iris Murdoch, The Sovereignty of Good 59 (1971).
38. Deirdre McCloskey, The Bourgeois Virtues: Ethics for an Age of Commerce (2006).
39. A different and more manageable question is whether a statute on its face reflects animus against an unpopular group. That is a familiar question of statutory purpose, and so the Court has managed to address it without attempting to search anyone's heart. When the Court has attributed a bare desire to harm gay people, it has been reviewing unusual statutes that, on their face, lashed out wildly and indiscriminately. See Andrew Koppelman, Beyond Levels of Scrutiny: Windsor and "Bare Desire to Harm," 64 Case Western Reserve L. Rev. 1045 (2014); Andrew Koppelman, Romer v. Evans and Invidious Intent, 6 Wm. & Mary Bill of Rights J. 89 (1997).
40. See Jonathan Haidt, The Righteous Mind: Why Good People are Divided by Politics and Religion 170–77 (2012). The concern with sanctity and pollution is, however, not only found among conservatives. It is reflected on the left in the moral impetus for the environmental movement, the market for products that purge the body of "toxins," and the aversion to genetically modified foods (15).
41. The term was originally coined by George Weinberg in an effort to invert the then-conventional notion that homosexuality was a mental illness, by

arguing that the aversion to homosexuality was itself pathological. George Weinberg, Society and the Healthy Homosexual (1972).

42. The 1968 Fair Housing Act includes the so-called Mrs. Murphy exemption, excusing dwellings with four or fewer units if the owner lives in one of the units. 42 U.S.C. §3603(b). It has had no discernible effect on the availability of housing. Yet it has been attacked, because its persistence "announces that our nation still tolerates discrimination." James D. Walsh, Reaching Mrs. Murphy: A Call for Repeal of the Mrs. Murphy Exemption to the Fair Housing Act, 34 Harv. C.R.-C.L. L. Rev. 605, 607 (1999).

43. See Andrew Koppelman, Why Jack Balkin is Disgusting, 27 Const. Commentary 177 (2010); Martha C. Nussbaum, Hiding from Humanity: Disgust, Shame, and the Law (2004).

44. Rod Dreher, Heads LGBTs Win, Tails Christians Lose, Am. Conservative, May 21, 2015; Jewelry store sign prompts same-sex couple to ask for refund, CBC News, May 16, 2015.

45. Samuel Fleischacker, Being Me Being You: Adam Smith and Empathy 159 (2019).

46. I am only aware of one case raising such a defense, but had it succeeded there obviously would have been others. See *Newman v. Piggie Park Enters., Inc.*, 256 F. Supp. 941, 944 (D.S.C. 1966), rev'd, 377 F.2d 433 (4th Cir. 1967), aff'd per curiam, 390 U.S. 400 (1968). No commentators suggested at the time that such views be accommodated. See James Oleske, The Evolution of Accommodation: Comparing the Unequal Treatment of Religious Objections to Interracial and Same-Sex Marriages, 50 Harv. Civ. Rts.—Civ. Lib. L. Rev. 99 (2015).

47. It played an important role in the election of Trump in 2016. Alan Abramowitz, The Great Alignment: Race, Party Transformation, and the Rise of Donald Trump (2018).

48. Andrew Koppelman, Gay Rights, Religious Accommodations, and the Purposes of Antidiscrimination Law, 88 S. Cal. L. Rev. 619 (2015).

49. Shannon Gilreath and Arley Ward, Same-Sex Marriage, Religious Accommodation, and the Race Analogy, 41 Vt. L. Rev. 237, 256–57 (2016), citations omitted.

50. Koppelman, Gay Rights, Religious Accommodations, 628.

51. Ibid.

52. Gilreath and Ward 277.

53. Shannon Gilreath, Not a Moral Issue: Same Sex Marriage and Religious Liberty, 2010 U. Ill. L. Rev. 205, 220 (2010).

54. Gilreath and Ward 257, quoting Koppelman, Gay Rights, Religious Accommodations, at 653.

55. Shannon Gilreath, The End of Straight Supremacy: Realizing Gay Liberation 252 (240), quoted in Gilreath and Ward 240 n.8.

56. Gilreath, The End of Straight Supremacy, 252.

57. Antigay violence is correlated with the belief that violations of traditionally gender roles are threatening, and is typically perpetrated by groups of young males, who are thereby demonstrating their toughness and heterosexuality to their peers. For a review of the scholarly literature on violence against gay people, see Dominic J. Parrott and John L. Peterson, What Motivates Hate Crimes Based on Sexual Orientation? Mediating Effects of Anger on Antigay Aggression, 34 Aggressive Beh. 306 (2008).

58. Alex Vandermaas-Peeler, et al., PRRI, Emerging Consensus on LGBT Issues: Findings From the 2017 American Values Atlas (May 1, 2018).

59. Quoted in Ira Katznelson, Fear Itself: The New Deal and the Origins of Our Time 90 (2013).

60. Ibid., 180.

61. Quoted in Chester M. Morgan, Redneck Liberal: Theodore G. Bilbo and the New Deal 250 (1985), and "He Died a Martyr," Time, Sept. 1947, 15.

62. See J. G. Kosciw et al., The 2017 National School Climate Survey: The Experiences of Lesbian, Gay, Bisexual, Transgender, and Queer Youth in Our Nation's Schools (GLSEN 2018).

63. The U.S. Department of Health and Human Services estimates between 575,000 and 1.6 million homeless and runaway youth annually. Available research suggests that between 20% and 40% of these are LGBT. Nicholas Ray, Lesbian, Gay, Bisexual and Transgender Youth: An Epidemic of Homelessness 1 (2006).

64. Ibid.

65. Russell Moore, Should the Church View Homosexuality Like Divorce?, Aug. 16, 2016, https://www.russellmoore.com/2016/08/16/church-view-homosexuality-like-divorce/. See also Russell Moore, What If Your Child Is Gay?, June 6, 2014, https://www.russellmoore.com/2014/06/06/what-if-your-child-is-gay/.

66. Russell Moore, On Weddings and Conscience: Are Christians Hypocrites?, Feb. 23, 2014, https://www.russellmoore.com/2014/02/23/are-christians-hypocritical-on-weddings-and-conscience-protection/.

67. He is a signatory on a statement, signed by more than 75 religious leaders, opposing such protection because of its impact on religious liberty. Preserve Freedom, Reject Coercion, Dec. 2016, Colson Ctr. for Christian Worldview, http://www.colsoncenter.org/freedom.

68. Andrew T. Walker and Russell Moore, Is Utah's LGBT-Religious Liberty Bill Good Policy?, Ethics & Religious Liberty Commission, Mar. 6, 2015.

69. Sharon Groves, Is the Southern Baptist Church Having an Identity Crisis, or Am I?, Huffington Post, Oct. 31, 2014.

70. Quoted in Rob Howard, The Great Divide, Gayly, May 2015, 32.

71. Zack Ford, Inside The Southern Baptists' New, Media-Savvy Approach to Homosexuality, ThinkProgress, Oct. 31, 2014.

72. Sarah Pulliam Bailey, Evangelical Leader Russell Moore Denounces "Ex-Gay Therapy," Huffington Post, Oct 28, 2014.

73. Shannon Price Minter, Belief and Belonging: Reconciling Legal Protections for Religious Liberty and LGBT youth, in Religious Freedom, LGBT Rights, and the Prospects for Common Ground 38 (William Eskridge Jr. and Robin Fretwell Wilson, eds. 2018).

74. Quoted in Avishai Margalit, On Compromise and Rotten Compromises 178 (2009).

75. W.B. Yeats, He thinks of Those who have spoken Evil of his Beloved, in Collected Poems 75 (2d ed. 1950).

76. See Jeremy Waldron, Mill and the Value of Moral Distress, in Liberal Rights: Collected Papers 1981-1991, at 115 (1993).

77. Ibid. at 120.

78. Ibid. at 125. Waldron's more recent call for restriction of hate speech is in tension with this argument. See Andrew Koppelman, Waldron, Responsibility-Rights, and Hate Speech, 43 Ariz. St. L. Rev. 1201, 1215–21 (2012).

79. This is one reason why the protection of dissent is so central to the free speech tradition. See Steven H. Shiffrin, The First Amendment, Democracy, and Romance (1990).

80. Andrew Koppelman, Veil of Ignorance: Tunnel Constructivism in Free Speech Theory, 107 Nw. U. L. Rev. 647 (2013); John Durham Peters, Courting the Abyss: Free Speech and the Liberal Tradition (2005).

81. See Carlos A. Ball, The First Amendment and LGBT Equality: A Contentious History (2017); William N. Eskridge Jr., Gaylaw: Challenging the Apartheid of the Closet 93–96, 116–23 (1999).

82. It probably was not original with him. See Barry Popik, A Liberal Is a Man Too Broadminded to Take His Own Side in a Quarrel, Big Apple (Dec. 6, 2009), http://www.barrypopik.com/index.php/new_york_city/entry/a_liberal_is_a_man_too_broad_minded_to_take_his_own_side_in_a_quarrel/ [https://perma.cc/R3MF-X3EE].

83. Andrew Koppelman, Unparadoxical Liberalism, 54 San Diego L. Rev. 257 (2017).

84. On the relation of censorship and solipsism, see Andrew Koppelman, Another Solipsism: Rae Langton on Sexual Fantasy, 5 Wash. U. Jurisp. Rev. 163 (2013).

85. Seana Valentine Shiffrin, Speech Matters: On Lying, Morality, and the Law (2014).

86. See Andrew Koppelman, You're All Individuals: Brettschneider on Free Speech, 79 Brooklyn L. Rev. 1023 (2014).

Chapter 9

1. Avishai Margalit, On Compromise and Rotten Compromises 2 (2009).

2. Ibid., 23.

3. Ibid., 73.

4. Ibid., 49.

5. Ibid., 5.

6. This possibility is explored in Robin Fretwell Wilson, Bathrooms and Bakers: How Sharing the Public Square Is the Key to a Truce in the Culture Wars, in Religious Freedom, LGBT Rights, and the Prospects for Common Ground 402 (William Eskridge Jr. and Robin Fretwell Wilson, eds. 2018), and Frank S. Ravitch, Freedom's Edge: Religious Freedom, Sexual Freedom, and the Future of America 91–92 (2016).

7. This is the only way that California allows businesses that serve the public to accommodate employees who are religious objectors. *North Coast Women's Care Medical Group v. Benitez*, 189 P.3d 959 (Cal. 2008).

8. Amy E. Knaup and Merissa C. Piazza, Business Employment Dynamics Data: Survival and Longevity, II, 30 Monthly Labor Rev. 3 (Sept. 2007).

9. *State v. Arlene's Flowers, Inc.*, 389 P.3d 543 (Wash. 2017), vacated and remanded, 138 S.Ct. 2671 (2018); aff'd on remand, 193 Wash.2d 469 (2019); *Klein v. Ore. Bur. Of Labor & Indus*, 410 P.3d 1051 (Or. App. 2017); *Gifford v. McCarthy*, 137 A.D.3d 30, 41 (N.Y. App. Div. 2016); *Craig v. Masterpiece Cakeshop*, 370 P.3d 272 (Colo. App. 2015), rev'd on other grounds sub nom. *Masterpiece Cakeshop, Ltd. v. Colorado Civil Rights Com'n*, 138 S.Ct. 1719 (2018); *Elane Photography v. Willock*, 309 P.3d 53, 59 (N.M. 2013), cert. denied, 572 US 1046 (2014). In other claims for religious exemption, courts have held that the interest in eradicating discrimination is compelling. *N. Coast Women's Care Med. Grp., Inc. v. Superior Court*, 44 Cal.4th 1145, 1158–59, 81 Cal.Rptr.3d 708, 189 P.3d 959 (2008); *Swanner v. Anchorage Equal Rights Comm'n*, 874 P.2d 274, 281–83 (Alaska 1994); *Gay Rights Coal. of Georgetown Univ. Law Ctr. v. Georgetown Univ.*,

536 A.2d 1, 31–39 (D.C. Ct. App. 1987); *State v. Sports & Health Club, Inc.*, 370 N.W.2d 844, 852–54 (Minn. 1985). The only authority to the contrary that is sometimes cited is a Kentucky court that held that a printing company could refuse to print T-shirts for a gay pride event. *Lexington Fayette Urban County Human Rights Commission v. Hands on Originals, Inc.*, 2017 WL 2211381 (Ky. App.). The religious liberty claim was not addressed by this decision, which held that the state statute did not prohibit the refusal to publish words with which the vendor disagreed.

10. I haven't discussed the federal RFRA, because there is no federal law banning sexual orientation discrimination in public accommodations, and so courts will not confront the question whether RFRA creates an exception. The Equality Act, which passed the House of Representatives in May 2019, would amend the Civil Rights Act of 1964 to prohibit discrimination on the basis of sexual orientation or gender identity in a number of areas, including public accommodations. It specifically exempts itself from RFRA. H.R. 5, 116th Cong., 1st sess. (2019). Another bill, the Do No Harm Act, would amend RFRA to make clear that it does not apply to antidiscrimination laws. H.R. 3222, 115th Cong. (2017); S. 2918, 115th Cong. (2018). If the Supreme Court decides that LGBT discrimination is sex discrimination under the Civil Rights Act of 1964—a question pending as this is written, in *Bostock v. Clayton County*, Georgia, No. 17-1628—religious exemptions would be baked into that decision. The statute permits religious associations, corporations, educational institutions, and societies to discriminate based on religion in a range of ways that other entities may not. 42 U.S.C. §2000e-1(a); 42 U.S.C. §2000e-2(e)(2). Employers may also discriminate based on sex if that discrimination relates to a bona fide occupational qualification that is reasonably necessary to the normal operation of their businesses. 42 U.S.C. §2000e-2(e)(1).

11. Frederick Schauer, Playing By the Rules: A Philosophical Examination of Rule-Based Decision-Making in Law and in Life (1991).

12. 2016 Miss. Law HB 1523 §2.

13. Quoted in Warren Richey, In Mississippi Gay Rights Battle, Both Sides Feel They Are Losing, Christian Science Monitor, July 14, 2016.

14. *Barber v. Bryant*, 193 F. Supp. 3d 677 (S.D. Miss. 2016), rev'd on other grounds, 860 F.3d 345 (5th Cir. 2017), cert. denied, 138 S.Ct. 652, 138 S.Ct. 671 (2018).

15. Richey, In Mississippi Gay Rights Battle, Both Sides Feel They Are Losing.

16. See generally Memorandum from Public Rights/Private Conscience Project, Columbia Univ. in the City of N.Y., to Interested Parties, State & Federal Religious Accommodation Bills: Overview of the 2015-2016 Legislative Session (Sept. 20, 2016), https://perma.cc/3H2L-AHB3 (collecting and summarizing all religious accommodation bills introduced in state legislatures between Obergefell and Sep. 2016).

17. Kan. Stat. Ann. § 60-5312, effective July 1, 2016.

18. Columbia memorandum, 3.

19. I quote from the latest version. See letter of Robin Fretwell Wilson, Thomas C. Berg, Carl H. Esbeck, Richard W. Garnett and Edward McGlynn Gaffney Jr. to Hawaii State Sen. Rosalyn H. Baker, Oct. 17, 2013.

20. Taylor Flynn, Clarion Call or False Alarm: Why Proposed Exemptions to Equal Marriage Statutes Return Us to a Religious Understanding of the Public Marketplace, 5 Nw. J. L. & Soc. Pol'y 236, 238–39 (2010).

21. She also inconsistently argues that accommodation is unnecessary because so few claims have arisen. Ibid. at 247–48.

22. Elizabeth Sepper, Gays in the Moralized Marketplace, 7 Ala. C.R. & C.L. L. Rev. 129 (2015).

23. The difficulties are further explored in Alan Brownstein, Gays, Jews, and Other Strangers in a Strange Land: The Case for Reciprocal Accommodation of Religious Liberty and the Right of Same-Sex Couples to Marry, 45 U.S.F. L. Rev. 389, 414–22 (2010), Mary Anne Case, Why "Live-And-Let-Live" Is Not a Viable Solution to the Difficult Problems of Religious Accommodation in the Age of Civil Rights, 88 S. Cal. L. Rev. 463, 470 & n. 28 (2015), and Shannon Gilreath and Arley Ward, Same-Sex Marriage, Religious Accommodation, and the Race Analogy, 41 Vt. L. Rev. 237 (2016).

24. Keith Bardwell, a Louisiana Justice of the Peace, refused in October 2009 to perform an interracial marriage. He resigned in disgrace soon afterward.

25. Elane Photography v. Willock, 309 P.3d 53, 59 (N.M. 2013), cert. denied, 572 US 1046 (2014).

26. See Andrew Koppelman, A Free Speech Response to the Gay Rights/Religious Liberty Conflict, 110 Nw. U. L. Rev. 1125 (2016).

27. Russell Nieli, Gay Weddings and the Shopkeeper's Dilemma, Pub. Discourse, Dec. 17, 2014.

28. See Koppelman, A Free Speech Response, 1141–42.

29. The following facts are drawn from the complaint in Phillips v. Elenis, no. 1:18-cv-02074 (filed Aug. 14, 2018).

30. Verified complaint, Aug. 14, 2018.

31. Masterpiece Cakeshop v. Elenis, order denying in part motion to dismiss, Jan. 4, 2019.

32. The logic in favor of settlement was anticipated in Eric Segall, It's Time for Colorado and the Masterpiece Cakeshop Owner to Reach a Deal, Slate, Jan 7, 2019.

33. Third Discrimination Suit Filed Against Masterpiece Cakeshop, CBS Denver, June 6, 2019.

34. Elizabeth Anderson, The Imperative of Integration (2010); Douglas S. Massey and Nancy A. Denton, American Apartheid: Segregation and the Making of the Underclass (1998).

35. See Andrew Koppelman with Tobias Barrington Wolff, A Right to Discriminate? How the Case of Boy Scouts of America v. James Dale Warped the Law of Free Association 26–31(2009).

36. Steven D. Smith, What Masterpiece Cakeshop Is Really About, Public Discourse, Oct. 24, 2017.

37. Douglas Laycock, Religious Liberty, v. 3: Religious Freedom Restoration Acts, Same-sex Marriage Legislation, and the Culture Wars 836–37 (2018).

38. Daniel DellaPosta, Gay Acquaintanceship and Attitudes toward Homosexuality: A Conservative Test, 4 Socius 1 (2018).

39. Douglas NeJaime and Reva Siegel, Conscience Wars in Transnational Perspective: Religious Liberty, Third-Party Harm, and Pluralism, in The Conscience Wars: Rethinking the Balance between Religion, Identity, and Equality 209–15 (Susanna Mancini and Michel Rosenfeld eds. 2018).

40. Elizabeth Sepper, Zombie Religious Institutions, 112 Nw. U. L. Rev. 929 (2018).

41. Frederick Mark Gedicks and Rebecca Van Tassell, RFRA Exemptions from the Contraception Mandate: An Unconstitutional Accommodation of Religion, 49 Harv. C.R.-C.L. Law Rev. 343 (2015)

42. See, e.g, Gerard V. Bradley, John Finnis and Daniel Philpott, The Implications of Extending Marriage Benefits to Same-Sex Couples, Public Discourse, Feb. 22, 2015, https://perma.cc/EM2Z-L6N8.

43. Ronald G. Ehrenberg and Robert S. Smith, Modern Labor Economics 273–78 (6th ed. 1997).

44. S. 815, 113th Cong., 1st Sess. (2013).

45. See Chris Johnson, House Panel Rejects Last-Ditch Effort to Pass ENDA, Washington Blade, Dec. 3, 2014.

46. See House Report Accompanying H.R. 5, 116th Cong., 1st sess. (2019), Rept. 116–56, 21–22.

47. H.R. 5331 (116th Cong., 1st sess.).

48. *Corporation of Presiding Bishop of Church of Jesus Christ of Latter-day Saints v. Amos,* 483 U.S. 327, 341 (1987) (Brennan, J., concurring in the judgment), quoting Douglas Laycock, Towards a General Theory of the

Religion Clauses: The Case of Church Labor Relations and the Right to Church Autonomy, 81 Colum. L. Rev. 1373, 1389 (1981).

49. For this reason, when the model statute was proposed in Illinois shortly before the legislature enacted same-sex marriage, I opposed it. See letter of Profs. Dale Carpenter, Douglas NeJaime, Andrew Koppelman, Ira Lupu, and William P. Marshall to Hon. Michael Madigan, Oct. 15, 2013, available at http://www.volokh.com/2013/10/30/religious-liberty-ssm-response-concerns-illinois/. Earlier, I endorsed similar proposals because, like many others, I was focused on the public accommodations issues and overlooked the model statute's implications for terms of employment. See the letters collected in Laycock, Religious Liberty, v. 3, 769–793.

50. Laycock, Religious Liberty, v. 3, 766.

51. Douglas Laycock, Afterword, in Same-Sex Marriage and Religious Liberty: Emerging Conflicts 200 (Douglas Laycock et al. eds., 2008).

52. See Ira C. Lupu and Robert W. Tuttle, Same-Sex Family Equality and Religious Freedom, 5 Nw. J.L. & SOC. Pol'y 274, 303–305 (2010).

53. *Estate of Thornton v. Caldor, Inc.*, 472 U.S. 703, 710 (1985), quoting *Otten v. Baltimore & Ohio R. Co.*, 205 F.2d 58, 61 (2d Cir. 1953) (per L. Hand, J.).

54. This point was raised in conversation by Douglas Laycock.

55. See, e.g., Minn. Stat. Ann. § 363.01 (barring sexual orientation discrimination, applicable to all employers); N.Y. Exec. Law § 292 (barring sexual orientation discrimination, applicable to "all employers with more than three employees"); Vt. Stat. Ann. tit. 21, § 495 (barring sexual orientation discrimination, applicable to "all employers").

56. Rod Dreher, What Hill Do We Die On, Then?, Am. Conservative, Sept. 4, 2015.

Index

For the benefit of digital users, indexed terms that span two pages (e.g., 52–53) may, on occasion, appear on only one of those pages.